Education Without Impact

Education Without Impact

How Our Universities Fail the Young

George H. Douglas

A Birch Lane Press Book
Published by Carol Publishing Group

A Birch Lane Press Book
Published by Carol Publishing Group
Birch Lane Press is a registered trademark of Carol Communications, Inc.
Editorial Offices: 600 Madison Avenue, New York, N.Y. 10022
Sales & Distribution Offices: 120 Enterprise Avenue, Secaucus, N.J. 07094
In Canada: Canadian Manda Group, P.O. Box 920, Station U, Toronto, Ontario M8Z 5P9
Queries regarding rights and permissions should be addressed to Carol Publishing Group, 600 Madison Avenue, New York, N.Y. 10022

Carol Publishing Group books are available at special discounts for bulk purchases, for sales promotions, fund raising, or educational purposes. Special editions can be created to specifications. For details contact Special Sales Department, Carol Publishing Group, 120 Enterprise Avenue, Secaucus, N.J. 07094

Manufactured in the United States of America
10 9 8 7 6 5 4 3 2 1

Library of Congress Cataloging-in-Publication Data
Douglas, George H., 1934—
  Education without impact : how our universities fail the young /
George H. Douglas.
        p. cm.
  "A Birch Lane Press book."
  Includes bibliographical references (p.)
  ISBN 1-55972-124-3
  1. Education, Higher–United States—Aims and objectives.
2. Education, Humanistic—United States. 3. Education, Higher—
Politiccal aspects—United States. 4. College Students—United States.
I. Title.
LA227.4D68 1992   92-26270
378.73—dc20   CIP

To W. W. Watt

Contents

Acknowledgments   ix

Preface   xi

Part I

    Higher Education: The Question of Style

1   Higher Education: Trouble at the Heart's Core   3

2   Two Cheers for the Old-Style College   9

3   The Double Wound   19

4   The Poisons of the Ph.D. Octopus   27

5   The Lost Essence of Undergraduate Education   35

Part II

    Passion Denied: The Professor and the System

6   Professors Under Fire   47

7   How Professors Weaken the Bonds to the Shared Culture   61

8   The New Druids and the Poisoning of the Humanities   68

9   The Indifference of the Ivory Lab   78

10   Do They Publish or Perish?   90

Part III

    The Poisoned Well of Learning

11   Defreighting the Curriculum: The Legacy of the Sixties   105

12   Lost in the Wilderness: The Undergraduate Course Today   117

13   A Fallen Giant of the Curriculum: Freshman
        English   127
14   Wars Over "the Canon"   137
15   The Penumbra of Liberal Education   149

Part IV

        Student Life in an Impoverished Community
16   Toward a Rejuvenation of College Life   163
17   Students: The Lively Lonely Crowd   168
18   *In Loco Parentis*—Then What?   183
19   Old Wine in New Bottles   196
        Bibliography   215

Acknowledgments

This book is dedicated to W. W. Watt, wit, teacher, and energetic man of letters, who gave me an idea of what a liberal education is all about when, as a college freshman, I was just barely old enough to understand.

My readers will perceive quickly that this book is an essay and not a treatise. It is the result of many years of contemplating the ups and downs, and sighs and grunts, of higher education in America. It has grown from a number of earlier articles and essays that I have written on the subject, and expresses themes that I have been refining and developing for a good long time. However, I would like to thank a number of individuals who are responsible for helping this project get off the ground. I would like to thank, particularly, a number of well seasoned philosophers and historians of education who either read the manuscript in its entirety or otherwise aided me with the principal idea. I owe a special debt of gratitude to Paul Violas, Foster McMurray, Mary Ann Wells, and Ralph E. Smith. Several colleagues of mine who read the manuscript and offered valued criticisms were Arnold and Charlene Tibbetts and U. Milo Kaufmann.

I should also like to thank Mr. Allan J. Wilson, editor at the Carol Publishing Group, for having faith in this idea and helping me to see it through to completion. Equally important, I would like to thank India Cooper for doing a superlative job of copyediting the manuscript and pointing out places where my meaning was obscure or otherwise confusing.

Needless to say, no book of this sort can be written without indebtedness to a great many individuals who have plowed the same ground for many years and even centuries. I believe that in the text I have adequately expressed indebtedness to most of those who have influenced my thinking, although it is hardly necessary to say that the particular stance and the thrust of arguments found herein are strictly my own.

Preface

O<small>VER THE LAST</small> several decades heaping cartloads of books and articles have proclaimed that there is something drastically wrong with American colleges and universities. All sorts of things have been found responsible for this alleged decline in our system of higher education. Some critics have said that universities are elitist, which is to say, not sufficiently democratic. Others have said that they are *too* democratic. Some have blamed professors for being self-serving pedants, or for being too wrapped up in research to pay attention to their students. Others have blamed poor preparation of students by high schools, an excess of specialization and technology, warped moral values, or the decline of the family. Some have whipped tired old horses like "progressive education." Some have blamed the lack of funding by state and federal governments. Coming in for more than their share of blame from time to time have been television, permissive parents, the drug culture, the war in Viet Nam—and so on, ad infinitum.

To most of us it may seem strange that the American educational establishment has been found guilty on so many counts. Around the world friendly observers continue to be amazed at the scope and the high quality of our institutions of higher learning. The Japanese, for example, who lately have been scornful of how things are done in American business and industry, continue to send thousands of their students to the United States to receive an American college education. Japan, in spite of its great wealth and its homogenous society, has not yet found a way to fully meet the educational needs of its population. Recent news stories have confirmed that the

Japanese have even tried to buy up American colleges—admittedly, tiny institutions on the verge of bankruptcy, not prestigious institutions with the sort of high-tech programs most of us would expect Japan to pursue. Still, their very interest and admiration of our achievements testify to the attractiveness of the system of colleges and universities we have in place. American universities, on the basis of their enormous size and diversity alone, continue to be the envy of the world.

I am a professor in a large American university, and I should say immediately that I, too, find a lot wrong with our system of higher education. Like a great many others who have written books on higher education recently, I keep telling myself how much better things were back in the 1950s when I was in college. I sometimes tell myself that this is nothing more than the nostalgia of a typical middle-aged curmudgeon. Things always appear brighter and more cheerful as one looks back to the days of one's youth. Many of my colleagues and agemates—and this includes most of the those people writing books about how bad things are—believe that higher education went to pot in the 1960s. And undoubtedly that decade gave a bone-jarring twist to the historical course of higher education. It was a time that allowed dark prophets to declare the existence of an official "crisis" in education. There is nothing that Americans love more than a crisis—or, more precisely, the freedom to shoot off fireworks and stink bombs announcing a crisis. And the 1960s was a great time for that. Clearly, though, the 1960s did not create, but only dramatized, the ills of our system. In the 1960s troubles were grievously piled upon troubles—the loads of straw that broke the camel's back, so to speak. But the straw had been piling on for a long time.

On the other hand, it is far fetched to say that what is wrong with America's colleges and universities constitutes a kind of crisis. These institutions are not really in crisis; they have never been in crisis. They suffer instead from a kind of lethargy, a tediousness, a middle-age disease of some kind—something like arthritis, shall we say, or any disease that ebbs and flows. Our colleges and universities are gouty and stiff; they have fed on the wrong diet for too long. But they are not close to falling into anarchy. And in most of the ways that outsiders can observe, they fare very well.

My own basic analysis of the problems faced by the American university is not revolutionary. Like other recent critics, I believe that a failure to provide a liberal education, an education for citizenship, is the principal defect of our mammoth educational system. Even though this has been said often enough, I find that it is very easy to forget that a liberal education is a peculiar thing. It does not confer itself automatically on people who simply take liberal arts courses. From my experience as a teacher in this area, some of the people crowding through liberal arts courses in the nation's universities have had virtually no brush with the genuine article itself, have often spent their time feeding on a carcass having no meat. A liberal education is a matter of style and substance, and if it is lacking in either (and often what goes under this label is lacking in both), it never really comes to life.

Unfortunately, liberal education is a rare and delicate plant; it needs to be cultivated profoundly and at leisure; it can be neither spoon-fed nor mechanically administered. Because it has to do principally with ways that a person lives in the world and responds to the world, and because it requires a highly individual response to learning, no mere transfer of information is going to bring it about. Our universities, alas, are presently not in a very good position to provide the type of human setting that brings about a liberal education. They are too big, too full of hustle and bustle, too busy doing society's work, to be the sort of place where a vital human transaction can take place. There is something seriously wrong with our universities as communities, as places for learning. Insofar as they are merely factories for producing specialized expertise or for imparting information in a routine and unimaginative manner, they are not serving our most important national needs.

Once again, the situation is not as dismal as it may seem, since people can and do create their own educational experience while in college—often in spite of their formal courses, which may lead far away from the heart of a vibrant and personal education. In fact, in the most important sense a liberal education is always what you give yourself, not something piped in from outside. And since a true liberal education involves a fierce independence of mind and a highly individual style, it is likely that at no time in history did any large number of individuals find the means to acquire it. On the whole the public has looked for quite different things from education; we Americans usually look for things that pay off in tangible ways. We like to hear cash registers ring whenever the word *education* is mentioned. We want to fit people for jobs in a technically complex society; we look to universities to split the atom, study social trends, develop better hybrid corn, or tell us what is wrong with the State Department's policy in the Middle East.

Even though it is easy to expect too much from our institutions of higher learning, and many critics have expected a college education to do more than it possibly can for the number of people processed by the system, there is still reason for concern that American colleges and universities have followed paths that are at cross-purposes with the spirit of liberal education. Many of the academic personnel who are expected to keep the spirit of the liberal arts education alive—professors of literature, philosophy, and the arts—have turned out to be among its deadliest enemies.

Insofar as this is true, it is because of the pressures our system of higher education has put on them. As a society we have often asked the wrong things of our universities and have developed an educational style that may meet the technical and commercial needs of society but not the needs of human beings, not the most fundamental needs of a republic. Viewed in totality, our institutions of higher learning are a long way from being failures. Whenever conditions offer a certain amount of leisure, freedom from want, and an opportunity for the imagination to play, a small number of truly educated people will arise in any society. Nonetheless, the present style of higher learning in America is antithetical to the pivotal mission of liberal education. One fears that frequently the flame of learning is extinguished needlessly in many individuals who, with a little luck, might be able to keep it burning.

Part I

Higher Education: The Question of Style

1

Higher Education: Trouble at the Heart's Core

HIGHER EDUCATION, it is called in these United States—education beyond high school. Not so many years ago one used to hear about the pleasures, the privileges, and the benefits of going to college or of receiving a college education. Nowadays a great many Americans aren't really all that excited about the college experience. They view college education only as a conduit leading to something else—law school or a professional training school, perhaps. A job, certainly. At one time undergraduate education was an end in itself, something having its own rewards; today it tends to be swallowed up in a large sea of indifference. It takes its place as another prosaic link in the educational chain or in the chain of life.

Somehow or other the wonderful thing that used to be a college education seems to have lost its luster. It seems to have become routinized in the lives of most Americans. It doesn't evoke the kind of excitement and exhilaration it once did. A college education may well be "higher" in the sense that it represents a higher rung on a ladder than other rungs down below, but that is a trivial sense of the word *higher*. All of the rungs on a ladder, after all, are pretty much alike. There was a time when most of those who went to college believed that they were going to get off the tiresome educational

3

ladder and step out upon a cloud, leaving behind all of the dull tasks and unsavory ordinances that had been dogging them since their earliest school days. Not any more.

American college education has become rather stale and careworn. This does not mean that a half century or more ago everyone who went to college was seeking to have a serious encounter with learning. In the 1920s the youth of Scott Fitzgerald's generation went as often as not to play football, to meet flappers, to spin uninhibitedly along some country road in the tin lizzy, or to drink wood alcohol in remote roadside dance halls. A giant serving of freedom, independence, and pure physical liberation has always been a major requirement in the diet of young people between the ages of eighteen and twenty-two. But the colleges that catered to the flappers and their gay blades in raccoon coats back in the twenties received them in something of the same youthful spirit. Today our colleges and universities are too busy doing the world's work to care much about the young. They want the young to become productive as soon as possible; they want to make them experts in something, and, failing that, they want as little to do with them as possible. Grant them their highjinks, grant them their fun, but keep it well apart from the laboratory or the seminar room. Come to college prepared to swallow knowledge as required—yes, just as you did in high school. Play in a playpen; get drunk or sound off somewhere else. Develop as a specialist or an expert with us; develop as a person on your own time.

Not too many years ago, most people connected with higher education in America—professors, scholars, administrators, researchers—knew that undergraduate education was the principal function of a college or university. Now they believe otherwise; their gods are those of the guild or specialty instead. It is in the more lofty graduate and professional schools that things really begin to happen. Undergraduate education is something to be gotten over or gotten through, as a cat shakes its paw to get rid of a few drops of water into which it has unfortunately been obliged to step. To professors and students alike, undergraduate education is one further phase of preparation and spoon-feeding, like the experience down below in high school. College education is no longer a step onto a cloud; rather it is merely one more wearisome step on a ladder that, the student has been promised, leads to a better life.

During the 1960s, when many college students began to agitate about the quality of the education they were receiving, a number of thoughtful critics wrote books that seemed to say the students had justifiable reasons for complaint. More often than not, as one might expect, the student leaders had not made a correct diagnosis of what was bothering them. Why should they?—*they* were not the educational sages, after all. But in their belief that they were being neglected, shunted aside, they had hit upon an important truth, and a great many educators, grown to maturity in a more mellow age, recognized the validity of their complaints. The students were correct in their belief that they were being shortchanged; that most large universities, even a great many small colleges, were not there for them; that those schools were now mainly serving their own goals as institutions of specialized research.

In allowing undergraduate education—call it general education, if you like, or liberal education, or education for human-being-ness—to trail in the dust, to take a backseat to other and frequently bogus aims of education, American universities have cheated the nation of a valuable commodity. Undergraduate education was at one time the keystone in the arch of higher education. When that keystone was lost, and replaced by goals spun out by the graduate and professional schools, by the needs of vocational training (and all the so-called scholarly subjects are viewed in a vocational light nowadays), the heart was cut out of it from the students' point of view—and perhaps from the professors' point of view as well, although they may not have realized it.

Some will ask, isn't liberal education still abundantly available in America? Can't students still take "liberal arts" courses in most universities? Quite so, but this completely misses the main point. The traditional liberal education was not just a matter of following a so-called liberal arts curriculum. Students of engineering can conceivably receive a rich liberal education, and students in the so-called College of Liberal Arts can remain cultural illiterates. At the heart of the liberal arts is a *style* of education; specific content, although important, is not the key issue. Traditionally an undergraduate college education involved a student in a community of scholars, a fellowship of learning, shall we say. The college campus was a place where the mature and the immature were bound together in a quest for common knowledge, a place where student and teacher touched one another in significant ways.

In *The Aims of Education*, famed British philosopher Alfred North

Whitehead pointed out that universities of higher learning are not justified if they are nothing but schools of learning and schools of research. "Both of these functions could be performed at a cheaper rate apart from these very expensive institutions. Books are cheap and the system of apprenticeship is well understood. So far as the mere imparting of information is concerned, no university has had any justification for existence since the popularization of printing in the fifteenth century." Whitehead might well have added that most of the functions of large research universities could be more cheaply and efficiently performed by think tanks or publicly funded research centers. But while the functions of research and teaching are capable of being performed in cheaper and more efficient ways, the main impetus to the establishment of universities has come since the fifteenth century. What could have been perceived as the need for such institutions? To Whitehead the answer is to be found in the nature of the community of learning:

> The justification for a university is that it preserves the connection between knowledge and the zest for life, by uniting the young and the old in an imaginative consideration of learning. The university imparts information, but it imparts it imaginatively. At least this is the function which it should perform for society. A university which fails in this respect has no reason for existence. This atmosphere of excitement, arising from imaginative consideration, transforms knowledge. A fact is no longer a bare fact; it is invested with all its possibilities. It is no longer a burden on the memory: it is energizing as the poet of our dreams and as an architect of our purposes.

An ideal university serves its purpose by kindling the imagination, and it does this not just for the young but for professors, who themselves need to be refreshed, reinvigorated. Teachers must act on their students—this is obvious—but for the imaginative transaction to take place, students must also act on their teachers. If the link between the two is merely perfunctory, merely the implacable mechanisms of examinations, lectures, the delivery of bundles of information, then the community of learning will be sickly and feeble. Only an imaginative community of learning and the zest for life that comes out of it will result in true education. Said Whitehead:

> Youth is imaginative, and if imagination be strengthened by discipline this energy of imagination can in great measure be preserved throughout life. The tragedy of the world is that those who are imaginative have but slight experience, and those who are experienced have feeble imaginations. Fools act on imagination without knowledge; pedants act on knowledge without imagination. The task of the university is to weld together imagination and experience.

Usually, though, in our typical modern universities, there is no such welding together of the young and the old in an imaginative consideration of learning. Professors gladly retreat into the depths of their various specialties, leaving students stranded. They teach "at" students but seldom engage their attention, to say nothing of their imagination. Students who enter college at the age of eighteen are not looking for, and do not need, one more educational experience that only "imparts" information. They need to exercise their minds and develop their sense of individual identity. They need to synthesize their knowledge. Late adolescence is a time of asking fundamental questions about the universe, a time of coming up with one's own answers. College students hope to be able to ask such questions in the company of their professors, and they were usually able to do so in the colleges and universities of an earlier day. Today their professors have little interest and concern for students' youthful questions and remove themselves to safer, quieter, and less unsettling precincts.

Many recent critics of education have agreed that a decline in the quality of undergraduate education—a failure to produce a bond of learning—is harmful to students. But it has been less readily apparent that the same failing has a negative effect on the people at the other end—the scholars, researchers, and professors themselves. It is assumed that they are secure and healthy in their erudition and their achievements. But if the essence of a college education lies in a community of learning, and this community reaches out to society as a whole, professors, too, have suffered badly by the decline in the undergraduate teaching function; they have become more narrow in their outlook, more pedantic, more parched, more astringent, and, above all, less imaginative and venturesome.

Those who defend the research functions of the university usually make the excuse that professors can involve themselves in teaching in a tangential way, that they may stand upon Mount Olympus, and still light paths for undergraduates. Professors are useful and brilliant, admirably suited to what they do in the study or laboratory. Their work meets the larger needs of the community and society. And their eminence will rub off on students through some magical alchemy—or at least so goes the argument. So what if they are not scintillating lecturers or classroom teachers? So what if they disdain the company of callow undergraduate minds?

The response to these facile assertions is not as cheery and encouraging as apologists for the research university would have us believe. By neglecting the primary functions of education professors also impoverish themselves, draw narrow and constricting parameter of pedantry around themselves. Under ideal circumstances scholars should belong not to their specialty alone but to a wider world of learning and to the general public. They should keep themselves in perpetual renewal, reinvigorated, lively of imagination, through contact with the young. Undergraduate students, after all, are one of their strongest links to the general culture, since such students have not yet been stamped out in the mold of the university, have not surrendered to the academic mind-set. So in withdrawing from the young, in becoming important personages with careers as "specialists," professors lose much of their authority as citizens. They dilute their qualifications as intellectuals and citizens of the world.

In order for universities to do something big for society—and I assume that mere technical accomplishment and specialized expertise are not big enough—they need a transfusion point between themselves and society at large. Once upon a time undergraduate students provided it, keeping the university's lifeblood flowing. Today that vital fluid is clotted and viscous; it circulates only sluggishly. American society is much the worse for it.

2

Two Cheers for the
Old-Style College

Most of us who write books or pound the table about the woeful state of college education do so while conjuring up some lofty image, some noble ideal, of what a college education really ought to be like. It is not the weary labor of the think-tank university that we bring to mind. What is it, then? Somehow nearly all of us harbor an idea—reinforced by ivied walls, which can be found even on the very largest and most impersonal campuses—that there is something arcadian, something restful, something refreshing, about the college experience. We believe that under perfect circumstances higher education removes us from the agitation of daily life, of getting and spending, and puts us in another realm, a realm of reflection, a realm where the mind can be at play and not at work.

We look for something pure; we yearn for something simple. Almost all of us have heard at one time or another that an ideal college education need consist of nothing more than "Mark Hopkins at one end of a log and a student on the other." This is a beautifully stated ideal, no doubt, but the teacher of whom it was said—a nineteenth-century professor of philosophy at Williams College—was never a backwoods sage, nor did he ever teach from a log or a wooden bench. Indeed for thirty-six years he was president of

9

Williams, which was then, as it is now, one of the nation's distinguished small colleges. Even the oft-quoted remark is inaccurate. The original statement was contained in a speech by General (later President) James A. Garfield, who spoke at a dinner for fellow alumni of Williams at Delmonico's restaurant in New York on December 28, 1871: "I am not willing that this discussion should close without mention of the value of a true teacher. Give me a log hut, with only a simple bench, Mark Hopkins at one end and I on the other, and you may have all the buildings, apparatus, and libraries without him."

Of course, the general was surely not suggesting that the library and the scientific apparatus of Williams College be thrown away, or that there was no need of such things. It's just that something in all of us wants to pare things down to some shimmering ideal, some essence. Curiously, where our colleges and universities are concerned, even when our alma mater is an urban institution of glass and nickel construction strung out along crowded city streets, our image of the ideal college is something simple, bucolic—something on a grassy knoll, some acres of wooded ground—above all, a place with no tone of urgency or frenzied productivity. The well-known Canadian humorist Stephen Leacock captured this vision with whimsical perfection in his frequently reprinted essay "On the Need for a Quiet College":

> I would need a few buildings, but it doesn't take many—stone, if possible—and a belfry and a clock. The clock wouldn't need to go; it might be better if it didn't. I would want some books—a few thousand would do—and some apparatus. But it's amazing how little apparatus is needed for scientific work of the highest quality: in fact "the higher the fewer."
>
> Most of all I should need a set of professors. I would need only a dozen of them—but they'd have to be real ones— disinterested men of learning who didn't even know they were disinterested. And mind you, these professors wouldn't sit in "offices" dictating letters on "cases" to stenographers, and only leaving their offices to go to "committees" and "conferences." There would be no "offices" to my college, and no "committees," and my professors would have no time for conferences, for the job they would be on would need all eternity and would never be finished.

Well, as we all know, Leacock's quiet college is far too utopian to exist in the real world—at least as we encounter it in the twentieth century. Such a college would have no football stadium, no records, no buildings with modern plumbing, no fleet of cars and vans, no faculty of commerce, no courses in sales management or glassblowing or child-rearing. There would be no committees, no fights over tenure, no way to "check up" on professors as though they were stockroom clerks. There would be no "hire and fire," no "publish or perish," no "standards," no "norms." Standards of quality would be hazy and ineffable, completely determined inwardly by the scholar, not by the bookkeeping methods of some "live-wire" administrator or businessman.

So yes, we all know that no such college exists in present-day America, nor could it. Leacock's fantasy college is nothing more than that, and defenders of today's institutions of higher learning will point out that our highly complex and segmented society needs big buildings, up-to-date apparatus that works, big laboratories, system, accountability. It needs to turn out thousands of well-trained young people ready to meet the requirements of a highly technical workplace. Not one, not a hundred, not a thousand sleepy, ivy-covered colleges could produce such for us.

On the other hand, neither is it precisely correct to say that Leacock's dream college was never a reality. We hearken to the sounds of the rustling trees, we see the peaceful green lawns, because early American colleges, perhaps right down to the end of the nineteenth century, tended to be not very much different from this bucolic world. The colleges that had their footing in colonial times were certainly disinterested and detached from society. A person didn't need to go to college to become a bond trader or an insurance salesman. For that matter, a person didn't need to go to college to be a doctor or a lawyer or a newspaper editor. Aspiring doctors followed other doctors around for a while in their buggies and shays; youthful lawyers read the law in somebody else's office for a few winters and went out in the fields in the summers; a young newspaperman burned shoe leather, sharpened pencils, and set type by hand for a few years before coming into his own.

There were exceptions to this: Back in colonial times people wanting to become ministers went to college in preparation for that holy vocation. In New England especially, it was thought that a minister needed to be a learned man. Accordingly, most of the colleges chartered then were founded by churches or religious denominations, a heritage most of them kept until the twentieth century. Other than those training for the ministry, however, a young man who went to college—there were no women's colleges then—did so because he had the leisure time to do so, or perhaps because he had some scholarly aspirations. He didn't go to become a playboy or a sportsman; neither of those pursuits had pull in early times. The colleges of our nation's infancy had very little of the practical and the useful about them; they had some faint, glimmering, indefinable essence of dignity and intellectual value, but that was all. You didn't go to college to become a success.

Thus the ideal of the detached and nonutilitarian "quiet" college is far from being a dream. It is what most of the old small colleges aspired to be for more than a hundred years. And something about that ideal lingered as colleges and universities grew and changed their characters. Even when huge institutions grew up in the years just before the turn of our century, persistent efforts were made to keep something of that essence of the small ivy-covered college—otherwise we wouldn't have erected universities with Georgian or "collegiate Gothic" buildings, with quadrangles and shaded paths. We would have stopped planting ivy. So yes, something deep inside us made us want to continue to believe that the college or the university was somehow set off from the realm of utility. Even though we no longer know how to build such an institution, we still pine for it.

All of a sudden everything changed. After the Civil War the United States moved rapidly—some would say with precipitous, lethal haste—from an agrarian nation to one of commerce and industry, of business. Almost immediately a new dimension entered the picture: Colleges and universities must produce something, just as factories produce things. This dimension was accompanied by a kind of compulsive force: There is something that we must be doing, somewhere important we must be going. One thinks of the White Rabbit in Lewis Carroll's *Alice in Wonderland*—"I'm late, I'm late, I must be going, I must be going."

Does all this mean that the dream college that we see in our mind's eye, that we yearn for in moments of sleepy nostalgia, represents the ideal for higher education? Well, of course, the answer isn't all that simple. Those most inclined to condemn the arcadian college, with its elms, its dotty and distracted professors, its moldy books, its leisurely atmosphere, dilapidated laboratories, will quickly point out that the old-time college wasn't really all that good. The modern university, they will insist, dispenses education of all types and at all levels with more rigor, more substance, and more authority. Are our instincts correct, or should we believe our current, prevailing belief?

The answer, as it usually does, lies somewhere betwixt and between. There was a certain grandeur in the more modest college of yore, although doubtless its elusive qualities cannot be justified in the hard-driving and fragmented society that has grown up in America since the Civil War.

One noticeable advantage of the bucolic colleges that persisted down through the middle of the nineteenth century was that their very smallness and their limited curriculum made for a kind of cohesiveness and personal unity lacking in the university of today. It was easy to think of them as true communities of scholars because when students and teachers did talk to one another they talked about the same things. Their frame of reference was circumscribed, but it was manageable. Today we Americans, or so foreigners like to tell us, are lovers of bigness and complexity; we are believers in the limitless expansion of all our aspirations. But there are manifest advantages to simple, personal, and gentle objectives, so that our early institutions of higher learning may have functioned better with their own diminutive resources than ours of today do with grandiose ones.

The colleges founded in colonial times, and those that grew up in the early years of the republic, had the advantage of needing to provide for only a limited number of goals and perspectives. Inevitably they brought together people of similar interests. Nearly half of the graduates of colonial Harvard would become ministers; a number of others were "gentlemen" who might one day be teachers, lawyers, or statesmen. Instruction in engineering or business or agriculture was in the far-distant future. Except for the ministry, college certification was not essential for any field of endeavor known in the United States. In fact one could be a "gentleman" without going to college—so that if a gentleman went to college it was that for some reason he wanted to be there. Of the first twenty-five American presidents (that is, up to 1900), only ten held college degrees. Our present compulsive style was distinctly lacking in the atmosphere of the early college.

What about the quality of the curriculum in these early colleges? For undergraduates in the first half of the nineteenth century (the "graduate school" in the present sense had not yet appeared) the curriculum was extremely rigid. A standard "classical" course of studies was followed, and by and large it was neither rigorous nor demanding. By modern standards the most obvious characteristic of the pre-Civil War college was its apparent lack of intellectual urgency. Students were given a run through a series of "classical texts," most of them in fact unappetizing and indigestible. Here, taken from a college catalogue for the year 1855–56, is a sampling of the courses a freshman was likely to encounter:

FIRST TERM	SECOND TERM
Livy	Odes of Horace
Xenophon's Anabasis	Herodotus
Loomis' Algebra	Loomis' Geometry
Latin Prose Composition	Greek Prose Composition

By his senior year things would be little better; but the student even by this time would not have encountered a single important contemporary idea. He would be taking (there was no such thing as an elective in most colleges):

FIRST TERM	SECOND TERM
Astronomy	Plato
Evidences of Christianity	Political Philosophy
Alexander's Moral Science	History of Greek
English Literature	Literature
History of Latin Literature	Butler's Analogy

Such a roster of courses, manifestly unmodern as it must have looked even to the students of that day, gives support to the view that in the formal sense the offerings of the early American college were limited and uninspiring. The attraction that drew young people to commit four years of their lives to such a college must have lain elsewhere than in the musty curriculum.

In his excellent study of the land-grant university movement, Allan Nevins gives us a picture of the world of higher education as it existed throughout most of the nineteenth century. When President Lincoln signed the bill creating the land-grant universities in 1862 there was, says Nevins, no such thing as a modern university anywhere in the United States.

> Henry Cabot Lodge tells us that when he entered Harvard in 1867, the winds of the revolution were about to sweep away its ancient musty-ness. "I went in," he writes, "under the old system, and came out under the new. I entered the college of the eighteenth century with its 'Gratulatios' and odes and elegies in proper Latin verses...the college with the narrow classical curriculum of its English exemplars, and came out a graduate of the modern university." Brander Matthews, who entered Columbia College in 1868, found it a place of almost incredible isolation, stagnancy, and eighteenth century primitivism. He was treated like an unruly schoolboy; he never walked into the college library of fewer than 15,000 volumes; and he, too, perceived a change. He listened to Henry N. Rood deliver a truly useful set of lectures on science. At Yale, Thomas R. Lounsbury finished his four years without once hearing mention of any English author—and Yale did not change.

This is a fair but devastating critique of the old-time college by several who were liberated by the fresh winds that began blowing after the Civil War. No doubt the criticisms are just—at least in a certain sense. On the other hand, in spite of the antiquated curriculum, in spite of the sleepy quality of everything having to do with the old-time college, there was something to be said for the leisurely ambience of the educational transaction in those days. What was it?

The principal advantages, of course, were the size of and relative homogeneity of the institutions. All colleges in the United States were small before the Civil War: As late as 1872 the freshman class at Harvard contained but 200 students; Yale had 131, Princeton 110, Dartmouth 74, and Williams 49. Students in these classes were a close-knit group, of course, and they were held together by more than this smallness of number. Their preparatory educations had been similar; they had read most of the same books in school, were steeped in certain classics of literature. They knew the Bible, which, whatever its present perceived defects, served as a focal point of a shared worldview. Not only did the students of a given class come to know one another intimately; they shared a common culture, and doubtless a uniform notion of what a college education was supposed to be about.

Education requires some kind of harmony between the young and the old, and in the small pre–Civil War college almost all of the students knew and had regular contact with the faculty, and vice versa. The professor was unhounded by professional obligations, and although he had quite sufficient leisure for writing if he chose to employ his leisure in productive scholarship, he also had more than enough time to talk to students in an atmosphere of genial informality. It was more than just likely, it was almost universally expected, that the professor would live right on the college campus, very often in a house provided him by the college. Students were encouraged to follow the professor home from the library, borrow his books, perhaps sit rocking for a time on his front porch, joining him for a smoke or savoring his wife's homemade preserves. Here the talk did not need to be of the musty curriculum but of whatever struck a commonality of interest, whatever there might be in the world of learning or public affairs that might spark the imagination.

Today, of course, we know that the professor seldom lives among the students. Invariably he or she lives in the suburbs, or even out of town; the campus precincts are big, noisy, and disruptive. Intimacy or fraternity between faculty and students, while not discouraged, is not a characteristic of college and university life. It is not at all unusual for students to have no direct human contact with their professors, who are very often hitting the road to do "consulting," or making the rounds of professional meetings attended only by other professors, with perhaps a scattering of Ph.D. students.

It was not only the personal bond between teacher and student that gave the old-time college its appeal; the community as a whole had a tendency to draw students into the mood of learning. Student life in the early days had some backbone to it—it was not limited to partying, beer-drinking, pot-smoking, or demonstrating. The typical small college of the nineteenth century was well endowed with intelligent (but not necessarily stuffy) student organizations—glee clubs, literary and debating groups, oratorio societies, rowing clubs, and all the rest. Today most college students see such organizations as childish or conformist or sissy; they seek out instead student groups of the "let's be free" or "let's thumb our noses at the establishment" variety. Outside of the standardized curriculum, today's students learn as much from bull sessions or rap sessions (sadly with the professor absent) as they do from formal lectures and classes. And well they should, for such experiences have always come close to being the pure gold of education.

This does not mean that the college students of the nineteenth century were mere "old men" in the making. This might be the facile belief of many of today's undergraduates who would give the Bronx cheer to literary societies and glee clubs. Quite the reverse is true. College students of those times were volatile, playful, and mischievous, more mischievous in fact than today's students, whose antics more often than not are flat, insipid, and stereotyped. College students were never quiet in the so-called quiet college. They took a lot out of the experience, but they put just as much in. And what they put in was by no means trouble-free. A study of college newspapers and records of the period shows that the elders of the college treated their charges as charming but unruly schoolboys, whose deportment had to be monitored with care.

Every conceivable kind of behavior in those days had to be governed by a book of rules and regulations. There were rules against singing, defacing the walls, keeping of animals or firearms, fornication, cockfights, striking an instructor, playing cards on Sunday, and the like. The rules were often ineffective, of course, for this was before the day when athletics and the cult of exercise drained off the excess juices of adolescence. College students were a boisterous lot and presented a far more serious threat to the physical property than students of today. Minor vandalism was common; hardly a week would go by during term when students failed to find something to smash or overturn. Thick coats of tar might be spread on the statuary; a bust of the founder might be spirited away; above all there was the firecracker, the student's favorite form of eloquence, which reverberated in the halls of the dormitory by night and day. The professor's house might be unsafe on Halloween.

Kid stuff? Yes, college students in those times seemed more childlike, more rowdy, more tempestuous than those of today. In spite of the popular view expressed in the press about any current crop of students being more troublesome than those of the past, the record shows quite the opposite. Our present students mostly pass benignly through our institutions of higher learning without making much of a nuisance of themselves. They do erupt sometimes, but when they do, it seems, it is in joyless and grim-faced ways. Students seen bearing signs in front of the administration building on today's university campus are usually pursuing some aim that gives them little joy and to which they may have been drawn without much real commitment, and certainly by no flights of the imagination. The quiet college could afford to have occasional unquiet, even ribald, behavior, which was always taken for what it was: an expression of adolescent high spirits, not the activity of young old fogeys in training.

In the quiet college the young were young, not old. They were young because their minds were still ready to receive; they had not yet accepted the heavy burden of knowing how to set the world straight. Even though they played jokes on their professor, perhaps threw a firecracker up on his porch, they knew they had his approval for some adventure in learning, and they were ready to undertake such an adventure now and then, when the spirit moved them. So much more boisterous but so much more mature than the college students of today, their luxury was that they were set down in an environment suitable to learning, to the play of the imagination.

The prime advantage of the quiet college of people's nostalgic memory was its leisureliness, its openness, its vague, amorphous quality. The curriculum may have had little substance, but the total educational experience, augmented by a shared belief in a fellowship of learning, had a value today's gargantuan universities lack. Today students find much information placed before them—a mile-long smorgasbord to feed on—perhaps far more than they can digest. A hundred years ago college students were given less but were guided along the way. What is more important, in the leisure given them they were free to create the overall pattern of their own educational experience. They were principal players in the drama. They weren't *in* the educational system, they *were* the educational system.

3

The Double Wound

I**N THE YEARS** that followed the Civil War our nation underwent a series of traumatic, soul-wrenching changes. The old republican America, the old agrarian America, quickly slipped away, replaced by a bold new nation—its economy and its social life driven by business and industry, by huge population spurts, by the spread of cities, and by the development of an urban lifestyle. In the 1870s and 1880s, as the United States was discovering the power and sometimes frenzied misdirection of big business and of corrupt urban politics, it was also developing an overpowering interest in education. The sometimes cynical and fiercely individualistic John Jay Chapman, who grew up in those years, recalled that "the terrible savage hordes of America waked up in 1870 to the importance of salvation by education," presumably as the notion of salvation by grace was on the wane. Universal education was *in*. Everyone must be touched by the magic wand of education, whether the magic itself could do the person any good or not.

The rise of education and the rise of big business need not have been simultaneous in American history. Perhaps a bit of chance had something to do with it. Furthermore, these great new national forces might have arrived on the scene simultaneously, although driven by separate causes. To a large extent, however, there was an undeniable linkage. These two phenomena lent coloring and substance to one another. Their styles were probably more akin to one another than they should have been for the health of education. It would have been much better for America if education had not developed a sense of grandiosity, of raw power and compulsive achievement; it would also have been better if large educational institutions (whether huge urban school systems or giant universities) had not been modeled on the corporation, with its zest for profit and production, its bureaucratic hierarchy of administration, its competitive urges, and, above all, its sense of specialization and fragmentation of talent. All of these qualities brought a quick and brutal death to the time-honored and leisurely ways of education; certainly to the old-style college.

In the 1870s a wholly new kind of educational institution began to make its appearance in America: the university. Before the Civil War the word *university* usually referred to any college that had one or more professional schools connected with it. Sometimes it referred to a state-controlled institution, such as the University of Georgia. But all of these so-called universities were no bigger than most of today's small colleges; in fact, they were invariably smaller. But the universities that burgeoned after the Civil War changed all that. Their educational missions would differ from place to place, but all would have grandiose ambitions. By and large the new universities struck out for achievements that would lend prestige to themselves and luster to their founders.

The founders, at least of the private universities, were from the new capitalist classes, and they wanted to see great monuments rise—cathedrals of learning, edifices of stone, granite, or marble that would be undisguised memorials to themselves. Indeed, not a few of these institutions took the names of their founders. Johns Hopkins University in Baltimore was founded by a man, probably the wealthiest in the city, who had amassed a fortune as commission merchant, banker, shipowner, and largest individual stockholder in the Baltimore & Ohio Railroad. California railroad buccaneer Leland Stanford founded the now famous university at Palo Alto, naming it for his son, Leland Stanford, Jr.

Sometimes these wealthy philanthropists took over small existing institutions with a promise of largesse in exchange for adopting the name of the benefactor. Thus the tobacco king James Bucannan Duke turned sleepy little Trinity College in North Carolina into

Duke University. He gave millions. Sometimes, though, the well-endowed citizens who founded institutions of higher learning managed to get their names tacked on after offering only pitiful amounts of cash. Rascally old Daniel Drew established the institution that bears his name by tendering a note, which later turned out to be worthless. On the other hand, in 1891 John D. Rockefeller, stingy in handing out tips and gratuities to porters and cab drivers, gave ten million dollars to found the University of Chicago. It was a huge sum in those days, but Rockefeller did not insist that the institution bear his name. None of these men was a college graduate himself; most had little or no schooling.

The new universities were to be monuments, show pieces—but not merely to the achievements of men of wealth. Indeed nearly all were founded in a spirit of strong idealism. Booster universities they might be called. They were going to turn out something special to call attention to themselves, to their community, and to the world of learning. This element in education was not precisely new in the 1870s and 1880s. Daniel Boorstein, historian and former Librarian of Congress, pointed out in his excellent history *The Americans* that the "booster" idea preceded the Civil War, especially in the Midwest, where the tiniest communities had established their own colleges (sometimes no more than a rickety frame building) as a way of attracting fame and building local pride. They did so in much the same spirit in which they had established railways with their names in them—the Puddletown and Western, for example. It was a way of putting themselves on the map. Hundreds of these booster colleges died ingloriously by the end of the nineteenth century, some without attracting a single professor. But these institutions gave a dimension to higher education that was unknown in Europe: a desire for self-promotion and competition.

But then there were the large universities that came on the scene in the 1880s and 1890s, and of these Johns Hopkins made the most immediate impression on American higher education. When Johns Hopkins offered seven million dollars to found the Johns Hopkins University and Hospital in 1876, he was acting out of a spirit of generosity but also from some well-considered personal motives. He and his founding president, Daniel Coit Gilman, were determined to establish a university along German lines, with high priority given to research and intellectual discovery. Gilman and nearly all of his newly appointed professors had studied in Germany, where they had been impressed by the hard burning light of German science. (The German word for science, *Wissenschaft*, referred not only to what we call the sciences but to a certain approach to all subject matter and to a particular cast of mind.) They hoped to produce a university with a strong focus on graduate studies and a correspondingly diminished emphasis on what had long been the mission of the old-style college—broad learning, a sense of human community. In the traditional American college the prevailing spirit had involved the cultivation of civility through human interaction; the Germanic model of education called for stern dedication to a particular line of inquiry. The student was now called upon to create something, to push forward the bounds of learning, to turn out intellectual manufactured goods. Daniel Coit Gilman stated the ideal of Johns Hopkins quite well when he wrote that this approach to learning would provide the student with "the unique experience of having contributed some tiny brick, however small, to the Temple of Science, the construction of which is the sublimest achievement of man."

In addition to a very strong faculty, Johns Hopkins almost immediately attracted some of the brightest students in the land— young men like the California Josiah Royce, who, like another early arrival, John Dewey, went on to become one of the country's foremost philosophers. Among the others to arrive in the bright early years of Johns Hopkins were Thorstein Veblen, Joseph Jastrow, James Cattell, Newton Baker, Frederic Howe, Walter Hines Page, and Charles Homer Haskins. These young men found themselves greatly moved by the spirit of scientific learning. Those who had already made a pilgrimage to Germany were wont to liken their experience to that of Göttingen or the University of Berlin. Some of them would wind up in other rapidly growing national universities dedicated to specialized learning at the graduate level—Harvard, Columbia, Clark, Chicago, and finally the state universities that decided to take on this same coloration: Michigan, Wisconsin, Minnesota, California.

Those who were there at the beginning shared Josiah Royce's enthusiasm for this new spirit of university life, so far away from that of the meager denominational college with its pedantic professors and antiquated curriculum. "Here at last," he wrote, "the American university had been founded. The academic life was now to exist for its own sake. The 'conflict' between 'classical' and 'scientific' education was henceforth to be without significance to the graduate student. And the graduate student was to be, as we told ourselves, the real student."

The original graduate classes at Johns Hopkins—or Harvard or Columbia for that matter—were small. Graduate schools in the beginning were extremely close-knit communities. For the time being these communities were totally lacking in the element of compulsion, of rigid structure, with requirements, requisites, prerequisites, examinations, all sorts of hurdles to overcome. One felt that one could produce in this kind of environment, but production was not the be-all and end-all.

Unfortunately all this changed as more and more students poured into graduate programs. (In the 1870s the number of graduate students attending American universities was not more than a few score; by 1900 there were some 2,872.) In evidence by the 1890s was the problem of masses of individuals entering graduate work whether fitted for it or not. To discourage those who had only come to fritter away their time, Hopkins and most other universities introduced the Ph.D. degree as a way of providing certification of academic accomplishment. This degree, and not dispassionate inquiry, soon became the impulse behind graduate programs. The Ph.D. was adopted in part because of a strong call from lesser colleges and universities for "certified" scholars trained in the new mode; alas, these urgings slowly but inexorably moved the graduate ideal away from its original inspiration and toward another. New forms of narrow specialization would arise, as well as new kinds of pedantry—different from those of the denominational colleges, but just as stultifying in the long run. To embark upon the Ph.D. quest one had to give up the free spirit of inquiry in favor of hardened curricula and protocols. Altogether this represented a diminishment in the kind of openness that marked Johns Hopkins and other such places in the first few years. Priority now went to producing the standardized product.

There was much to worry about in this new development. The turning out of standardized graduate students for utilitarian ends (mostly that of accepting teaching positions at other institutions aspiring to have their own day of glory) was something of a departure from the ideas behind the German Ph.D., and in the American milieu it was to result in a much different kind of university.

One of those early Johns Hopkins pioneers who saw trouble brewing was Thorstein Veblen. Veblen left Hopkins, received a Ph.D. at Yale, and later held a number of university teaching positions (at the University of California and Stanford, for example), most of which were unhappy experiences. In his 1918 book *The Higher Learning in America*, Veblen tried to explain what had gone wrong with the founding ideals of the universities. His critique will seem dated to some today, perhaps because it was written at a time when the daily affairs of universities were strongly monitored by the captains of industry who supported them; Stanford, for example, was run as something of a personal fiefdom by Leland Stanford and his wife, both of whom believed that they had the right to fire any professor who incurred their displeasure. Much of Veblen's book is devoted to explaining how during the late nineteenth and early twentieth century the wings of learning were clipped by governing boards and by businessmen presidents and deans, all wielding the power to stifle dissent and control the personal and professional lives of professors who were, in effect, their "employees."

But Veblen also had a complaint that is more timeless and more subtle. The captains of industry and their administrative cat's-paws inflicted on the academy an even greater wound, a certain cast of mind, a business enterprise notion of the university. It was not just a matter of control; in a few decades, especially after the founding of the American Association of University Professors in 1913, actual reins of control were loosened, but the businessman had already put his stamp on the university, now a place that must show results and turn out standardized products. It wasn't only their edicts that bothered Veblen; he abhorred the fact that the captains of industry had foisted on the universities their crude utilitarian cast of mind, their predatory and competitive tactics, their desperate clamor for "output." Under the model prescribed by the business ethos, the university was quickly transformed into a place of animalistic struggle where the tone was set by the spirit of business management, that is, the insistence upon the techniques of salesmanship and boosterism.

The hallmark of the university, then, is no longer unfettered inquiry but rather bureaucratic mechanisms, committee work, office management, cost control, public relations. A tone is set of activity, bustle, intrigue, and internecine competition—all in an environment, as Veblen so well put it, of "quietism, caution, compromise, collusion and chicane." In this kind of environment professors, reduced to mere hirelings, are required to spend an inordinate amount of time climbing the ladder of success, making a good account of themselves and their work, above all, clawing their way through a system of academic politics that is as deadly to learning as it is to human civility. The mood of academic politics is certainly not conducive to flights of the imagination or the cultivation of the mind; just as important, it reduces the social milieu to the impersonal, the standardized, the mechanical.

Historians of the American university will point out that the old legacy of the captains of industry was driven out of academia a long time ago; professors believe themselves to be, by and large, free and independent thinkers not held to account by benefactors and boards of trustees. This, of course, is nothing more than a happy illusion— delusion, shall we say. The captains of industry have retreated to their own turf and no longer keep their fingers on the pulse of things; they seldom seek to censor the ideas of university scholars and researchers. But in fact by the 1880s they had already passed along their genes and set up the university in the image of the corporation. Control of academic careers now is through the specialties, but the style of this control is essentially the same as that long ordained by the men of business and their administrative sidekicks. Professors may think that they are "free," but actually their environment is extraordinarily restrictive, hemmed in by rigid professional practices, old-maidish politics, cast-iron habits of mind, ruthless conformity to the edicts of the guild, obligatory intellectual fads, relentless competition, perpetual obligations and expectations. It is all a far cry from the arcadian college of yore, and just about as far away from the joyful spirit of the graduate schools of the first few years.

There was, then, a kind of double wound inflicted on the university as it began its great growth spurt in the 1880s and 1890s. The first wound was struck by the strong arm of bureaucracy, leading to the constant irritations of academic politics, the wearisome need for aggrandizement, and the ceaseless push toward productivity. The second wound was brought about by the proliferation of the Ph.D. and the impetus toward bolt-hole specialization. Today these two wounds may be taken as having the same result, since institutions use bureaucratic mechanisms and business practices to force scholarly products off a conveyor belt, to insist that professors "produce." The products of research are counted, checked for standardization and quality, and eliminated if they don't satisfy the "bottom line."

If the American universities had been spared these two wounds they would be in a much healthier state today, and it is likely that we should be hearing many fewer complaints about the perilous condition of our institutions of higher learning, the faltering curriculum, and all the rest.

4

The Poisons of the Ph.D. Octopus

In a delicious moment of pique, Edmund Wilson, one of our most distinguished men of letters, once remarked that the United States would have been much better off if, during World War I, it had junked the Ph.D. degree as just another Germanic atrocity. Anti-German feeling was strong then; even German words were being rooted out of the dictionary—hamburger was being changed to Salisbury steak, schmierkase to cottage cheese, and sauerkraut to liberty cabbage. So it might have been an appropriate time to drop all the mechanical appurtenances of German scholarship.

Of course, it wasn't precisely the German element that had made mischief with the Ph.D. In Germany that degree had meant something quite different; throughout the nineteenth century it had never been used to construct a Procrustean bed for subject matter specialization; it had never been used for institutional puffery and aggrandizement; it had never been a means of bureaucratic control and stratification. The German universities that were lovingly admired by the wandering American scholars of the nineteenth century had never aspired to become factories of learning. They remained aloof, for the most part, from the state and industry. The rector of a German university was not a mover and shaker, a builder of buildings, an arranger of trusts. He was an eminent individual of the faculty in whose mind the idea of "management" never dawned, and he gave over his hours to composing his *Rectorsrat* or some other peroration, not to the hiring and firing of professors or the purchase of steam fittings or floor tile. The management of his university as a physical plant was assigned to some *über*-janitor or other glorified factotum who had no relation to matters academic. In other words, although German ideas of higher education were imported into the United States, they never arrived intact; they were broken up into little pieces and reassembled in a new and completely different form. For this reason we are a bit unfair in blaming the Germans for our educational woes.

But skeptical concerns about the Ph.D. and the development of graduate and professional training cannot be passed over lightly. What Americans did with the Ph.D.—the terminal degree of the scholar of researcher—continues to be a strong source of anxiety, and has been so since the time in the late 1890s when universities began to convince themselves that higher degrees, sprinklings of letterings after one's name, were necessary to the success of a college professor, and that the acquisition of such title-bedecked individuals was essential for any college or university that aspired to "distinction."

One individual who agonized long and hard over the growth and spread of the Ph.D. mania was William James, who retired as professor of philosophy at Harvard University in 1907. In his later years James was undoubtedly America's best-known philosopher, and he possessed tremendous influence not only among others in his field but with the general reading public. James's ideas about the goals and purposes of a college education attracted a good deal of attention in their day, and they are still worth serious consideration, although, as it turned out, they did little to affect the course of educational history. American universities wanted graduate degrees, and they wanted elaborate graduate schools to dominate their intellectual life, so the resistance of James and others to the new tendencies proved to be unpersuasive. But because this resistance came at such a crucial and sensitive juncture in the history of higher education, it continues to be illuminating.

During the last few years of his tenure at Harvard, James became increasingly dissatisfied with the way things were going under

President Charles W. Eliot. Eliot had attempted to move Harvard along the same paths as Johns Hopkins and the other "graduate" universities; indeed by 1900 he had probably been even more successful in assembling the building blocks of a great research university than Daniel Coit Gilman at Hopkins. But Eliot had not at the same time neglected Harvard's older traditions, so his university lost little of its appeal to undergraduates. Even so, James thought things weren't moving in the right direction. Education in the highest sense was being sacrificed for something of unproven worth.

James believed that the purpose of a college or university education was to allow people to discover their own directions in a congenial and close-knit environment, not to get them to assemble a cast-hardened set of ideas for public approval. He always believed that it was the undergraduate college and not the graduate school that should be the center of focus in the university. In the undergraduate college one has a chance to touch the young when they are still fluid, still ready to receive ideas in a mood of creative play and enjoyment—an opportunity that rapidly fades in the graduate school. James himself preferred to teach in the undergraduate college at Harvard, and although he did take on graduate students, the idea never occurred to him that teaching of this sort was more "prestigious."

James seems to have come by his attitudes naturally as the result of his own eccentric and highly individualistic upbringing. William and his brother Henry James, Jr., soon to become the famous novelist, along with a sister and two other brothers, were raised in an atmosphere of free expression and nonconformity. Their semi-invalid father, Henry James, Sr., a lecturer and religious philosopher who had inherited a considerable fortune derived from the Erie Canal, devoted a great deal of his time to providing education for his family both at home and abroad. The children's formal education was spotty, since the family spent much of its time traveling in Europe. But at home in Concord, where they were friends and neighbors of Ralph Waldo Emerson and Henry Wadsworth Longfellow, education proceeded at a high level through spirited dinner table conversation. The elder James believed that education should unfold in an mood of spontaneity and uninhibited expression, an attitude that survived in his philosopher son.

James's higher education had the refreshing air of a desultory walk in the woods. He attended Harvard as an undergraduate but never took his degree. For a while he studied painting and had his father's blessing for an artistic career. Later, however, he entered the Harvard Medical School, where in 1869 he took the M.D. degree, although he never intended to practice medicine. He joined the Harvard faculty, where he taught anatomy and physiology for a few years before moving into psychology. In this latter field he eventually won an international reputation; he was, in fact, largely responsible for setting American psychology on its feet as a specialized discipline. But he never believed that psychology was an isolated discipline—he never believed in any isolated disciplines—and the 1890s found him a professor of philosophy. In his last years he was even more famous as a philosopher than he had been as a psychologist, so there were few who had the temerity to challenge this intellectual waywardness, as they surely would today. In 1900 such a curious mix of accomplishments did not seem as peculiar as it does now.

As he approached the end of his life James became seriously alarmed that the young who sought an academic career were being required to tread an undeviating path, the gift of the Ph.D. programs that were spreading throughout the land. He believed that the spirit of education lay in a different direction. James called his own philosophy "pragmatism" (a term actually coined somewhat earlier by his friend C.S. Peirce). Some people have interpreted "pragmatism" to mean that ideas should be judged entirely by their usefulness or cash value. Nothing could have been further from James's intention. He meant rather that the world of thought is in flux, that ideas need to be caught on the wing, so to speak, put to good use for one's current intentions, made to work in the context of one's present experience of life. The philosopher (any scholar, for that matter) should not be a man with a bag of specialty parts slung over his shoulder wherewith to batter down the opposition; rather he should be looking at the broader picture, discovering the creative potential of ideas at play.

One of those who remembered James as a teacher was Dickinson S. Miller, who himself spent a short time in an academic career. Miller was among the many students who listened to James's lectures on psychology at the old Lawrence Scientific School at

Harvard in 1890. He remembered James as a man with a vigorous, playful air, his bronzed complexion and brown tweeds giving him more the appearance of a sportsman than a professor. In that class in psychology the already famous James had to put up with some arrogant graduate students who tossed him questions that were really nothing other than disguised criticisms, but he endured it all with humor and seemingly inexhaustible patience. After class, students followed the professor up Kirkland Street toward his home. He continued to answer questions, apparently entertaining all ideas, however annoying or shallow.

What marked James above all else, said Miller, was an air of openness and receptiveness. "He almost never, even in a private conversation, contended for his own opinion. He had a way of falling back on the language of perception, insight, sensibility, vision of possibilities. I recall how on one occasion after class, as I parted with him at the gate of Memorial Hall triangle, his last words were something like these: 'Well, Miller, that theory's not a warm reality to me, yet—still a cold conception'; and the charm of the comradely smile with which he said it."

James's philosophy of teaching and of scholarship seems to have been that both are the product of direct human interaction, and that in the new research university this interaction would be purged; you would be setting up artificial barriers between people, forcing them to fight their way through a dense jungle of pedantic fustian, of bureaucratic edicts and impediments, all of which would have the effect of making real learning—the genuine, spontaneous expression of ideas—cumbersome and painful. Above all, after Harvard's graduate school got in full swing and began grinding out Ph.D.'s, James frequently let it be known that he didn't approve of this process of turning young men into old. He thought that the generation of philosophers produced at Harvard since the establishment of the graduate school (and Lord knows how many more at lesser places) were for the most part tedious and uninspiring hacks. In 1905 he wrote to his colleague George Santayana that nothing could be worse than "the gray-plaster temperament of our bald-headed young Ph.D.'s boring each other in seminaries, and writing those dutiful reports of the literature in the *Philosophical Review*." He found the "overtechnicality and consequent dreariness" of these young/old men to be positively alarming. Much of the output of graduate scholarship, which he called "desiccating and pedantify-ing," gave him more than a mild fright.

In his 1903 essay "The Ph.D. Octopus," James had already laid down his objections to the spawning of the German monster. Some of them arose from his democratic sensibilities, from a suspicion of titles, honorifics, all sorts of conferred benefices that smacked of the tired caste systems of Europe. Americans, he believed, ought to go at the world with their own achievements; these foolish academic knighthoods need not be adopted to establish merit. James feared that the original American suspicion of honorifics was quickly fading away under a new impulse to bespangle pages of the college catalogue with Ph.D.'s, S.D.'s, and Litt.D.'s "as if they were sprin-kled over it from a pepper caster." He felt that this compulsion to wallow in vanity degrees flew in the face of our best traditions of equality of opportunity. "America is…as a nation rapidly drifting towards a state of things in which no man of science or letters will be accounted respectable unless some kind of badge or diploma is stamped upon him, and which bare personality will be a mark of an outcast estate." We must rouse ourselves to the danger of this grotesque and decadent tendency before it runs out of control. "Other nations suffer terribly from the Mandarin disease. Are we doomed to suffer like the rest?"

Of course, James acknowledged that the main impetus to the cancerlike spread of the Ph.D. disease came from the nation's colleges and universities, especially inferior universities that needed to show some tangible evidence of possessing a superior faculty. But to James the badge of the degree was not evidence of anything beyond itself, and it therefore could do great psychological damage to those upon whom it was conferred. Bestowing Mandarin status on individuals would likely lead to a lifelong career of inactivity and highly cultivated pedantry. Since the qualifications that were needed to get past the Ph.D. barriers took no note of an individual's moral, social, and personal characteristics, the degree offered not the slightest evidence that the honoree would make a successful teacher. Indeed the most likely assumption is that elevation into the Man-darin caste would tend to establish a wide rift between lowly student and elevated professor.

James's strongest objection to the proliferation of the Ph.D. and the creation of a professional academic caste was that it would set up whirring, clanking machinery between person and person, between person and idea, between teacher and student. For James the best ideas come out of plain old human nature, when people relate to one another in equality and with spontaneous interest. Everything in the new university, and everything in the "Doctor-monopoly," was leading the other way. "The institutionalizing on a large scale of any natural combination of need and motive always tends to run into technicality and to develop a tyrannical Machine, with unseen powers of exclusion and corruption."

Altogether it was a strong indictment. The Ph.D. octopus, if allowed to swim unchecked in academic waters, would harden academic categories and restrain creativity; it would encourage bureaucracy, cheap politics, and corruption in the universities; it would lead to silly and mindless boostering on the part of all institutions of higher learning; it would have a depressing effect on teaching, widening the gap between the out-of-the-guild student and the in-the-guild teacher; it would chain one to one's "specialty" in the way a prisoner is chained by the ankle in a dungeon; above all, it would force man, bare man, "man thinking" as Emerson put it, into a straightjacket—a straightjacket made of all the forms, protocols, and petty annoyances of the doctoral apparatus. Instead of confronting the world directly with the force of imagination and intellect, the "Doctor-man" would seek salvation in the machinery provided for him, he would always gravitate back to preset and stereotyped forms and conventions. Worst of all, he would attempt to pass these forms of the dead hand onto the younger generation.

It is interesting to note that James's bitter prophecy—which we have seen more than fulfilled in our time—was not an isolated cry in the first few decades of the twentieth century. Many of his contemporaries expressed similar ideas, sometimes in equally trenchant language. From outside the academy—from writers, independent intellectuals, and men of letters—there was plenty of scoffing at the heavy apparatus of scholarship, as one might expect. But for a number of years, even in aspiring and aggrandizing freshwater universities where the Ph.D. had become an article of veneration, there was much complaint about the rigidity and staleness of the doctoral machinery from professors themselves.

For example, in the great public land-grant universities—which were originally intended to capture the free spirit of the people, where knowledge was believed to be open-ended, where the professor wasn't afraid to put his hand to the plow—the Ph.D. was an object of suspicion until booster deans and presidents forced the issue and insisted that only the doctoral process, only competition and rock-hardened professionalism, could bring status and prestige to their institutions. But for many years the best professors in these universities remained skeptical. Fred Lewis Pattee, sometimes credited with being the first professor of American literature, a field he developed at Pennsylvania State University starting in 1909, characterized the then virulent Ph.D. mania as "dry rot." At the University of Illinois Pattee's friend, English professor Stuart Pratt Sherman, probably one of the best-known American academics of his day, came down even harder on the Ph.D. straightjacket. Sherman was busy handing out Ph.D.'s to Illinois farm boys by 1915, but he had a low opinion of those who submitted themselves to this churlish labor. "The very best men," he wrote, "do not enter upon graduate study at all; the next best drop out after a year's experiment; the mediocre men at the end of two years; the most unfit survive and become Doctors of Philosophy, who go forth and reproduce their kind."

One view that all of these early critics of the Ph.D. seem to have in common is that the process, and the dominance of the graduate school mind-set that went with it, could not really be attractive to the most youthful and vigorous talents; that the long, tedious, mind-deadening process—the requisites, examinations, orals, the narrowly focused research—had the effect of repulsing those who really ought to be devoting themselves to serious thought or flights of the imagination. It encouraged mediocrities instead of first-rate minds. Worst of all, the graduate schools had this appalling habit of turning vigorous young men into tedious old men. The Ph.D. mind-set took most of the joy, and probably much of the value, out of what used to be college education.

5

The Lost Essence of Undergraduate Education

CLARK KERR served as president of the vast University of California system during the 1960s, when student disruptions at Berkeley began to draw the public's attention to problems of higher education. Occasionally in those years Kerr was asked to explain the ideal function of a large American university such as the one over which he presided. As can be expected, he attempted to describe a university that included everything currently on view in the academic firmament, a university that would offer all the richness and diversity that experience had shown to be necessary to the educational diets of the young and were believed to be beneficial to the public at large.

Kerr's formula for the great public university was stated this way: "A university anywhere can aim no higher than to be as British as possible for the sake of the undergraduates, as German as possible for the graduate and research personnel, as American as possible for the sake of the public at large—and as confused as possible for the whole uneasy balance." Well, by the late 1960s there was widespread agreement about the confusion, but what of the other elements of the formula?

At this point we should not be in a quandary about what Kerr had in mind by speaking of the "Germanic" function of the university. He was referring to the research functions of the graduate school, to the doings of Think Tank U., to the laboratories, to the scholarly activities of the faculty within their specialized disciplines, and of course the ancillary functions of training graduate students, scholars, researchers, experts in the making. In short, the "German spirit" in higher education is to be found in the activities of the graduate school and the professional schools.

The "American" function of the university is also easy to divine. Kerr had in mind the extended service functions of the university: the university's commitment to extension; to vocational training; to the smorgasbord of courses in everything from weed control to child-rearing, from pot-making to certified public accounting. Perhaps he would also have included under this rubric athletics, study-abroad programs, the sale of beer, candy, and computers, the operation of fleet vehicles, the provision of infant care, the running of conference centers, and whatever other arms and wings of the modern university may come to mind. It is clear that these ancillary services, many of them unknown in universities around the world, are a great source of pride to the American public; certainly they do constitute the mark of the American style of higher education.

Ah, but that leaves one element of Kerr's formula to account for: "as British as possible for the sake of the undergraduates." What could that possibly mean? Undoubtedly the notion will bring to mind the style of those great institutions of medieval origin, Oxford and Cambridge, with their steadfast and occasionally antiquated traditions. We think, perhaps, of education for citizenship, for civility, not for trade and utility. But alas, Oxford and Cambridge are universities in a sense only dimly understood in the United States today. Oxford and Cambridge were institutions made up of a collection of independent colleges—not colleges of business or engineering or pharmacy, but rather colleges made up of fraternal individuals who seek a particular style and quality of life. The college within the university conceived in the British way is not so much a place for congeries of specialization; rather it is a kind of community of people who have sought one another out, who live, eat, think, and work together.

The British tradition of learning is built around a highly individu-alized style, not productivity and divisions of learning. The college—the undergraduate college—is a place where you learn to be a civilized member of society, a gentleman, let us say, although I hate to use a word, that has no real equivalent in the American language and would offend some in our coeducational environment. It is a place where one savors a highly eccentric charm, a place where one takes meals with one's fellows, in halls with timbered ceilings, presided over by paintings faded with age—paintings often of small merit but maybe of certain suggestive power. It is a place where one can adjourn to the rooms of one's "tutor" with wainscoting on the walls, with tarnished silver and bric-a-brac, with scrolls, medallions, and ancient coats of arms. A place where one may choose to attend lectures or laze away long afternoons under an alder tree on a river bank. It is a place where they seem to be having tea all the time. It is a place of intimacy and strongly personal motivation. Whatever there is of learning is breathed in, infiltrated through the pores; it is not doled out in quantifiable increments as so many credits for graduation, so many examinations to be taken or so many courses for a major.

Certainly it was this British element in education that men like William James believed to be in peril back in 1900, when graduate schools were proliferating at an ugly rate and it looked as if undergraduate education and liberal education would take a backseat to professionalism. Harvard—the Harvard that James had known in the 1870s—was born of the British tradition, like most of the small and sleepy colleges of the nineteenth century, even though for the most part they had been poor imitations of Oxford and Cambridge, harnessed to a rigid classical curriculum and often hobbled by a narrow denominationalism.

Of course, there are vestiges of the British tradition in today's higher education in America. The flame burns in some good small private colleges and at least flickers in many others. It certainly burns brightly at many of the better women's colleges, especially those that have managed to keep their distinction as all-female institutions. And of course the tradition persists at the large private universities, like Harvard, Yale, Princeton, and Stanford, which do a somewhat better job of ministering to undergraduates than many large public universities. Harvard, for example, never went all the way down the path William James dreaded in 1903; it was never completely swamped by the graduate school ethos. Indeed, even

Charles W. Eliot, in determining to battle it out with Johns Hopkins for supremacy as a graduate school, never turned his back on the undergraduates, never dreamed of creating a "graduate only" institution. Eliot was always well aware that "Harvard College" was in a very important sense the anchor of the university, and his successor, A. Lawrence Lowell, president of Harvard from 1909 to 1933, devoted much of his time to girding up the British tradition at Harvard—developing the system of undergraduate living units or "houses" and fostering more personalized teaching through the agency of tutors and fellows.

Cynics may remark that places like Harvard or Yale are obliged to do more to meet the needs of undergraduate students than the state universities because of their frighteningly high tuitions, and because they continue to exude an elitist aroma, or because they are under constant pressure to do so by all-powerful donors and alumni groups. But in general an ever so slight gravitational pull exists toward the British style in those universities, even though many professors can't see why it is necessary. A few years ago a Princeton professor complained to me because his university had taken over the stately old Princeton Inn and turned it into an undergraduate "house" of the Harvard type, a place where freshmen and sophomores may be "coddled and wet-nursed," as he put it. The professors who object to such coddling naturally believe that freshmen and sophomores ought to be thrown live into the specialty disciplines just as a lobster is thrown into boiling water. Accordingly, it is not entirely clear how many distinguished full professors, even at Princeton, can be coerced to tread the halls of these coddling houses for undergraduates. One suspects that many "research' professors believe them to be sops to the parents, a perfunctory nod to the antiquated demands of gentility rather than bona fide expressions of an educational philosophy. But at least efforts are made. If a large freshwater university indulged in a similar essay in personalization, it would likely be little more than a show of smoke and mirrors.

The difficulties the modern American university has in maintaining even a weak semblance of the British tradition—and by this one does not necessarily mean a mirroring of the British social system but only a fundamental faith in the possibilities of an intimate community of learners—can be traced to a faulty notion of the educational process that has its roots in the poisoned soil of the

Ph.D.–graduate school model. In this model the main essence, sometimes the only pure essence, of the university is the expert, the compartmentalized subject matter specialist. It is along the leading edge of some field—the classics, nuclear physics, social psychology, foreign policy studies—where the principal work of the university is being done. If there is any community of learning worth paying attention to, it is that of subject matter specialists, all of whose loyalties are to those specialties, not to the institution that throws them a home.

This model of higher education brings us back to that old Germanic vision of a ladder of learning, with great sages at the top and minor thinkers, usually the undergraduates, far down below. Maybe the imagery of the ladder is not the best; perhaps we should think instead of some kind of gravity chute, much like that used to feed livestock. The subject matter experts at the top are in possession of rich storage lockers of feed, which they dump down the chute to the hungry and as yet poorly nourished neophytes. The young, callow undergraduates are passive receivers of information waiting to have their gaping maws filled from the pipeline above.

Needless to say, no view of education is more mistaken and destructive than this. Whether we use the analogy of the ladder or the feeding system—perhaps it all goes back in Western thought to Plato's analogy of the cave, or to some other conception of the "pure" or enlightened intellect—no view of education is satisfactory if it makes a division into givers and receivers of knowledge, into those who pour materials downward and those who are poured upon. Learning is never such a purely intellectual transaction; it grows out of a person's desires and interests; it is spawned in a pool of psychic energies. It may well be, and it often is, that the older, supposedly more mature scholars lack these psychic energies, that they are partly or completely burned out on the rich load of materials kept in the cerebrum. The beginner, on the other hand, may be ready and eager to step out on some new adventure; at this stage, one does not want to be a mere receiver of all the accumulated wisdom of the world and can do much better, in fact, without having huge bundles of information dumped on one's head.

Under an ideal set of circumstances in a university, the desires of the student and the desires of the teacher are bound together in a sympathetic union. Each must be a teacher in some sense; each must be a student in some sense. When this ideal union doesn't coalesce, you don't really have a transaction that is suitable for higher education. You have a stale and inept community, an impure essence of some kind.

And that, unfortunately, is what has come about in the American university over the last several generations. Under the trickle-down theory of education—where up above there is higher learning, and down below hungry mouths to be given morsels from the table— you get something about as far as imaginable from Mark Hopkins and his student at two ends of the log. Teacher and student are not sharing the feast, the British ideal in education. The student is getting the leavings from the table.

Consider an example of a more tangible nature. In the typical large university, undergraduate students are processed in large lecture classes or perhaps mechanically taught in smaller classes by teaching assistants who in the main are drudge-elves attempting to ape the behavior (and usually the worst traits) of their senior professor mentors. More often than not, the elementary or survey courses at a university are the worst the institution has to offer—when they should be the best. And the reason for this is clear. For the most part, professors, especially "star performers," will avoid teaching such courses as if they were a kind of penal servitude. And why should they not try to avoid them? This is lowly work, drudge work. Why should a professor of psychology, let us say, besmirch himself or herself teaching people who know nothing about Psychology? That job can be left to almost anybody on the premises. To be sure, it is understood that such courses are necessary; they may, after all, be responsible for creating an interest in the field of psychology and eventually gain converts to the field. On the other hand, all the other students, those who are there to fill gaps in their general education, are mere ciphers, mere blanks, sheep to be prodded over the fence. Little can be or is done for these sheep. They receive no answer to any of the really important questions they may ask, such as why study psychology at all, or how does psychology relate to their own lives or to the other things they are learning at the university? The professor will drop a small number of eggs in the students' basket, hoping against hope that students on their own will be able to get them to hatch.

In the large research universities of America, where undergraduate students are subjected to a series of routine lecture courses and seldom encounter the "star" professor, who is being saved for other things, the kind of personal bonding that is needed to give any life or spirit to education never develops. Notice I don't precisely say that students get nothing at all in the research university; they may indeed get a good education in spite of the system and because they have the leisure to read, enquire, and think, and if they use this leisure wisely they will surely educate themselves. In the end, though, they have not gotten the kind of education that is rooted in human relationships and for which they have paid money. At the hands of the university they have had various forms of pablum spoon-fed to them, and that is all.

If I have sounded terribly pessimistic about the quality of liberal education for undergraduates in the American university today, I ought to add that the picture for higher education as a whole is not as gloomy as it might seem on first glance, since there are still a large number of institutions, mostly the older small colleges, that nourish the liberal arts, that see education not as the function of experts but of general personal development and human interaction. In these institutions there are still many teachers, perhaps thousands of them, who live among and interact with students—yes, who actually *teach* them in the primoridial sense of the word. Such institutions, although often in perilous straits in our society, offer the brightest hopes and promises of higher education.

I should probably also not neglect another development of the years since World War II: the vast network of public community colleges, which also have their share of good teachers and, just as important, good teaching environments. To be sure, many of these institutions have had to accept the heavy burden of vocational education—providing specialized training for radiologic technicians, dental hygienists, and data processors, some of it on a rudimentary plane. On the other hand, the majority of students attending these institutions are pleased with them, seem at home there, whereas the undergraduate students at some nearby research university often feel like outsiders.

As the community college movement spread, it received a certain amount of criticism from higher intellectual circles. These colleges were said to be low-voltage institutions, "high schools with ash trays," it was jokingly said. Many feared that undergraduates who spent time there might not be prepared to integrate into four-year colleges if they chose to do so. But experience has shown that such is not the case. As a longtime teacher at a state university I found that I could not easily make a qualitative distinction between students who had spent their first two years at the university and those who had come from community colleges, although I think if I had to choose from my position in the humanities, I probably would give a slight edge to those who began at community colleges. Certainly I would give a wide edge to those who had transferred from private four-year colleges.

Not too long ago I had an opportunity to talk to a professor emeritus from the University of Illinois who, upon setting foot in the green pastures of retirement, decided to take some courses in art at a nearby community college. I asked how he was enjoying himself. He told me he was thrilled with the experience—he had taken courses in painting and pot-making—and even assured me that the teaching was much better there than at his own university. What was more important, everybody seemed to be enjoying things over there. There was "more whistling in the corridors"; students seemed to have bright, happy looks on their faces, not the crabbed, frozen, or petrified look of so many at the university. It was great, my friend observed, to get away from the snobbish "big wheels" at the university, all plugging away at some contrived, self-serving game. There was a sense of fresh industry at the community college; everybody was pulling on the same oar. It was just a tincture of the British style in education, however modest and unassuming.

Interestingly enough, a century ago the large state universities (of course, they were not very large then) gave pretty much the same face to the world that the community college does today. There was a triumphant sense of community. There were all these new un-discovered dimensions to education, and they were exciting, refreshing. There was co-education, there was this idea of education for all social strata; there was this idea of service to society. All participants, teachers and students alike, felt as if they were moving together toward some shared goal. Those were the reasons for the spontaneous feelings of affection for these institutions, emotions that lingered even after the schools grew large, sodden, and unwieldy.

Back in 1870, twenty-six-year-old Nathan Herman Ricker arrived at the University of Illinois with experience as a master craftsman. He had $750 in savings and wanted to take a course in architecture, which was listed in the catalog but in fact didn't exist. He arrived at midnight one cold January day and slept on the dormitory floor. The next day the president (then regent) of the university, John Milton Gregory, arranged for Ricker to work with a civil engineering professor who might know something about architecture. In time this very able student was put in charge of the carpentry shop in the engineering college. Some time after, Gregory induced the board of trustees to offer a scholarship to Ricker for the study of architecture at the Bauakademie in Berlin, after which the young man returned to the university to become head of the Department of Architecture.

That, you see, was adventure. That is what for a while the new American style of higher education was all about—the mutual discovery of talents, interests, and desires. Alas, there is little room for adventure (for either teachers or students) in the huge, atherosclerotic universities of today. Today one can find one's talents and desires only by threading one's way through the educational machinery, by learning how to deal with hidebound bureaucracies, by shifting through deadweight or worn-out curricula, by learning to imitate the sounds and the higher mumblings of one's betters and ape the views of the current tribalistic intellectual fads.

William James was clearly right about the dangers of developing a Mandarin class within the American university. The university Mandarin wants to keep all his wealth for himself. Furthermore, the Mandarin element is unsavory in the land of a democratic people; it leads to a kind of deadness of spirit. This is what has happened to the large, overreaching university of today. That original sense of adventure has been lost. Human relations between teacher and student have become hardened and sluggish; youthful spontaneity is suppressed. Perfunctory handing down of information is antithetical to the spirit of higher education, which really survives only in an environment of free exchange of ideas and belief that each individual is attempting to establish a body of knowledge that is useful to him, that shapes and informs her own peculiar intellectual style. The university instead has become a place of learning and standardized habits of thought, making higher education dismal, and perhaps also somewhat dangerous.

Part II

Passion Denied: The Professor and the System

6

Professors Under Fire

I'VE ALREADY SAID something about the steady stream of books and articles critical of higher education that have flooded the market in the last few years. It may seem surprising to find that these books not only take aim at the mission or value of the university as an institution, but that most of them have also complained vigorously about the academic style, the academic way of life, most particularly the professor's way of life or quality of mind. Once upon a time, in the age of the freewheeling boards of control, or in the grim interlude of the McCarthy witch-hunts, the usually expressed fear was that if the university had enemies, they were on the outside. The foes were the Huns and Vandals beyond the gates of academe. Inside the ivied walls the lamp of disinterested learning burned with a steady and unquenchable flame. Or so it was thought. Now, however, there has been a rising tide of anxiety about some of the university's own—the professors!

The reading public was given a rude shock in 1987 when Allan Bloom's book *The Closing of the American Mind* waged a frontal attack on the professorate of the last several generations. To be sure, Bloom's book made a sweeping analysis of a great many tears and fissures in American culture—everything from sexual permissiveness, to television, to the failure of our original constitutional values, to rock music, to student lifestyles, to all manner of intellectual

47

fancies and quackeries—but its bitterest broadsides were saved for the custodians of university education. For Bloom, the professors had been guilty of abandoning liberal education because it is too much of a burden to administer; they had trashed the traditional curriculum without having anything better to put in its place; they had grasped wildly about, seizing upon perverse intellectual fads and imports; they had turned inward to their specialties and abandoned the general culture and the ills of American democracy. The professors don't really care about what happens to the university as a whole, said Bloom. Accordingly, here you have these great universities, richly—almost disgustingly—well endowed, which can split an atom, or send people to the moon, or find a cure for mysterious diseases, yet "cannot generate a modest program of general education for undergraduates." Professors are so busy doing supposedly "big" things that they don't have time for the really important little things such as educating the young.

A few years later the public found the heat being turned up quite a few degrees in another book, *Prof Scam*, by a journalist named Charles J. Sykes. Sykes's book, subtitled "Professors and the Demise of Higher Education," indulges in a bit of overkill, and it certainly makes a mistake in gathering all the blame around professors when in fact Bloom, and other recent critics of higher education, have been more nearly right in seeing the problems of the colleges as growing from a multitude of causes—mass public education, difficulties surrounding the fragmentation and cheapening of knowledge, a weakening of the shared culture. Nonetheless, Sykes's harsh indictment of professors is not altogether misplaced, even when expressed in the manner of a muckraker.

The professors, says Sykes, have a lot to answer for. They are "overpaid, grotesquely underworked," and the architects of a vast empire of waste. They avoid their teaching functions and to the typical undergraduate are "unapproachable, uncommunicative and unavailable." They emphasize research over teaching, and whenever possible, they turn teaching chores over to an underpaid and overworked academic underclass. They issue thousands of articles and books written in "stupefying and inscrutable jargon," which masks the vacuous and trivial nature of much of their research. In a shameful lust to advance their academic careers they have filled libraries with "masses of unread, unreadable and worthless pablum."

American universities have largely been factories for "junkthink," their professors devoted to woolly-headed theorizing that is of virtually no value to the general population. Furthermore, they have twisted the ideals of academic freedom so as to stamp out original thinkers and nonconformists, those who don't fit any of the approved molds. In doing these things they are essentially accountable to no one. So says Sykes.

Well, no doubt there is some truth in these allegations. Of course, many of these charges have been repeated over and over again in only slightly less indignant language; some have been around as long as there have been universities. From the perspective of the outsider—especially, I suppose, the brisk, pencil-behind-the-ear newspaperman—the occupation of "intellectual" or "thinker" will probably always be an object of scorn, and charges to this effect, even without evidence to support them (and Sykes surely has plenty of evidence), will probably continue to be made by a great many Americans outside the university.

The professor, we might almost say, has always been a rather uncharacteristic and perhaps comical figure in American folklore; in a society that places so much emphasis on success and productivity, or at least the hype that surrounds them, it has always been easy to see the professor as an idler. At any university in the country, the building janitor or physical plant electrician regards the professor, sitting comfortably in an office, puffing on his pipe, or shuffling her books and papers, as an unproductive and leechlike member of society. And most people outside the academic profession—the hard-driving used-car salesperson or securities dealer—would probably agree with Sykes's judgment that the professor is underworked. The professor does not seem to be a "doer."

On the other hand, as a person who has been on intimate terms with professors for the better part of a lifetime, I have never found this way of putting things very convincing. I have never been drawn to the conclusion that professors are underworked. They are, in fact, full of both drive and activity—a good deal of it misplaced and trivial, perhaps, but I think it is a mistake to assume that the professor's hours are filled with inactivity and idleness. It might in fact be better if professors had less to do, if they had more time for speculation and flights of fancy. No, professors keep busy; the problem is not exactly lack of effort; it is a matter of the direction of effort. Critics like Sykes might have been more precise in pointing out that professors spend an inordinate amount of time spinning their wheels (and wheel-spinning requires effort, let there be no doubt about that), exhausting themselves with the trivialities of academic politics, of hewing the party line of their specialty, of attending committees "for the sifting of sawdust into" (as Thorstein Veblen so aptly put it), of building bridges, of cultivating friends and isolating enemies, of giving manufactured evidence of scholarly productivity that often just isn't there. In spite of the views of the college janitor or the bustling journalist, professors are not freed from the American work ethic. They are, if anything, shackled to it.

So it goes with some of the other charges commonly raised against them. It is said that they have too much freedom, too much license, and thus can run roughshod over students, inferior colleagues, those with unfamiliar or unpopular ideas. The truth is more likely that professors have not too much license but too little. They themselves have not created the academic hierarchy, the rigidities of professionalism, the safe and trivial bromides of a special discipline; rather they are lashed to those inevitabilities like a miscreant boatswain lashed to the mizzenmast in a driving rain, and with little more freedom of action. They do not create storms; they are constantly looking for ways to avoid them. And that invariably requires painful labor.

The professors' alleged pedantry and jargon-laden language, their love of the minuscule, of tiny little packages of abstruse learning, is nothing new to report, although it is certainly worth saying again. The vision of the woolgathering and pettifogging professor does not belong to the United States alone but has been around as long as there have been professors. In all popular mythologies professors, almost by definition, are people who surrender to materials they regard as bigger and more important than themselves; they tend to be, as H. L. Mencken once put it, characters of "trivial and unromantic achievement." The professor portrayed in the movies or the funny papers is often a pinched and lackluster man who when young doesn't get the girl and who when old evokes the image of a doddering old fool.

Undoubtedly there has always been an antipathy between the scholarly mind and the mind of vigorous imagination—poets, bawds, troubadours, drunken metaphysicians, painters, and all those unfathomable damage to these institutions. In Veblen's day the university factory, often dictatorially run by men of business or their sycophantic deans and chancellors, had the effect of making the professor a hireling, an employee, a timid individual, living in an environment of "quietism, caution, compromise, collusion and chicane." In those days the professor's environment was not one of freedom at all. To be sure, in our time, with tenure nearly universal, with plutocrats and boards of trustees removed from active control of academic life and no longer harassing professors who write about monopoly or the beef trust, the restraints upon freedom are clouded or unfathomable, but in essence they are just as severe and hobbling to the professor as they were early in the century. The university is still very much circumscribed in its activities by the funding provided by foundations and governmental agencies. And of course research universities continue to be dominated by the compulsion to produce, to turn out end-products, an urging forced upon them by the business ethos.

Books like Veblen's magnificent jeremiad or Upton Sinclair's vituperative 1922 tract *The Goose-Step* stressed the vulnerability of the professor to the prevailing ideological views of the business culture, or in some cases the forces of religious piety. In many universities at that time professors were subject to summary discharge; more typically they would be let out under vaguely genteel but inscrutable circumstances. Academic salaries were paltry and pensions often nonexistent, so that the ability to survive and keep one's family intact meant exactly what Veblen suggested: keeping oneself hidden, playing discreet politics, and uttering no ideas that would give offense to the power structure. When standing in the open jaw of a monster it is best to remain silent. Caution, restraint, and conformity are the best policies.

The Goose-Step portrays the professor as being forced to march in lockstep to the drums of the "hell hounds of plutocracy." To be sure, much of Sinclair's socialistic rhetoric seems heavy-handed and archaic today, but he provided no small amount of evidence that professors survive only when they "go along" and make no attempt to stand against the prevailing winds. Their goal was then, as it is now, to be as innocuous and standardized as possible. (Of course, many professors believe themselves to be nonconformists and freethinkers; they may howl against the establishment or against the

who see life in color. Scott Fitzgerald said that writers write for th
young of their own generation, for the critics of the next generatior
and for the schoolmasters of all the generations thereafter. Rea
writers or poets have always been outsiders in the university
although in some instances they may hang around for a bit of th
money. Generally the poet must be a solitary and not an institutional
figure. The deliciously antisocial rapscallion François Villon used
the medieval University of Paris as a good place to hide out, and
other writers have done so since. Occasionally the university has
been a suitable oasis for a community of merrymakers. On the
whole, though, the dividing line between poet and scholar, or
between artist and thinker, is the one so well expressed by William
Butler Yeats in his poem "The Scholars":

> Bald heads forgetful of their sins,
> Old, learned, respectable bald heads
> Edit and annotate the lines
> That young men, tossing on their beds,
> Rhymed out in love's despair
> To flatter beauty's ignorant ear.
>
> All shuffle there, all cough in ink;
> All wear the carpet with their shoes;
> All think what other people think;
> All know the man their neighbor knows.
> Lord, what would they say
> Did their Catullus walk that way?

So no, the complaints made against the scholar, the digger, the
searcher, are hardly new; they have been around as long as the species
has flourished. On the other hand, the presence of enormous
numbers of such individuals in gargantuan and powerful institutions of public learning, and a widespread belief that the scholar is
somehow identical with "man thinking," make the recently renewed
suspicion of the species an unsettling one.

The most irritating concerns about the professor and about
academic life continue to be those enunciated by Veblen in *The
Higher Learning in America*. At the heart of the Veblen's book is the
charge that the creation of universities in the image of a business, or
perhaps a factory turning out stereotyped products, has done

state of the nation, but only when the other professors around them are howling the same tune.)

A good part of Sinclair's book contained personal observations of Columbia University, where he had been a graduate student in the first few years of the century. Columbia was then, as it is now, one of the premier institutions in the land, although Sinclair seemed to find in it always a mood of fear and grim competition. In the few years that he was at Columbia, Sinclair wrote six novels—this was, in fact, not the beginning of his incredibly productive literary career, since he had already put himself through the City College of New York by writing dime novels. He was a close watcher of the campus scene at Columbia and continued to be so for several decades. He was especially fascinated by the intrigues of the university's president, the social-climbing Nicholas Murray Butler, whom Sinclair called Nicholas Miraculous. Butler was an empire builder, an erector of buildings, and very successful at it, like so many university presidents of that day. Most of his success, according to Sinclair, was due to his ability to butter up well-heeled benefactors like superbanker J. P. Morgan.

In his student days, however, Sinclair discovered that all of his best teachers—people of bold imagination and fierce independence of thought—were eventually fired or gently eased aside. Only the pedants and sly conformists survived. Among the teachers at Columbia who impressed Sinclair were George Edward Woodberry, writer, critic, poet, and professor of comparative literature, and Edward Macdowell, music professor and composer. Both were inspiring teachers and men of the first rank in their respective professions. (Macdowell is now universally accepted as one of our greatest American composers.) Both were pushed out. Sinclair was equally impressed by his professor of Latin, Harry Thurston Peck, but Peck, too, was canned and eventually committed suicide. "It was a very peculiar thing," observed Sinclair; "every single man who had anything worth-while to teach me was forced out of Columbia University in some manner or other. The ones that stayed were the dull ones, or the worldly and cunning ones."

President Butler got himself into a particularly nasty scrape with a number of his best-known professors during the World War I period. Among the celebrated professors whose leaving resulted in a public relations disgrace for Columbia was historian Charles A. Beard. But

by this time the American Association of University Professors had
been founded, and imperious presidents like Butler were beginning
to have their wings clipped. In Sinclair's opinion, however, most of
the really strong professors at Columbia had already departed. Some
great stars may have remained, but in Sinclair's mind they were men
who managed to elude all entanglements with administration, like
John Dewey, or who glittered in some other firmament, like the
man-about-town drama critic Brander Matthews.

What you then had at Columbia, according to Sinclair, "is a host
of inferior men, dwelling as one phrased it to me, in 'a twilight zone
of mediocrity'; dull pedants, raking over dust heaps of learning and
occupying their minds with petty problems of administration. They
have full power to decide whether Greek shall be given in nine
courses or nine and one-half, also whether it shall count for four
credits or four and a quarter. 'And we love that,' said one to me with
a bitter sneer."

With the passage of time, the vulnerability and terrifying vocational exposure of the professor began to fade. Procedures of tenure
came upon the scene, as did pension systems, appeal procedures, and
the many safeguards that mark the modern university and seem to
make it, at least on the surface, a secure place to spend a lifetime. The
interlocking directors and satrap presidents who so annoyed Veblen
and Sinclair might still be able to roar, but they would mostly have to
do so in their own cages. Similarly, the professor's livelihood and
prestige would improve greatly over the next four or five decades.
With the launch of the Sputnik, a mere forty years after the
appearance of Veblen's diatribe on professorial servitude, it seemed
that Americans were at last going to award the professor a place in
the sun. The specialist or expert was now to be revered and, what
was immediately more important, rewarded handsomely in gold
coin. When the Sputnik thrust into the stratosphere in 1958, very
few American professors were making ten thousand dollars a year;
within a scant few years that would be a *low* beginning salary.
Professors, it seemed, no longer needed to hide from the sunlight;
they gloried in it.

But had their lot really improved? And what is more important,
had they really become more valuable to the university, or to the
young who were placed in their charge, or to society at large? Most of
the recent books dealing with higher education have concluded in

the negative. There is reason to suspect, first of all, that security and affluence (often elusive but at least promised) have made the academic life more vulnerable than ever to the demands for conformity, uniformity, and standardized patterns of thought. At one time, certainly through most of the nineteenth century, the professor was a person of some Olympian detachment, even if not well paid. But the conditions that brought prosperity have also made academics more timid and wary of upsetting any apple carts. They may seem to stand up tall against the abuses of politicians or business leaders, or anything else from Wall Street to popular culture, but only after their methods of doing so have been sanitized by the leaders of the flock.

The distinguished American historian Richard Hofstadter, in his book *Anti-Intellectualism in American Life*, pointed out as early as the 1950s that it wasn't only the professors among the American intelligentsia but intellectuals everywhere who had been standardized, as they became comfortable and moved into positions of respect in the media, in government, in the mainstream of society.

> One hears more and more that the intellectual who has won a measure of freedom and opportunity, and a new access to influence, is thereby subtly corrupted; that having won recognition, he has lost his independence, even his identity as an individual....He becomes comfortable, perhaps even moderately prosperous as he takes a position in a university or in government, or working for the mass media, but he then tailors himself to the requirements of those institutions. He loses that precious tincture of rage so necessary to first-rate creativity in a writer, that capacity for negation and rebellion that is necessary to the candid social critic, that initiative and independence of aim required for distinguished work in science....We live in an age in which the avant-garde itself has been institutionalized and deprived of its old stimulus of a stubborn and insensate opposition.

The judgment that the academic intellectual has "tailor[ed] himself to the requirements of those institutions" refers not to the colleges and universities as collections of human beings, but rather to the standards and proprieties of the profession. This has been the route by which the professor has been "institutionalized." In the twentieth century the university intellectual has taken on the role of "expert," and by this means alone he or she acquires a reputation—not mainly by being on the faculty at Harvard or Berkeley or Slippery Rock. Professors are accordingly chased by a new set of hobgoblins. No longer under the threat of banishment by the beef trust or the village curate, they are instead harried, kept firmly in line, by their standing among their peers, who act in the name of remote higher administrations to enforce productivity of a new and different kind: publication, popular teaching, grant-getting, public service, endless committee work, or any number of other prescribed labors of a modern Hercules.

The demands placed on college professors in the last half of the twentieth century are every bit as cruel and relentless as those placed upon them at the turn of the century by Upton Sinclair's toadying presidents and interlocking boards of trustees. They make today's professor every bit as hobbled by lockstep movements as the professor of yore. The particular objects of Sinclair's attack have vanished, but his central concern is still applicable. Universities tend to make the professor as timid and unadventurous as ever. To the impartial observer, the professor's belief that he or she is now free of the constraints of the business ethos must seem somewhat comical. The professor's role in the American university was long ago shaped in the corporate mold. The academic ladder and system of promotions and intrigues is merely a cartoonlike version of the corporate lifestyle, dressed up (or down) with the comfy clothes of collegiality.

The mechanism that has renewed and continued the professor's servitude, and accounts for so many of the recent complaints about evasion of teaching or refusal to make a commitment to the larger issues of education (i.e., anything beyond his or her "specialty"), has been created, as it is not hard to see, by the spreading of the long tentacles of the Ph.D. octopus. The corporate ladder is replaced by a ladder of supposed scholarly productivity. The psychology professor or the history professor is not really concerned about learning in general, or what goes on in the minds or dormitory rooms of undergraduates, but only with what goes on in the psychology or history journals, or the latest esoteric rumblings at the meetings of the professional societies. This is especially true in the research institutions, although the same impetus is often felt in the small liberal arts college.

The field of one's Ph.D.—nay, not only the broader field, but the narrow area of emphasis—becomes the yoke the professor must wear for a lifetime. The new Ph.D. in psychology is invariably hired not only because of that degree but because of expertise in "physiological psychology" or "behavior dynamics." There will never be the chance (at least not in the large university) to change back to social psychology or counseling; ninety-nine times out of a hundred a life's commitment rides on one's Ph.D. thesis. That is where one gets one's start, and that is one's life sentence. Even though at one time the Ph.D. degree was supposed to signify only the ability to carry on research in *any* field, a professor of physiological psychology, shall we say, who decides to write a book on musicology or a life of Winston Churchill will be branded as a pariah. Engaging in such activities before receiving tenure results in being cashiered as quickly as a drunken paymaster; becoming involved in such vagaries after receiving tenure sends one to the bottom of the salary scale and requires moonlighting if one wants to send the children to college. Such antic behavior seldom develops, of course. The professor, not desiring the ostracism of colleagues, will invariably stay handcuffed to the lathe he or she chose as a graduate student.

It is important to keep in mind, though, that the charge made by a number of recent critics that the professor who has entered the tenured garden may sit back and contemplate it while lesser beings do the work is an illusion. The professors' problem is not that there is little to do, or that they may now relax while others do everything for them; the problem rather is that each is tied to a narrowly defined patch of ground and must use the same tools and the same maneuvers over and over again. It is these qualities, too, rather than bad will, or indifference to teaching, that are most likely to make them unsuitable companions for the young. The young possess suppleness of movement and seek freedom to romp. The professors have been forced to give up their suppleness, their freedom to move around the intellectual world. Of course, they frequently believe themselves to be free and playful—one can thumb one's nose at politicians or corporations, or indeed any group-selected targets of academic abuse; the only thing one is not at liberty to scorn is the most important thing of all, one's own workbench, to which one's wrist is always tied.

In recent decades the domination of professors by their specialty field has presented a clear and obvious threat to the university for an important reason that often goes unnoticed. If the professor is devoted mainly to his or her specialty, concern for any particular institution is greatly diminished. In their creative years, many professors do a cakewalk from one institution to another, usually with the justification that they are "bettering" themselves professionally. This is especially supposed to be true of the best, and therefore most competitive, talent, the so-called stars. Roving professors, seeking to better their salary and professional reputation, do not feel tied to the destiny of any specific institution and its highly individual problems. It you are at Michigan and get a better offer at Stanford, you pull up stakes and go. Your commitment to Michigan has been weak and provisional all along, your ties there dependent wholly on what your department could do for you there. Your actual interest in the institution of the University of Michigan—its history, its personality, its traditions, its student body—has been marginal at best. You have formed there only a weak notion of an intellectual community; in fact, you probably have never even contemplated what kind of meaning the words "a community of learning" might have. All that enters your mind is clusters and concatenations of specialties.

For this reason the critics of higher education have been correct in their condemnation of the professor as neglecting the primal functions of education. Education means the acceptance of highly personal transactions and interactions. But this should not be simply interpreted to mean that professors neglect the art of teaching or fail to make themselves popular with undergraduates—the only things university administrators can think about whenever this complaint is raised. Administrators invariably make spectacular and showy attempts to find out which teachers are popular with students, and they probably do find out, but such discoveries—or rewards emanating from them—have virtually no effect on the quality of teaching. The fundamental problem in the teacher-student transaction is that it exists in the wrong sort of environment, the wrong sort of community. The mandate that calls for the "expert" or the subject matter specialist results in a place more like a think tank or research center than what has historically been known as a university. The ideal of the university is, or was in the past, a place where students and teachers are rowing the same boat, not different boats; a place where they share intellectual concerns. As university teachers, we need to know what sorts of things our students should be studying, not only in *our* course, but everywhere else. We should know who our students are and understand their aspirations. We should be ministering to our students whether or not we see them as potential candidates for our specialty.

Similarly, students must be willing and anxious to profit by the knowledge of their professors (yes, even including expert knowledge, since there is nothing intrinsically wrong with expert knowledge, only with the misapplication of it). Students should be hoping for and expecting and insisting on more than a mere dumping of information from the professor. They should expect a dialogue and some kind of human encounter. Perhaps this means that students will also have to do more than they have in recent years to prepare themselves and stand open to the things the university has to offer. They bear some of the responsibility themselves for being merely processed. It may mean that under ideal circumstances they will have to know more and read more than they have, and that each will promise himself or herself to be more than a mere passive receiver of information, a role that has too easily satisfied both teachers and students in recent years. Above all, use of one's college education as merely a route to professional advancement is a distorted ideal for the student's, just as is devotion to narrow professionalism for the professor.

The traditional college education will work only if the teacher and professor are at some point at least talking the same language, and talking to one another. In our present system of higher education, most especially in the research-driven university, the professors— and the largest share of the blame must fall on them, since they are supposedly more mature and more knowledgeable—are responsible for finding ways to speak to their students and form a personal bond with them. In recent years professors have spent far too much time talking to restricted groups of co-specialists and engaging in the activities of allegedly high-powered coteries. This has not made them more highly productive, the perpetual excuse for intellectual activity being marshaled along specialty lines; rather it has made them more distant from the students they are called upon to teach.

Of serious concern to society at large, the inward-turning habits and specialized discourse of professors have had the effect of separating the academic community from the social life that we all have to share.

7

How Professors Weaken the Bonds to the Shared Culture

ONE OF THE RECURRING questions posed by the existence of universities is how such institutions are related to the cultural mainstream of the nation, how they fit into the fabric of ordinary life. By its very nature the university and the people in it are set off from the workaday world; professors and teachers are esteemed, at least in part, because of their traditional independence and isolation from the wider community. We don't really want the members of a university community to be at the beck and call of outsiders. For this reason, the never-ending urge to keep colleges and universities independent of church or clergy, of state, or of banks and corporations has always been a laudable and healthy one. We want our thinkers, scholars, scientists, and intellectuals to be free to work independently and to fulfill their own aims and desires, even if these are evanescent, indistinct, or not immediately profitable.

On the other hand, the independence that is provided to the university, the wide latitude that is offered to the professor to discover, invent, and explore, must somehow be balanced by the broader needs of society and the cultural life of the nation. The university needs to be independent of society but also responsible to it—responsible not so much in the way a factory or retail outlet is

61

accountable to stockholders, but in the sense that, for all its separation from daily life, the university and its members should have their feet firmly planted on the native soil. In a democracy especially, the university must be responsible to the society it serves. This does not mean that it should jump to every shout heard in the marketplace or respond to every popular rumble. It does not mean that a nation's intelligentsia should "do what the people want." A certain stubborn resistance to the popular will should always be an essential trait of the spirit of learning. On the other hand, every university in a democratic society has a moral obligation to integrate itself with the cultural mainstream of the nation. While set apart from the people, it must somehow also share the metabolism of the whole society. A nation is healthiest when its intellectuals are closely bound to the people as a whole and contribute importantly to society.

A common complaint about professors over the last several decades is that they are aloof and unresponsive to the demands and needs of students. Somewhat less frequently heard, but perhaps just as troubling, is the complaint that the professors are not responsive to the needs of the nation and the culture around them; that they give all their allegiance to the guild, to the demands of a specialized calling, and not enough to the needs of the rest of us. Professors, it is alleged, spend too much time talking to other professors, co-experts, and not enough time meeting a wider public. When they do create bonds of communication, it is only through journals or books of limited or special appeal, using language that is esoteric or even willfully abstruse. Professors of our time seldom seem to want to talk to the general public, let alone what is sometimes jocularly referred to as "the man on the street"; rather they want selfishly to horde a pile of specialized learning for those who speak their own language. Such an attitude is not a healthy one in a democratic nation.

The desire to mumble in "tongues" is one of the unfortunate byproducts of what William James referred to as the Mandarin disease. It is a trait that grows with the Ph.D. mentality—the notion that because scholars have worked their way through all the brutal procedures and secret rituals of the guild, they have somehow entered a world *above* that of ordinary mortals and should not consider it their main business to communicate with them. They should instead limit their communication to those who are similarly anointed and wear the same regalia. To be sure, the intellectuals or "experts" usually allege that their superior learning will somehow fall out, or sprinkle down, on everybody else in due course. But those who have been critical of our universities in recent years have questioned this fallout or "trickle-down" theory of learning. If learning is not a shared property, if it does not immediately touch the majority of people in society in ways that are readily intelligible, there is good reason to believe that it will never do so in the future.

A number of cultural critics and historians have suggested that one of the most pernicious traits of today's universities is that academics have largely removed themselves from issues of large public import, absented themselves from the cultural mainstream, abdicated responsibility for forging any bridge to society as a whole. This is an especially serious charge when made against the humanist, who, above all others, bears the responsibility for doing precisely that: building bridges between people, keeping alive the flame of learning all human beings share.

The inability of university intellectuals to share what they have, and to build bridges, was expressed forcefully in a recent book entitled *The Last Intellectuals; American Culture in the Age of Academe*, by Russell Jacoby. Jacoby's principal point is that at one time in America we were richly provided with "public intellectuals," individuals who aspired through their writing and thinking to make some kind of impact on society at large. They wrote good clear English, not gobbledygook; they attempted to reach out to their fellow citizens in intelligent but not specialized publications—magazines such as *The Atlantic Monthly, Harper's, The New York Review of Books, The New Yorker*, and *Commentary*. Among those Jacoby mentions as filling this role in recent decades are people as diverse as Lewis Mumford, Edmund Wilson, Max Eastman, Dwight Macdonald, Lionel Trilling, John Kenneth Galbraith, Arthur Schlesinger, Jr., Sidney Hook, and Malcolm Cowley. A great many others of a slightly earlier era also come quickly to mind—H. L. Mencken, Walter Lippmann, Upton Sinclair, Charles Beard, Henry Adams, John Jay Chapman, Van Wyck Brooks, Herbert Croly—all of whom go back to a strong "public letters" tradition that ran throughout the nineteenth century.

Looking around at his own generation, Jacoby was shocked to

find that few thinkers of this kind are still prominent in the life of the nation and few new ones are coming along. Most independent people of letters have died; some have lost their voice or a suitable forum for their ideas. Other recent independent intellectuals—one thinks perhaps of Tom Wolfe—have allied themselves mostly with the mass media or with the world of entertainment. So unfortunately there are few today who match the daring, erudition, audacity, or imagination of our older public intellectuals.

Jacoby blames this decline of the "general intellectual" on two things: the overweening power of the university with its tendency toward specialization, and the decline of the center city as a congenial and stimulating place to live and work. The first of these two points has had plenty of airing in recent years. Intellectuals who want to achieve success within the groves of academe can do so only in one way—by limiting themselves strictly to the demands and concerns of their specialty, their colleagues, and journals and publications directed to limited audiences. A professor who aspires to write for the *Atlantic* or *The New Yorker* risks being called a lightweight or shallow populizer by colleagues; from my own experience I know this to be true. An economist of my acquaintance assured me that John Kenneth Galbraith could not be a real economist (even though he was called such at Harvard University) since he appeared on television and wrote for the public prints! No economist worthy of the name would attempt to utter ideas that could be understood by the public at large.

Jacoby's other point, however, is more novel and quite thought-provoking. The professor of recent years, apparently, has sought out an academic career because it provides a comfortable, well-paid, middle-class environment with few risks and responsibilities. There is no need to hobnob with distant intellectuals within the confines of the trivial games of academic politics—certainly not for brisk dialogue and true intelligent competition. In days gone by, so much of the intellectual life of the nation (or any of the earlier nations of history) was carried on in the cosmopolitan and even bohemian quarters of cities, usually by hungry, shabbily dressed, but eager and vibrant partisans. The retreat from this older, "bohemian" way of developing and sharing ideas has a great deal to do, says Jacoby, with the decline of general culture and the loss of shared idioms of civilization.

Back in the 1920s, much of the intellectual life of the nation was centered in places like New York—especially in Greenwich Village, or perhaps the magazine offices or city rooms of the great metropolitan dailies. Here people were forced to put their ideas and their personalities on the line, and they wrote for each other. Even if perforce they wrote to *limited* audiences, they were also *real* audiences, not the purely hypothetical audiences of academic journals or "little, little" magazines, which are fated to repose, mostly unread, in the rear of the library's storage stacks. Then, intellectuals with authority had to learn to speak the common idiom because they rubbed up against one another. They took delight in getting on one another's nerves, in forcing one another into constructive combat. It is Jacoby's opinion that those who have forsaken city precincts and the uncertainties of bohemia for the comfortable and totally middle-class haven of the universities seldom develop an interest in reaching the general public, never engage in the rough-and-tumble part of the intellectual life.

There is, interestingly, a good deal of historical precedent for Jacoby's belief; we hardly need to limit our discussion to the twentieth century. In ancient Athens, Socrates expressed a very similar notion. In several of Plato's dialogues, Socrates, a singularly combative philosopher of savage wit who liked nothing better than to drag staid citizens into an argument while they were on their way to market, often expressed the opinion that he couldn't bear to live beyond the gates of Athens. Outside of them, he said, there was little intellectual challenge, no qualified wits with whom he could banter. In the pasture one grows pastoral, self-satisfied, complacent, perhaps bovine. Above all, *people* are missing. To be sure, the modern university might conceivably be the very sort of place that Socrates yearned for—walled off, modest-sized cities where strong minds can congregate. In fact they tend to become places where only discussion of a certain kind goes on. Yes, there is dialogue, but only of a standardized and presanctified type, carried on only among people who have agreed to keep to a specified wavelength, who don't want their apple carts and sacred idols upset by nonconformists and eccentric partisans.

Jacoby, it should be added, admits to being an old-style, left-leaning intellectual, and he professes to deplore the almost total lack of living, breathing, knock-'em-dead Marxists of the type that flourished, say, in the ping-pong rooms at the City College of New York back in the 1930s. There are still Marxists today, he observes, but they have mostly retreated to the universities, where they reside within tiny and impotent cells and communicate only in jargon. That is to say, they speak and write in specialized languages that are deadly, boring, and inaccessible, and, what is more important, they disdain to submit any of their ideas for general public consideration. Unlike the older disputatious and high-spirited Marxists of the thirties, they feast on a weak gruel of dead abstractions occasionally seasoned with obscure pomposities. The most telling indictment of the academic Marxists of today is that the public at large never hears anything about them, nor are university administrators and boards of trustees alarmed by them. They are much too somnolent and obscure to bother about. They have crusades, but only among themselves.

Perhaps it is not easy to pass judgment on Jacoby's belief that the decline of literacy and general culture in our society corresponds to the removal of intellectuals from cities and their resettlement in a sheltered and highly standardized university glade. Doubtless a number of factors are involved in this decline. But yes, considerable damage has been done to our shared intellectual world by the situation that has developed mostly since World War II: The idea of the "intellectual" has been primarily identified with that of the "expert" or "specialist," and experts are not expected to communicate with nonexperts and are even penalized for doing so.

The dangerous isolation of the academic class, the development of the Mandarin specialist, has not been healthy for society and for the university itself, which ideally needs to be a microcosm of society. It is not healthy because it results in the fragmentation of learning, and fragmentation means the failure to provide bridges of communication. A free people and an enlightened people need to build links between the various segments of the intellectual life, not set up barriers between them.

The new intellectual Mandarins, who have mostly appeared over the past forty years, have sought special privileges for themselves, privileges that really shouldn't pass muster in a free society; they not only hope to remove themselves from the mainstream and refuse to communicate their ideas in ways that mean something to the rest of us, but they also refuse to answer for this failure to communicate. Worse, many have set themselves up as active crusaders against the general culture—a crusade that is probably bound not to succeed in the long run, because the partisans have neither the fire nor the verse nor the creativity to succeed. Still, in the university setting, always so open to easy manipulation, they have done and continue to do a great deal of harm. Let us look at who they are and how they operate.

8

The New Druids and the Poisoning of the Humanities

THE CRITICS who have recently been diagnosing the ills of the university seem to be in almost universal agreement that it is the teachers of the humanities above all others who have been most perverse in forsaking the cause of higher education and the liberal arts. It is the humanists, the very teachers of literature, history, and philosophy, who have most shamelessly abandoned the traditional core of learning. It is these same individuals—long accepted as the custodians of books and ideas, long trusted as the keepers of the flame of erudition—who have most eagerly and carelessly fallen for all the cheap-tinsel intellectual fads that have come down the road, have glutted themselves on the latest manifestations of junkthink, have written the most bloated and bombastic academic prose. At one time it was the humanist who was charged with keeping the culture intact, but today some of the most allegedly prestigious intellectuals in the arts are the most clannish, introspective, and obscurantist in the academic zoological garden. Talk about the Mandarins—here one can find Mandarism in its most chilling forms, indeed almost a kind of intellectual solipsism, a belief that in the intellectual kingdom only oneself and a few other self-anointed individuals are capable of possessing and interpreting the true and the beautiful.

The poisoning, or at least the fouling, of the humanities has taken place slowly over time; it cannot be attributed to a single cause. But the primary cause is probably the sense of loss the humanists have felt in the twentieth century as the scientists have been in the ascendancy. The physical scientists, and to a much lesser extent the social scientists, fit smoothly into the molds that have been created by the so-called research university. Because there has been a widespread belief that the sciences provide the wherewithal to run a technologically advanced society, because scientists are richly rewarded for their triumphs, however trivial, they are clearly the monarchs of the large research-oriented university—or at least the dukes and earls. It would be hard to think of any large public university anywhere in the nation where the humanities are esteemed more highly than the sciences. Yes, it is true that in some large, privately owned universities like Harvard, Stanford, Yale, Columbia, where there are deeply entrenched traditions, or where undergraduate instruction remains important because it forges an indispensable link with the alumni and with major sources of funding, the humanistic disciplines are at least nominally on a par with the sciences. Such universities probably have the strongest humanities departments of any institutions of comparable size. But almost without exception, at the upwardly struggling freshwater university, the English or philosophy professor is invariably regarded by all around as a distinct second-rater when compared to even the most plodding and unimaginative scientist. The scientists are in the saddle; the humanists do all they can to hang on to the horse's tail as they are dragged willy-nilly down the dusty academic trail.

It is little wonder, then, that for the better part of the twentieth century the humanists have been attempting to ape the scientists or, at the very least, steal some of the gold dust from their saddlebags. The sciences are difficult, rigorous, demanding, so the humanities must be also. The sciences call for high specialization, so the humanists must have exaggerated specialization and compartmentalization also. Scientists speak and write only for other scientists, often in symbols or indecipherable scrawls; the humanist must do likewise. Let's say that you, a nice youngster, appear at the university with a love for history, or a great desire to read the novels of Charles Dickens or the plays of Shakespeare. Such activities may be enjoyable, even commendable. They may be enlightening, may be traditional, but the history or English professor would be remiss to allow you to go through college thinking that you can improve yourself by such desultory and enjoyable reading. No, that kind of pursuit would be considered "soft," unintellectual, undemanding. When you got out of college you might have enjoyed yourself, even improved yourself, but you would have little if anything to wow the groundlings, to make them think that higher education had given you real punch and authority. So the humanistic disciplines needed to set out to discover, or "manufacture," high-octane subject matter. They had to find ways to teach people to talk in "tongues," to evince proof of possessing esoteric knowledge that a mere reading of books would never confer. The humanistic disciplines had to resemble the sciences: They had to deal in concepts that are difficult of access; they had to pretend to uncover mysteries and solve puzzles; they had to elaborate theories and concepts that can be shared only by a few co-specialists.

Accordingly a new kind of deadly scholasticism came to infect the humanities. I hardly need to add that there are still a great many traditional humanists who have not been infected by this virus. It would be a little unfair to say that the humanistic spirit is completely dead in the universities, for surely it is not. It is just that it is under constant siege. It is in constant danger of being killed off by those who have attempted to retail one or more of the newly fashionable esoteric sciences or isms that have tended to go the rounds in departments of English, comparative literature, philosophy, some-times history—structuralism and poststructuralism, deconstruc-tionism, new historicism, gender studies, neo-Marxism, and a flock of other murky impostures that are smoke in the eyes of unwary and overbusy deans or guileless students.

These new isms and the practitioners who proclaim and jealously guard them are faintly reminiscent of the dark and sinister necro-mancy of the ancient Celtic Druids, although they are used today to give the long-neglected humanists of the American university a claim to the magical powers of modern science—a claim that will naturally never be fulfilled. Like the Druid priests of old, the present-day structuralists and deconstructionists shuffle around their darkening campfires, mumbling oaths and other incantations utterly without any human uses, yet obscure and pompous enough to dupe outsiders into believing they possess the cures for all the ills

of the world. Like the ancient Druids, the present-day sorcerers of
the humanities have their serpent's eggs, brightly colored, giving off
smoke and hissing sounds, used to scare away the timid and the
uninitiated. Like the Druids of old, the new Druids prefer to keep
their own counsels, look scornfully down on those who fail to be
impressed by their dark arts, terrorize their colleagues and the
young by whatever means are at their disposal.

The dark and murky critical sciences of today's humanities
departments do not impress older humanists or most young students, except perhaps the more gullible ones, or cunning graduate
students who feel that mumbo-jumbo will give them some extra
oomph in their job search. Many will snicker or roll their eyes as the
house theorizer passes by. On the other hand, so desperate are many
departments of literature or philosophy or arts to prove that they
offer a "high-voltage" curriculum, with really deep and esoteric
thinking going on, that the new Druids are seldom called to account.

For the person standing outside the humanistic theory camps—
and most general readers of this book are likely to be outsiders,
unfamiliar with the happenings on the so-called upper-level specialized studies in the humanities—a few brief words of introduction to the mind of the new Druids would be helpful. Literary
studies started to get themselves into big trouble back in the 1930s
and the 1940s when the self-styled "New Critics" began stressing
the importance of "close analysis" of literary texts as a way of
ensuring that literary studies were not superficial and easy of access.
You couldn't just read books and enjoy them or weave them into the
culture you already possessed. You couldn't see works of literature as
being an integral part of the author's life or of a particular epoch or
age. No, these works became "texts," that is, something belonging
only to professors. Students now had to look at the literary text as
something that needed close formal analysis. Careful scrutiny of any
literary work, with special emphasis on uncovering mysteries and
secrets that the untutored reader might not have been aware of, was
considered to be the route of escape from literary scholarship that
was imprecise, soft, and unchallenging. Doubtless the New Critics
did provide a strong corrective to older literary studies that seemed
to many to be nothing more than a hack through names, dates, and
canned opinions. Almost certainly this emphasis in scholarship put
literary studies on a more elevated plane.

Unfortunately, this tendency opened a Pandora's box in the years after World War II, especially in the 1960s. By the late sixties numerous forms of structuralism and poststructuralism were running amuck in the land, and these dragged literary theory right off its feet. The poststructuralists and their stepchildren, the deconstructionists, took off for Cloud Cuckooland, to borrow a term from the comic master Aristophanes. In opposition to the New Critics, these supertheorizers believe that even the text itself is unimportant; all that matters is theory and the devisings of conceptualizers. The theorist is everything. Indeed, whoever is at work in the field of criticism is bigger, more vital, and more important than the poet or novelist being discussed. Sometimes the literary text is made to disappear altogether by these "critical" prestidigitators. More frequently the so-called literary critic uses whatever writer or artist is useful to his or her purposes. If Shakespeare fits the need, Shakespeare is in. If Shakespeare doesn't fit, he is cast aside. Shakespeare is not often openly denounced or thrown on the dust heap of history, although even that has been tried on occasion. Usually that extremity is avoided because it would set off too many alarms. Typically the poststructuralist will choose the text of some obscure writer or poet whose reputation can be neither injured nor enhanced but whose work will serve as a sounding board for the "critic's" own opinions. Remember, now, it is the critic who has all the big ideas; the writer is a museum piece to be picked up and flashed around when it suits the critic's purposes. Accordingly the critic can select the work of some obscure writer whose ideas touch some chord, or who hasn't already been worked over by someone else, or who has some political or ideological notions the critic can exploit or borrow without any colleagues being the wiser or being inclined to protest.

Most of the fashionable new forms of criticism seem to have come from France and to be grounded in one or another of the forms of romantic existentialism that took root during World War II. The existentialism of Jean Paul Sartre, and of his German mentor Heidegger, seemed to postulate that only the self exists, and that any world of shared values—society out there, or a common rationality—is a mere shadow. Each "thinker" (perverse as that word may now seem) must shape and fashion the world for herself or himself. Such a notion worked quite well for the young intellectuals of the 1960s who wanted to show that everything approved by bourgeois society was phony or dead. You had to cast aside everything that had once been cherished or provided the underpinnings of culture. Waved aside were rational thought processes, the traditional canons of literature, all notions of individuality, of commonality of knowledge, and yes, heaven forbid, the antediluvian idea that literature should be *enjoyed* or its values appreciated by large groups of people. Maybe literature should be destroyed altogether or, failing that, encapsulated in these hissing Druid's eggs that are passed furtively around among the few, those who have pledged their allegiance to whatever necromantic "theory" might be in the ascendancy at the moment.

Roger Kimball, a critic of art and architecture and managing editor of *The New Criterion*, has written an interesting book on the new Druids entitled *The Tenured Radicals*. Kimball develops the idea that most of the recent gurus of "theory" are sixties-style radicals who have grown older and gotten tenure in American universities. It is no small coincidence that a great many deconstructionists and other birds of this feather tend to fall into the Marxist camp and use literary criticism as a way of passing on various leftist ideologies to what might otherwise be an immune younger generation. Marxism, after all, is fading around the world, even among the intelligentsia; it is more than a little amusing that even in France, where Marxist intellectuals were once as common as roadside wildflowers, and where deconstruction had its birth in the writings of Jacques Derrida, the Marxists have almost completely vanished into the ether. Columnist and conservative sage William F. Buckley recently remarked, with a certain delicious sarcasm, that in a few years there won't be any Marxists left in the world except in American universities, a notion that doubtless would be shared by Kimball. Kimball finds the Marxist-deconstruction types to be a positive blight on the culture, a view that may be a trifle overstated since they do not really have much influence outside the walls of the academy, nor can they ever. The Druid conceptualizers are not bothered by this fact, of course, because they don't believe that any thought exists outside the university; the priestcraft alone is in possession of wisdom.

Still, Kimball is correct in his analysis of the extent of the blight. As a serious student of architecture and architectural criticism, he has produced a mass of evidence that shows how deconstruction has spread to the unlikely field of architecture. Truth to tell, it has not really spread all that much to the major commercial architects or to workaday architects in general, but it has spread to architecture schools and, generally, to places where people sit around and spin theories about architecture. Naturally if the deconstructionist architectural theorists had their way, architects would be designing buildings specifically because they are uncomfortable to live and work in; they would design chairs that would give the average person, certainly the average "bourgeois" person, an anxiety attack, or at the very least a backache. And yes, there continues to be a strong antibourgeois (which is to say anti-American) sentiment among the deconstructionist-Marxists. At root they are more interested in tearing society down ("brick by brick" as they used to say in the 1960s) or being a burr under the saddle than they are in supplying any intelligible program for society. Even Marxist theorizing has been basically a kind of pompous front for ordinary garden variety Jacobins. Like Madame Defarge, the American-bred radicals hope to keep knitting their balls of fustian while a decadent America falls apart. Marxism as a grab-bag of ideologies gets harder and harder to sell to American college students, especially as Marxist governments fade in eastern Europe. But undoubtedly there will always be a little room for a brand of academic theorizing that includes the notions that what we already have is rotten, that old values must be thrown overboard, that tradition should be undermined, that the smug and comfortable world of parents, or of corporate executives, or of liberal education, should be trashed if at all possible.

The new Druids, though, are probably not as dangerous as Roger Kimball believes. In spite of the vast amount of material he presents concerning the field of architecture, he is not too convincing when he argues that the day-to-day work of architecture is going to be undermined by a few woolly-headed thinkers on the faculties of architecture schools, however well known their names are to fellow members of small coteries. Architecture will have to go its way creating buildings that people will actually want to buy, and in a generation or so the present theorizers will have passed from the scene, replaced by another generation of obscurantists who probably will be equally ineffective in shaping the way our towns and cities look.

That most of the present "theory class" in the humanities divisions of our universities is dominated by (perhaps we should only say infiltrated by) a kind of low-grade infection—sixties-style radicalism—is not the main reason for concern. The real worry is that the theorists fit so poorly into campus life. They are decidedly not young in mind or in spirit, although they frequently use their credentials as "radicals" to show that they are or once were young. Even if their radicalism had once been a sign of youth, it has been mummified with the passage of time and is completely unlikely to set fire to the youthful imagination.

More important, the new theorists are a bad influence on campuses because of their twisted and perverse Mandarinism. They have no desire to communicate with the world at large. They write their articles only for co-specialists, for coteries and tunnel workers. Accordingly they have never attempted to learn to write with style or wit or grace and are drained of those virtues in all of their human interactions.

The first thing that is observed about the "theory only" crowd is their dullness. To quote Dr. Johnson: "They are dull and they inspire dullness in others." Almost invariably they write deadly, pompous, and flatulent prose that few people would want to read; indeed the only readers of it seem to be students, who have no choice, and a few other kindred practitioners who want to belong to the coteries or to get published in obscure and insignificant journals. Their inability to reach out to any kind of wider audience is, of course, what will consign them to oblivion and assure that within another generation all of their work will be as dead as mutton.

The new Druids have made feeble attempts to show that they are tied to general culture, to the worlds that all of us share. Occasional structuralists or deconstructionists will dig into popular culture, will try to show that they are good sports by writing about Bugs Bunny or country and western music. For the most part this is merely a pretense, since it is impossible to imagine that anyone outside the poisonous in-groups would care what they have to say on such subjects. They will never be quoted in the daily paper or heard on television; it is inconceivable that the deconstructionist's view of

Bugs Bunny would provide much mirth or enlightenment even at the dullest and dreariest academic jamboree.

Any point at which the new Druids claim tangency with the outside world is probably a sham or a delusion. Some of Mr. Kimball's sixties-style radicals affect fancy proletarian dress or make an elaborate show of being interested in the fate of the poor and the downtrodden—although quite comically they never hobnob with the underdogs they champion and have virtually nothing in common with them; they only *talk* about liking them. Basically this is because they are extreme elitists or "priestcraft" types who use a series of ideological dodges to conceal an essentially aloof, solipsistic, and supercilious outlook on their fellow citizens. Marxism, for example, is an effective and perhaps a necessary disguise for the Druids since it gives them a ready-made suit of protective armor against the charge that they don't care about people. Marxism or other "love the common people" ideologies give them a prefabricated set of formulas to invoke against anyone who charges that they have no "heart," or lack interest in humanity, or are far removed from campus values and concerns.

Not too long ago I had the opportunity to attend a lecture delivered by a semifashionable Marxist-deconstructionist. He read his paper, a masterpiece of obscurantist and agglutinous prose, which anyone with even the tiniest vestige of a liberal education should have known could not be delivered orally any more than pages of mathematical symbols. He presented an argument that was so thick and incoherent that all of his listeners were nodding off after only a few sentences. Somewhere in the middle, however, he dropped the manuscript he was reading and began an impassioned plea, mostly in ordinary English, which was something he never used in his professional writing. In a howling lamentation he demanded that literary scholars pay more attention to the downtrodden, to trade unionists, to neglected black and women poets (whether they are competent or not), suggesting that somehow or other this would relieve him of the guilt of elitism. And perhaps it did in the mind of his more naive listeners. He attacked his fellow English professors (always an easy target since in the collegial environment they are required to be "open-minded"), traditionalists, and other selected bogeymen. That was good for at least a little feeble applause. But for anyone even slightly alert, this dodge would have trumpeted the essential isolation of the man. His actual "learned" paper as presented was more than sufficient proof that the thought processes behind his customary meditations were confused, disorderly, incoherent, even just plain unintelligible.

How wonderful it would be if the heavy-footed conceptualizers of today's humanities departments could actually make good on their extravagant promises, if they could really reach out to some wider community, if they *could* say something about literature or popular culture that people would want to listen to. Unfortunately they can't. And never will. These shuffling, ashen-faced Druids, attempting to impress the few with the faint aromas of their feeble necromancy, come away without any influence at all on the many. There is really little to fear from them as ideologues. On the other hand, so much of what they say and do is a drain on the resources of the university, which already has a hard enough time keeping a shared culture alive in our modern society.

9

The Indifference of the Ivory Lab

THERE IS A SICKNESS at the heart of liberal arts education: So one has heard over and over again in the last few years. On the other hand, the utter scarcity of complaints about the sciences is really nothing short of startling. Perhaps the people who write books on higher education (mostly educators themselves) are overawed by the sciences. Perhaps the scientists who *are* qualified to offer a critique of science in the college curriculum are not motivated to write much on educational issues—which may give us some inkling of one major weakness in scientific education. For the greater part of the twentieth century the scientists have been invincible. They are the knights of the academic world. Nobody questions what they do. It is just assumed that if left alone they will do the right things in their laboratories, and this is all we should really ask of them. Nobody wants to trouble them by asking nasty questions about the curriculum, or what they do in the classroom, or how they relate to the university community or the outside world.

In one very important sense it is probably true that the sciences are free of the gross impostures and perversities that plague the humanities. There is no room for the new Druids here; quacks and counterfeits may appear in the sciences on rare occasions, but the

78

force of the prevailing scientific body of knowledge and of scientific culture generally is such that the scientific field itself is seldom violated; in the humanities the various theory-spinners and junk-think merchants can infiltrate the very subject matters themselves and run wildly across the curriculum. Deconstructionist critics or literary flimflam artists can convince themselves and a small handful of others that they are great poets themselves or people of high imagination, all evidence to the contrary. But the pathology corresponding to this seldom infects the sciences. Looked at in their isolation and their unified integrities, the sciences, certainly the physical sciences, are in a far healthier state than the humanities in the present-day American university.

To be sure, the sciences have come in for their share of complaints from the public and from thoughtful outsiders. There have been vast public policy issues regarding the sciences, including any number of huge expenditures on projects of dubious merit or value. From time to time scientists have been blamed, inter alia, for being dupes of big business or mere foot soldiers of the military-industrial complex. They have been accused of waste and greed, of utter hostility to all public expenditures that do not line their own pockets. By and large, though, at least in the fairly recent past, the scientists have not had to spend much time making excuses for themselves. Occasionally they have complained bitterly that basic research is inadequately funded (as opposed to other projects that will elicit immediate cash dividends); more typically one particular scientist feels that his or her specialty, perhaps a marginal branch of science, is not being adequately underwritten. But the scientists these days never need to justify the merit of what they are doing; they never have to defend the utility of science itself. It is an enviable position to be in—certainly in a university environment.

On the other hand, there are burning educational reasons for being troubled by the kingdom the scientists have built up for themselves. First of all, the scientific mind, above all others, has surrendered to the rigid compartmentalization of knowledge. The scientific faction on the typical university faculty holds as an article of almost reverential faith that the production of "experts" in specialized fields is the sole business of the university. Some scientists may occasionally speak of the value of their scientific colleagues knowing something about literature or history or music, but these are increments, "nice to have's"; they are peripheral to the central educational goal, which is to produce men of science.

The typical university scientist in our time believes that the development of the scientific cast of mind and the cultivation of a tiny patch of specialized ground is the alpha and omega of education. His or her interest in the education of nonscientists, or in people who approach the sciences for some reason other than wanting to become a full-time participant in a specialty, is essentially nil. It is true that many scientific departments in large universities offer courses for nonscientists as part of their service function, but these courses are almost universally storage bins where students out on the flanks are processed. Nearly always, when such courses exist, they are taught by junior staff, rare eccentrics, second-raters, or people being punished for something. The idea of drawing in students not destined for the sciences is one that never dawns in the minds of the typical scientist. Insofar as the scientist is devoted to undergraduate teaching in research institutions, it is to guard the gate, which is to say, to identify and encourage the potential scientists and to give the bum's rush to everyone else.

Any person who passes through a large research university today can hardly fail to be aware of the abrupt and violent division of subject matter, to see that there is little if any communication between the literature professor and the astrophysicist. Yes, of course, these individuals may fraternize since they work for the same institution; their spouses may well be good friends; they may go to the same parties; they may be able to engage in small talk together, or even what might be called "middle-sized" talk. Obviously, though, neither has the slightest desire to tramp in the other's vineyards; all fields of specialized learning are hermetically sealed and kept apart from one another.

The walls between the various university disciplines went up slowly over time, although William James for one was aware of the phenomenon and troubled by it as soon as the rage over the scientific curriculum began in the 1880s. The existence of an unbreachable gap between the sciences and the humanities first caught the attention of a wider public in 1959 when English writer C. P. Snow published a lecture he had delivered at Cambridge University entitled *The Two Cultures*. Snow, who had been trained in the sciences himself but later turned to writing and achieved some

eminence as a novelist in Britain, observed that the university had
broken down into two camps, one might almost say two armed
camps: the scientists on the one side, the literari or humanists on the
other. Between these two camps, said Snow, there is "a gulf of
mutual incomprehension—sometimes (particularly among the
young) hostility and dislike, but most of all lack of understanding.
They have a curious distorted image of each other. The attitudes are
so different that, even on the level of emotion, they can't find much
common ground."

In the English educational system, Snow traced the development
of the two opposing cultures to the Oxford and Cambridge
scholarship examinations, much more rigorous than any of the
corresponding examinations in America, which forced the young of
the aspiring middle classes onto completely separate tracks. "Somehow," said Snow, in England, but in an only faintly different style in
America and elsewhere in the world, "we have set ourselves the task
of producing a tiny *elite*...educated in one academic skill. For a
hundred and fifty years in Cambridge it was mathematics; then
mathematics or classics; then natural science was let in. But still the
choice had to be a single one."

The most marked characteristic of these two separate and distinct
cultures is a lack of communication. The burden of becoming highly
expert in a single area is so great that it becomes progressively more
difficult for the scientist to learn anything in depth about the
humanistic disciplines. On the other side of the fence, the humanist
invariably becomes a scientific ignoramus. Snow was convinced, for
example, that not one individual trained in literature in a hundred
could say anything substantial about the Second Law of Thermodynamics. Whenever he raised this point at a gathering of people
nurtured in the "traditional culture," especially those who had been
carrying on with gusto over the "illiteracy of scientists," he received
a negative response together with an appropriately repressive stare.
Yet this question was the scientific equivalent of asking "Have you
read a work of Shakespeare's?"

But the situation was even more serious than that. What if he had
asked an even simpler question, such as, what is mass? or accelera-
tion?—equivalents of "Can you read?" "Not more than one in ten of
the highly educated would feel that I was speaking the same
language. So the great edifice of modern physics goes up, and the

majority of the cleverest people in the western world have about as much insight into it as their neolithic ancestors would have had."

Looked at from the other side, the situation is just about as bleak. Snow does not insist that scientists care nothing at all about the social, moral, or psychological dimensions of life. In fact they care very deeply about these things; it is just that they fail to see how history, poetry, or plays are relevant to them. The scientist is probably not as ignorant of Shakespeare or Yeats or of the history of our century as the typical humanist is of the Second Law of Thermodynamics; it is just that he or she believes that this side of learning is a kind of ornament, something nice to have, amusing, pleasurable, but incapable of offering any solutions to the problems of the world. The scientist can toy with the facticity, the thing-ness, of the arts but fails to make a rapprochement with their spirit, does not even understand what their spirit might be. (Snow excludes music somewhat, since among his scientific acquaintances he noticed occasional sensitivity to as well as in-depth knowledge of musical culture.)

The upshot is that two separate cultures with stone walls around them have grown up in the university community. Thirty years before Snow's lecture—in the 1920s, say—"the two cultures had long ceased to speak to one another; but at least they managed a kind of frozen smile across the gulf. Now the politeness has gone, and they just make faces." By 1959, with Sputnik shooting across the sky to the disgrace of American education, and with the scientists in the complete ascendancy, Snow was correct in observing that there was no reason for the scientists to make even a passing nod to the humanists. Even a mediocre scientist (and few universities even admit that there is such a thing as a mediocre scientist, because they have so completely sold the public on the notion that everything done by the scientist, however trivial, is contributing to the common good), that is to say, even the most plodding individual in the ranks, could be assured of a well-paying job in academia by the 1960s, while the young Ph.D. in history, if not driving a taxicab instead, was making 30 percent less than contemporaries in the sciences.

Snow's identification of the two-culture dichotomy, which he declared to be an educational disaster of the greatest magnitude, received a great deal of attention by the early 1960s. Snow even received some hate mail about it—certainly a large number of strident and overheated rejoinders. Some editors of newspapers and journals wrote to Snow asking him if he would absolve them of libel suits if they ran a particular review or comment. He had whipped up a tempest in a safe and settled world that doesn't like tempests. It was not as violent, perhaps, as the storm of calumny that followed the publication of Allan Bloom's *Closing of the American Mind* in the 1980s, but the situation was similar. Universities don't like to have their dirty laundry exposed in public, and they react violently to those who bare their secrets, even if the criticism is stated in a quiet, reasoned manner, as it was in Snow's lecture. Both scientist and humanist have come to accept the two-culture status quo; they have no desire to look into it or hear about it, since to do so might open up a Pandora's box, might lead to changes in the delivery of education—particularly undergraduate education—that would undermine a comfy ivory tower lifestyle that both have come to depend on. (In the case of the scientist, perhaps we should say "ivory lab," a term judiciously employed years ago by Jacques Barzun in his classic *Teacher in America*.)

While this is not the proper place to explore the question of the role of the sciences in the intellectual life of our time, inside the university community it is probably fair to say that since the separation and hardened intransigence of the two cultures, the scientists, far more than the humanists, have been indifferent, even hostile, to the fate of general education. In the large research university most scientists pay little attention to the content or quality of their own lower-level courses; all they care about is weeding out students unsuited to scientific work and preparing the elect for graduate or higher-level work. The scientists are the Vestal Virgins of our time. They care little what goes on in the humanities. They invariably want to be relieved of all burdens of higher education except their own. Their advice in deliberations over the language requirement or the teaching of ethics or modern history is seldom sought and almost certain to be of little value. As a teacher of writing I have frequently heard rumblings from those in the scientific fields that the English Department doesn't know how to teach "their" technical students to write (they are probably correct), but no attempt is ever made to inquire why this might be so. All such matters must be left strictly in the hands of those other fellows—it is their field, after all. Obviously, though, the use of language is the most widespread human concern, not the province of specialists alone.

It is easy to think that at least in one scientific area—the social sciences—there might be a strong impetus to build bridges to the broader culture and to evince an interest in general education. Alas, the social sciences have just as willfully built fixed barricades around themselves as have the physical sciences. Social scientists have insisted on writing in inaccessible jargon, have drawn a cloak of impenetrable technicality around themselves. Unfortunately, a feeling of inferiority to the so-called pure sciences has always plagued the social scientists, and they have always had to make superhuman efforts to pretend that their work has all the rigor and exactitude of the "real" sciences, which stand near the altar of the temple. But this timid and subservient approach has been disastrous for the social sciences, which would have been better advised not to ape the exact sciences but rather to use scientific expertise and methodology to establish a rapprochement between all the fields of learning and the larger world outside. They are *social* sciences, after all; how much nicer it would be had these social sciences met ordinary life head on, rather than elaborating a series of inward-dwelling and self-serving specialties. (Some social scientists believe that the politicization of the social sciences in the years since World War II is proof that they have brought about some kind of synoptic view of the world; in fact, it has led some critics to believe that the "social sciences" might better have been called the "political sciences.")

For a time, earlier in the century, it seemed as though the social sciences might one day offer a great boon to society; that they might unlock the mysteries of war, ignorance, poverty, human unhappiness, social unrest, mental disease—many of the perennial woes of the human condition. Certainly much was expected of economics back in the 1930s, when John Maynard Keynes had seemingly made economics queen of the social sciences, at least for the time being. Keynes, a highly cultured man who wrote in a crystalline English prose style, offered some hope of making economics accessible to the multitudes and fostered the belief that the vagaries and terrible effects of the boom-and-bust capitalist society could be cured by some heroic surge of theoretical thought. By 1950 economics seemed to be in the saddle, and economists were believed to be essential to the nation's health. Celebrated members of the fraternity held high government office; there was a presidential council of economic advisers. (President Harry Truman welcomed the breed into his inner circle, although he personally remained skeptical, once reputedly remarking, "What I need is a one-handed economist. Every time I ask an economist what to do, his answer begins, 'On the one hand this, and the other hand that.'")

By the 1960s and 1970s economics was no longer the queen of the social sciences; there were no queens and no kings. The economists by and large had settled into the dark recesses of academia, building mathematical models to tell you what was going to happen—although it seldom did. Economic advisers to presidents or to banks and corporations still exist, but their helpfulness has been so much the object of suspicion that even the best of the breed prefer anonymity. In academia most prefer to keep to themselves, torturing some quantitative subdivision of their specialty in ways that can be assured of certainty, even if their "certain" truths are not applicable to the world. In economics, as in numerous other fields of the social sciences, the painful truth is that the more scientific the findings, the less they refer to the real world; the more they refer to the real world, the less they are scientific and must fall back upon loose speculation.

The situation in most of the other social sciences is, if anything, even more abysmal. Undergraduate enrollments in the various social science fields have dropped considerably in the last several decades—in economics somewhat less so because of its closer ties to education for business and relevance to careers in business. In the mid-1970s nearly one million students were enrolled in sociology courses. By the early 1980s that number had shrunk by half. In 1974 thirty-three thousand degrees were awarded in sociology; by 1981, only seventeen thousand.

A great many students I have spoken to who were majoring in sociology have found their courses to be dull or trivial. Certainly a large percentage of the research that goes on in this area is trivial or lightweight, although dressed up with ponderous argot or spurious quantification. Not too long ago I received a questionnaire in the mail from a sociologist—the filling out of questionnaires is one of the many hidden burdens of a professor's daily life. Social science researchers think nothing, in fact, of sending elaborate ten-page questionnaires they expect to be filled out gratis in one's leisure, although they often give no idea of how the information will be used; they merely want you to accept their motives and methods on good faith. This questionnaire purported to deal with "Vehicular Utilization by Members of the University Faculty," which I soon perceived to mean that the researcher wanted to find out how often and for what purpose professors used their cars. I asked to receive the results of the study, which arrived in due course with various mathematical squiggles, as well as charts and graphs. Put in a nutshell it seemed to show that professors use their cars to go to work, to go to the grocery store, and occasionally for long trips! To help uncover this wisdom I had given over half an hour of my time.

As a teacher of writing I do a good deal of my teaching in individual conferences. I routinely ask students what their major is, and, if they are near graduation, I ask them how they have liked their major. The vast majority of the students who took sociology or psychology expressed keen disappointment. (Students of anthropology had a slightly brighter outlook by and large, perhaps because anthropology is more open to an interdiscplinary approach than most of the other social sciences.) Most psychology students, for example, described their undergraduate courses as boring or trivial. They had arrived expecting to learn something about the human world, but they had come away with big bundles of technical information that was neither interesting nor challenging, although sometimes made artificially difficult in order to create an aura of scientific exactitude.

Psychology has followed rather murky paths since it developed, in the words of James, from the confines of philosophy. Its contribution to general learning has been far from spectacular. In their desire to emulate the "exact" sciences, psychologists have spent too many years running rats through mazes, all with the promise that the knowledge so gained would eventually say something "big" about human nature—the trickle-down theory again. But the big windfall has never come. Sometimes there has been a small benefit to some of the still duller stepchildren of the field, such as educational psychology. But here the problem is not dullness alone: More than infrequently it is something near charlantry. Educational psychologists long ago saddled us with a series of veritable hoaxes, for example, that it is possible to measure intelligence by means of the so-called IQ test. But the IQ test is manifestly a fraud, as shallow and as silly as the pseudo-sciences of the Middle Ages psychologists now deplore, such a reading palms or counting the bumps on the back of the cranium. The mere fact that the IQ test provides quantifiable information does not rescue it from the dustbin of fads and quackeries.

The social sciences would have done much better in their nascent years to form alliances across the human spectrum rather than to make fatuous and awkward dances around the temple of the pure sciences. It would have been much more sensible, for example, to root the discipline of sociology in history—or at least in some wider panorama of humanity such as that envisioned by Auguste Comte, who invented the word (and the field) in the first place. (The vast majority of sociologists today, unfortunately, have never read a word Comte wrote.) The experimental psychologists, too, would have done better to use their independence and whatever scientific training they possessed to investigate human nature using some shared human idiom. Science, after all, need not imply the quantification of everything; the word *science* can also refer to any systematic and orderly architectonic of thought. The psychologist would have done better to use the already existing artifacts of language and culture to tell us how the mind works, what place religion or myth or poetry has in our lives, how we are shaped by cultural forces, how we are and are not imbedded in human history, how we are affected by art or the pageant of everyday life. In fairness to the field of psychology, we should, of course, add that many psychologists, especially clinical psychologists, have built up impressive bodies of knowledge about human behavior that has sometimes been used to good effect, although the clinical psychologists have never been the elite of academic psychology departments since they don't walk with their heads in the rarefied air of "real" science.

Whatever we may conclude about the actual contributions of the social sciences to the world about us, the evidence seems to show that the contributions of these fields to general education, to the undergraduate curriculum, have left much to be desired. The social scientists, alas, have been every bit as guilty as the pure scientists in developing a course of study that will draw interested persons into their fields and dump everybody else out. To be sure, the social sciences have accepted a huge burden in staffing and building up lower-level service courses in their areas, especially since they have always had to fight for their own turf in the university curriculum.

But their contributions to the liberal education of the young need to be called severely into question. For the most part, their efforts have been to get students on the technical track as soon as possible, to instill the mind-set and patois of the specialty, and to give a quick brush-off to all who do not share the inclination for it.

Return for a moment to the field of economics. Thousands of American colleges offer a course called Introduction to Economics, General Economics, or some such thing. Thousands and thousands of American students take these courses, yet we find that most college graduates—yes, even those who have taken such courses— remain economic illiterates. Few of them who have been processed through the survey course have the tools needed to understand the principal economic issues that are posed by presidential or congressional elections, a tragic failure, certainly, of our educational system. For citizens in a democracy to be able to make intelligent decisions about public policy, it is necessary for them to have a rudimentary knowledge about the national debt, the consequences of taxes, how the Federal Reserve system works, how to make sense of the financial pages of the daily newspaper. Millions upon millions of Americans don't know what money is and where it comes from— they believe that it is identical with hand-to-hand currency, that is, the paper money printed at the Bureau of Printing and Engraving. Millions of Americans, having taken courses in economics, hear on the news that the American dollar has fallen (or risen) against the Japanese yen, yet they really don't know in what practical way this is good or bad. The nightly news carries jittery spots about the trade deficit, yet the typical American has no way of judging in what sense this is or is not a serious problem. When the savings and loan institutions failed at the cost of billions to taxpayers, not one person in a hundred could give an articulate explanation of what had happened.

Why? Is it because the professor of economics says nothing about these things? Well, not precisely. It is just that when students come to college, professors attempt to draw them into the heart of the technical field of economics forgetting that the youthful listeners are still mainly undeveloped human beings, imperfectly educated, forgetting, too, that someday they will have to be adults and citizens of the republic. The students are looking for their bearings, to be given a map of the territory. They want to find out how their studies relate to things they already know. But the economists, who already have their bearings, want to get each student as quickly as possible up to their level. Now, of course, it is not impossible that a student can be pulled up, put on some kind of tech track—it is painful, but possible. The trouble is, it is not desirable. The liberal arts approach to education means a slow opening up of vistas; it means full use of knowledge that one already possesses. It does not mean that one should immediately begin spouting the nomenclature or mumbo-jumbo of economics, for this will result in passing over the basic knowledge that one needs and replacing it with a level of abstractions, a domain of knowledge that the college freshman or sophomore simply doesn't need.

Over the past half century, the segmentation of the sciences, along with their isolation from the shared idiom of general culture, has been one of the most serious defects of American university education. On the grounds that everything scientists do is worthy of admiration, the sciences have been supported royally and uncritically by the universities—and will probably continue to be so in the future. University administrations, with the full backing of society, have done everything possible to see that scientists are spared the nuisance of having to rub shoulders with scientific ignoramuses or with those whose scientific interests are secondary or peripheral. Scientists have been allowed to establish and maintain think tanks within the universities without having to bother about interests other than their own or having to offer an explanation to the rest of us for what they do. They have been the most ivory-tower-bound of all the American academics—ivory lab, if you wish. Their isolation may or may not have been good for themselves; it may or may not have been good for technology; it is much more clear that it has not been good for education or for the commonweal.

10

Do They Publish or Perish?

IF THERE IS ONE THING that the general public has heard about college professors, it is that they are somehow burdened with the necessity of publishing the results of their research. This notion has entered popular culture and folklore through the catchy and memorable phrase, "publish or perish." If you don't publish, you can't get promoted, and if you don't get promoted you can't, in most cases, keep your job. Which is to say, you perish. If you hold a Ph.D. in one of the fields like classics or philosophy, where there are no related jobs outside the university, perishing means that you wind up driving a taxicab or opening up a health food store at the age of thirty-five. Publication is the academic's route to success. Or at least so they say.

The truth is actually a little different. Anyone who has studied the promotion documents of a prestigious research university will be aware that a great many individuals manage to climb into the tenured ranks after publishing only a handful of articles and sometimes a single book, after which they can glide for the rest of their careers. The compulsion to publish is still there for a tenured professor but is considerably reduced. In days gone by very many people attaining tenured ranks published little or nothing in their later careers, although in most universities today a modest demonstration of activity seems to be required to keep getting salary increases, or sometimes promotion to the rank of full professor. In many small colleges the emphasis on publication is much less compulsive, and in some places the necessity of publication is almost nonexistent. The lack of pressure to publish in smaller institutions is sometimes seen as a sign of their mediocrity by those holding jobs in prestige universities, which may or may not be true. On the other hand, the claim of administrators in liberal arts colleges or other smaller institutions that they stress good teaching rather than publication also may or may not be true.

But the old edict "publish or perish" has something rather comical about it. For the most part, professors don't publish a great deal, but they usually don't perish either. (The buzzwords might equally well be "neither publish nor perish.") True, a fair number of people don't make it in the academic profession, but in recent decades most of them perish at the very beginnings of their academic careers. They fail to get tenure track positions and have to put in years as "temporaries" or "adjuncts," or they have to settle for positions in inferior institutions. In times when the job market is soft (nine years out of ten in academia), they get no job at all. Their Ph.D. degrees hang around their necks like a giant's overcoat on the body of a dwarf. They open gift shops selling objets d'art or gewgaws, or start some kind of consulting service. The word *tenure* comes from the Latin *teneo*, which means to hold or grip. The majority of professors get a grip pretty early in their teaching careers, gaining some kind of security as they grope their way up the academic ladder. They do this either through publication or through some other kind of effort.

The other kind of effort can involve any of a number of things. As a fledgling professor, you learn very early in your career that you can get by without having to publish a great deal. You can't get by without any effort at all, since the university marinates in the juices of the American work ethic. Professors are supposed, as they say, "to build reputations for themselves," but this can be accomplished in a multitude of ways. Most typically it is accomplished by a spirit of "collegiality," which means learning the art of "getting along" or "being in the swim." Collegiality means learning the art of academic politics; it means serving on the right committees, buttering up the right people, looking properly askance at any views or persons currently out of favor. It means attending professional meetings and making much of oneself there, above all latching onto those who are either well known or powerful in the discipline. It means filling out forms and questionnaires on time (and the typical professor spends a great deal more time on filling out forms than on scholarly activities). In short, it means the same kind of backing and filling that goes on in the corporate office, although it is carried out in a slightly different style.

Professors keep busy; they do not, as some recent critics believe, spend long hours peering out the windows at the green lawns or ivy-covered buildings of the quadrangle. Much of this activity is arduous but, alas, unproductive. Much of it is mere academic bustle—I keep in mind here the delightful definition that the great Dr. Johnson gave to the word *bustle*: "mounting horseback on board ship." Somehow professors really don't get all that much done; as I said, if you look at dossiers typical of professors at the end of their careers, chances are you will find that they have each come up with a book or two and a smattering of articles, most of which will probably be forgotten by the time of retirement. This is true, by the way, even at the leading universities. Many people believe that at Harvard or Stanford all of the professors are almost certain to be great or well-known scholars, but a look at the roster of any department at these universities shows this is a long way from being true. Still, whether in the mediocre or great university most professors manage to *convince* the higher powers that they have been "productive."

Doing so is something of a high art, perhaps even bordering on magic. At most universities with which I have been acquainted, the professor every year has to fill out some kind of "activity" sheet, showing what he or she has done to deserve a raise. When the proper moment arrives, the same is done to secure a promotion. These activity sheets—puff sheets, they might be called—bring out all that is best (or worst) in the art of academic maneuvering. It takes the new young faculty member a while to get a deft hand at it. The puff sheet can make you look good, even if you really haven't done much of anything. It gives you an opportunity to list "research in progress," a category with almost inconceivable opportunities for puffery. You can provide your dean or department head with the names of your "working papers," or "conference papers," or "seminar papers." You can supply the names of committees served upon, extramural activities, public service, and any number of other evidences of bustle. I have in my hand an annual report form used at a research university. It asks the busy professor, among other things, to list papers, reviews, lectures, editorial duties, items for publication not yet submitted, items for publication submitted but not yet published, professional honorary societies, evidence of professional consulting, administrative service on departmental, college, and university-wide committees, teaching achievements such as dissertations and theses supervised, tutorials, independent students, teaching committees—and many more.

The professor quickly learns to water and bloat these categories to offer proof of productivity. Let's say that a professor in history decides to get up a piece about Gladstone's relationship with Queen Victoria. This can be listed one year under "research in progress," another year under "working papers," the next under "papers submitted," and so on ad infinitum. None of this is taken as hype by higher-ups, most of whom have practiced these arts themselves in their own days in the trenches. Unfortunately one of the great inhibitions on academic publication is this frantic need to "show" current productivity rather than actually achieve it in the long run. Probably it would be better if professors were given few forms to fill out, no officials to appease, just a blank check to follow their scholarly bent. The person who wanted to work on Gladstone would better be left alone to read, to meditate, to write—for ten years if necessary—relieved of the burden of showing "evidence" every year, and in the end might come up with something really good. Instead of thinking and working in spurts and tiny droppings, he or she might eventually be able to come up with a grand and lusty panorama. Having to deliver butter and eggs on a regular basis like a milkman with a white cap has the effect of making professors into miniaturists, consigning them to that level of pedantry; above all, it keeps them from doing something for themselves, which in the end has the best chance of leading to work of lasting value.

Many other things also tend to inhibit academic publication. There is the matter of bolt-hole specialization, which we have already discussed at considerable length. The professor in a research university is invariably consigned to one little patch of ground in his or her scholarly career—and, we might almost say, chained to it. One who steps away from this little patch of ground may well fall into oblivion, since doing so is usually looked upon as "inappropriate" or unseemly for the scholar. Sometimes, though, keeping to one of the patches of artificial turf created by the university's organizational chart is a near impossibility, requiring the most tortuous of labors.

Imagine yourself a young Ph.D. in English with your dissertation in some area of Old English. You get a job in a university under the expectation that you will become their "old English scholar." You must paw that turf for the rest of your life, whatever your alternate desires and inclinations. The trouble is that the literature of Old English is small; it has been worked over time and time again by other experts. The little plot of ground is fallow, and the subsoil is infertile. It is nearly impossible to get anything new to grow there. Very few scholarly journals are looking for material in this area, so the competition to get into the few is great.Of course there are the university presses, about which more shortly, but a scant few of these want to publish things about Old English. If a really earthshaking book in the area comes along—well, perhaps. But most are not earthshaking; rather they tickle and readjust some of the already well worked issues.

Then, too, academic articles and books are judged and evaluated by other specialists—in this case the tiny handful in the world certified to pass judgment on Old English scholarship. These, by the way, are the very people most likely to have their knives out for the work of any young upstart hoping to make a name in the field. I've always believed that a manuscript dealing with Old English should be sent to an evaluator in some other area of literature or anyone who is simply qualified to read it to see whether it is interesting or not. When you send it to the co-specialist, you get the expected amount of pettifogging; your manuscript will be dribbled upon, pawed over; flyspecks will be removed or added, and supercilious judgment pronounced. But your friends and colleagues in the field (just as likely they are enemies) will not be your only obstacle to publication, since you will finally need some journal or university press editorial board to pass on your work as well, and the process of getting a book or even an article published might take years—and usually does. In the end your book might be rejected because it is not "marketable," so that even a good word from an expert might not be enough.

Because the field of Old English as understood in a typical university is a tiny plot of ground that cannot be expanded like a scientist's field (all of the material in Old English literature is in place; no more will be written), as a narrow specialist in it you walk a very thin line. For you everything works *against* productivity. Everything works against any major attempt at upsetting the whole field and coming up with something new. And the specialist is not permitted to escape the field. A major part of your effort, accordingly, must be directed at gently and quietly ingratiating yourself with those in control of the field when you come into it. There are the aged gray heads to be placated and buttered up—you must become known to them before you dare to submit an article. Accordingly, for years and years you must attend the right meetings; you must meet and interact with the "older" authorities, write them letters of flattery, ask for their opinions on trifling points, send them "working papers" of articles for approval, perhaps advanced chapters of books. Instead of working your field, you work the experts in your field. It is a process not unlike getting your Ph.D. all over again. It means toadying, backfilling, and genuflecting. In brief, it means years of unavoidable business and wasted effort.

The academic publishing business is essentially a kind of tread-mill—"a treadmill to oblivion" to borrow the wonderful title of the autobiography of the late radio comedian Fred Allen. It is an activity with a lot of sweat connected to it, made doubly onerous because there is a vast array of rules to be learned. Typical professors, certainly in the fields of the humanities, must spend years in the production of professional sweat, which bears little relationship to genuine inspiration. Instead of using their imagination and inge-nuity, the scholarly qualifications which the Ph.D. degree sup-posedly testifies that they have, instead of discovering new things, venturing forth, making their own mark in the world, they are shackled to what is already in place. Whether they are productive or not will seldom be questioned. All that will really be asked is whether they put in their time.

Now, as far as this business of getting published is concerned, it must be obvious that most of the organs of scholarly publication are extensions of the universities. Most professional journals and most university presses do their part in ensuring that the things published by professors will be narrow in scope and duly certified by other experts or authorities. They will ensure that such publications will not be of interest to the general reader, that for the most part they will be timid, cautious, and unadventurous.

Let's consider for a moment the activities of the university presses, of which there are several dozen in the United States. These presses were set up and have proliferated over the years to assist in the publication of research that is considered too specialized or esoteric to be published by general trade publishers. Their books are printed in such small quantities that they will rarely make money either for the press or the author. Since the sale of university press books is invariably small, most of them are being subsidized by the publisher, which makes them, in a sense, vanity books—a term that gives a horrifying jolt to the university scholar but is nonetheless at least partially appropriate. Most university press books won't enjoy a brisk sale, so they have to be paid for by an angel, which is usually the university itself or sometimes a foundation.

University presses are hardly new; they are not a twentieth-century product of the American multiversity, as some might think. But they were not originally conceived as gristmills for compulsive academic publishing. Presses for the production of scholarly books were established at a number of European universities in the late fifteenth and early sixteenth centuries. Among the pioneers were those at the Sorbonne in Paris, Oxford and Cambridge in England, Leipzig in Germany, and Leyden in Holland. It was to be expected, during an age when there was a joyful surge of interest in printing, that printers and kindred graphic artisans would gravitate toward universities where there was a natural affinity between lovers of the written word and the new arts of typography. The idea of a university administration controlling various printing functions and having an imprint in its own name began at Oxford around 1690.

In the United States, Cornell University established a small press in 1869, but the forerunner of the American university press as we know it today was one established at Johns Hopkins in 1878. The Hopkins press was conceived from the beginning as an extension and arm of the graduate college. Within a few years of its founding it was publishing the *American Journal of Mathematics* and the *American Chemical Journal*. No books were published until 1887, but by this time it was perceived by Johns Hopkins and other universities that many kinds of specialized books simply would not be undertaken by commercial publishers; if universities wanted such books published, they would have to provide their own means of doing so.

The university press concept established itself firmly within a few years, especially in the well-endowed research universities. When William Rainey Harper opened the doors of the University of Chicago with the aid of the Rockefeller millions, he had as one of his immediate goals the establishment of a press that would be "an organic part" of the university's mission. The press that he established published books and journals, but it also worked as an all-purpose university printer, doing the much-needed production work of the university's own business: calendars, bulletins, catalogs, and miscellaneous publications. (Many universities maintained their own printing facilities in the early days, and some still do today, although characteristically most university presses now contract out their books to commercial printers, just as do commercial or trade publishers.)

By 1948 there were several dozen university presses in the United States, thirty-five belonging to the Association of American University Presses. Twenty years later this number had more than doubled, actually tripled if one considered a number of marginal presses that produced only a few books a year. In 1948 university presses produced 727 titles; in 1966 approximately 2,300. This was an increase of 319 percent, a good indication of the pressures that had been building up in those years to find outlets for scholarly books, especially books of a more specialized nature.

An early impetus to the growth of the university press in America was the need to find a way to get Ph.D. dissertations published. For a long time universities required publication (or at least "printing") of dissertations, although this requirement was later replaced by inexpensive reproduction methods or microfilming. Today most university presses want nothing to do with dissertations and are as wary of them as an evangelical preacher is of a lady of the night. They want books that are scholarly but lacking in the pedantic vices and other stale aromas of the thesis, that is, presumably higher in quality, although it is not always easy to say higher in what sense. Editors of university presses all yearn for the day when a best-selling book will come their way, or at the very least a book that will make a respectable profit. Such books are few and far between, except for a few of the most prestigious presses such as Oxford or Harvard, which stand in the borderland between scholarly and commercial publishing. Far and away the largest number of university presses issue books in exceedingly small press runs—sometimes only five hundred or a thousand copies—which ensures that they will make no money either for the press or the author, even with excessively high prices. The most important customers for university press books are university libraries, which are presumably well heeled enough to afford the inflated prices of the books. More precisely, they are obliged to buy them at top price.

The authors of university press books (most of the time, professors) often do not receive royalties for their work, although this usually does not trouble them: The publication of one's book may bring a raise of several thousand dollars, which raise continues year after year, thus making the publication of a book with no royalties quite worth the effort. Some time ago I acted as an outside editorial reviewer for a university press, for which chore I received a small stipend of two hundred dollars. As I typed my review, I had occasion to reflect that the author of this book would probably not receive a dime from the proceeds of its sale. As an outside reviewer I got paid. It is one of the many sordid ironies connected with this business of academic publishing.

In any case, decisions about what to publish at a university press have little to do with the salability of the work, although such considerations do affect ultimate editorial decisions when budgets are short or subsidy funds otherwise unavailable. Decisions are made by outside "experts," supposedly people in an author's field. As editor of a university press, you may have a great longing to publish beautifully written books, or books that have a widespread appeal, but for the most part your hands are tied: You have to go by what outside experts think about a particular book. Very often you may have to publish a book you instinctively suspect to be a mountain of pedantic trash.

Not too long ago, I talked with the editor of a university press that recently had put out a collection of "deconstructionist" essays, which was certainly bound to be read by no one except a few of the new Druids and cast-iron conceptualizers. When the book came out, I noted that it was reviewed in a respectable old-line literary journal with a one-sentence notice: "This book weighs four pounds, thirteen ounces." I asked the editor why he published the book. His answer was that the compiler was on his editorial board. Also, the material was so specialized that none of the editors was able to make any sense out of it; accordingly he had to rely entirely on the views of co-specialists. Since for their safety and survival the Druids have their own tightly knit band of individuals ready to put an imprimatur on books written by others of their flock, it was inevitable that the book would be given a green light. To have passed the manuscript outside the coterie (which is precisely what should have been done) would have violated the silly notion of coterie approval that is the driving bugaboo of the university press.

The university press, then, reinforces the mind-set of the research university and acts on the philosophy that the best books are those safely and securely fixed in the niche of some subfield of learning. Go into a public library and look around for university press books. There will not be a great many in a public library, but characteristically you can expect to find titles like these: *The Growth of the Liberal Party in England Between 1886 and 1905; Fragments of "The Logic" in the Early Theological Writings of Hegel; The Origins of the Anti-Saloon League; Plantation Life in Alabama During the Early Civil War.* These are not real titles of books—I have just made them up. But they are characteristic of what might be in the latest list of a university press.

Why, you might well ask, did the author of the first book not write the whole history of the Liberal party in England? Too big a job for a lifetime? No, certainly not. The scholarly book must suggest narrow and sharp focus, not appear to be a book that an ordinary citizen would want to read. Its toughest audience, those who are going to be scrutinizing it goes to the publisher, will not be general readers but people who already know a great deal about the Liberal party of England, who have probably written their own books on the subject, and who will examine his work with a microscope, presumably in a mood of dyspepsia or malice. This is all to ensure that the book is composed of nine-tenths perspiration and one-tenth inspiration. It is to ensure that the writer has muddled over the material for years, cleared things with authorities, not stepped on any toes. It is to ensure that the writer didn't actually try to enjoy the process of writing. Again, this does not mean that there are no breakthrough books, no revolutionary books, from the university press gristmills. There are. They are just few and far between.

By a curious twist of irony the compulsion to publish, whether in university press books or specialized journals, has the very opposite effect of what is intended. University deans and administrators almost all believe that when they place the burden of publication on their professors, they will ensure greater production—more titles of books and articles, more "linage" of written material. Actually, as a professor you spend so many years being careful, precise, mindful of prestige and tradition, that you are wary of going into publication too soon. You would get hurt. Accordingly, you incline toward underproduction rather than overproduction; you turn out only a few books in your entire academic career. If left completely to your own devices, if not required to show evidences of fruitfulness, if not forced to create within a system of "credentialing," you might well become a far more productive and happy scholar.

People outside the walls of academia often ask why there seems to be this compulsive need to publish in the first place. And this question is sometimes joined with another: Is there really an obvious relationship between research and teaching? Needless to say, all administrators, and most researchers themselves, take these to be dumb questions. The answers are obvious or taken for granted. Publication is as much the end of academic labor as the pursuit of the Holy Grail was to the Knights of the Round Table. The logic goes something like this: The best teachers will obviously be the leaders in any field of endeavor, the people on the cutting edge of the creative process. And how do you identify the most creative figures in any field—the big-name figures, the "stars," as they are sometimes called in research universities? They are those who have "produced," that is to say, published in "refereed" journals or in books that have the imprint of a university press.

There is an obvious fallacy in this line of reasoning. Certainly the claim that the best teachers will be the most inspired has a kind of specious plausibility, but, alas, the whole argument falls apart when we perceive that in the present-day research university "inspiration" is defined in terms of speciality-oriented publication, which means the tame, cautious, and more often than not ponderously written works of the kind usually associated with the university press or the narrowly focused academic journal. In the end, the argument that the "inspired" researcher will be an inspired teacher founders on the key notion of inspiration; there is more than a little doubt that the majority of works of academic publication are inspired in any of the usual senses of that term. They are more likely to be filled with evidence of sweat, of precision, of attention to detail, of sensitivity to what is politic, of what is approved and sanctified, than of what we call inspiration, which is a product of largeness of vision, true flights of the imagination, surges of creativity.

Simply looked at from the angle of ordinary human experience, it ought to be evident that students in a university have found little truth in the idea that big-name professors are necessarily their best teachers—this leaving entirely aside the question of whether they will even come into contact with these usually well protected and isolated individuals. In his recent and challenging book *Killing the Spirit: Higher Education in America*, Page Smith casts serious doubt on the old academic shibboleth that the great scholar must of necessity be the best teacher. "Everyone who has attended a college or university has known famous or, one step down, 'distinguished' scholars who were the bores of the world as teachers. In their laboratories or studies they might be able to communicate to their students the inner spirit as well as 'methodology' of their researches, but as far as conveying anything but the most routine information to large groups of passive listeners, they were washouts."

The whole trouble is that in the research university the search for quality starts off on the wrong foot. It is assumed that quality is somehow related to intellectual activity of a certain sort. This is a reasonable assumption, but when it is insisted that the activity be publication or output, another and very suspicious dimension has been slipped in. Page Smith is quite accurate when he writes that "research defined as purposeful intellectual activity is certainly a legitimate requirement for a university teacher. Research necessarily resulting in production is quite another matter," and as often as not in the American university it has been vitiating and destructive, because it forces specialization and narrowness of outlook. As Smith puts it so well: "The best research and the only research that should be expected of university professors is wide and informed reading in their fields and related fields. The best teachers are almost invariably the most widely informed, those with the greatest range of interests and the most cultivated minds."

Alas, this is precisely where the American university has failed us. It has not sought to produce what it has both the time and resources to produce, that is, the most highly cultivated and best-informed people who are well versed in their own fields and related fields as well, people anxious to share this cultivation. Instead it has sought to produce the narrow-track expert, who can tortuously inch forward along some narrow line of thought or inquiry and add a few more layers of dust to the heap of learning. Yes, to be sure, in the universities there are some, perhaps quite a few, who break loose from these narrow lines and strike out on their own. Sometimes they produce evidence of this in publication, sometimes not. Sometimes they manage to chuck the narrow-track attitude and begin something splendid on their own a few years before retirement (which may be one of the hidden benefits of the tenure system, perhaps its greatest benefit). But the frantic compulsion to produce specialized works, to exhibit publication linage, has not, for the most part, led to the turning out of individuals of the broadest cultivation, individuals who play with knowledge as well as grapple with it, individuals uplifted by knowledge rather than harnessed to it.

These people of the widest and most joyful learning, then, are also the people who will be the most effective teachers. Unfortunately, the compulsive goals and inhibitions of the modern American university have not created the kind of congenial environment needed to produce them. As presently constituted the university is not set up to give us people of the widest concerns, but rather quantifiable end products, that is to say, so many students prepared to take jobs or enter the professions, so many professors manifesting the tangible evidence of research—publication and just plain sweat. These segregated functions, the ideal of the professor as a workhorse and the ideal of the student as an end product, are not healthy for the university community. Accordingly, we waste energy when we worry about whether the professor has tried to avoid teaching. The root of the problem, despite what many recent critics have assumed, is actually deeper. The fruits of the publication treadmill—the academic style and the drive toward productivity—cripple the community of learning in such a way that simply bringing professors back to the classroom wouldn't do very much to improve the quality of higher education.

Part III

The Poisoned Well
of Learning

11

Defreighting the Curriculum: The Legacy of the Sixties

SOMETHING BIG, something revolutionary, perhaps even catastrophic, happened to the American university during the 1960s. But what actually went wrong in those years? According to the educational critics of the time, and to many since, the university had become politicized, the campus a place of political ferment and intrigue instead of a place of learning. Rather than reading books, students were crusading against the war in Viet Nam, erecting roadblocks and barricades, staging sit-ins in the office of the president, destroying property, howling at corporate recruiters, building shantytowns, sometimes calling for the overthrow of the government.

It is unfortunate that these are the main things that are remembered about the sixties, because focusing on them distracts us from a revolution of even greater significance that was occurring at the same time. Not that the political rumblings were of only minor importance: They were endured at great expense by the universities; they cost millions of dollars, most of which could have been much better spent elsewhere. They were a severe drain on the energies of students, faculty, and administrators. But something else was brewing that was much more destructive to higher education. It did not go

105

completely unnoticed at the time, but its importance was invariably obscured by the political storm clouds that were drifting overhead.

The 1960s was the decade when the universities made the complete adjustment to the masses who had arrived since World War II. The traditional college education was pummeled, shrunk, detoothed, if you like. The universities found a way to trivialize undergraduate education; faculties discovered ways to defreight the traditional curriculum so that students could be passed along to law or professional school or to the job market painlessly and without complaint. Professors discovered ingenious techniques for keeping the shell of the traditional curriculum on museumlike display, while cutting the heart out of it in reality. This surgery freed the professors for further self-absorption in their own work; giving students an easy ride gave teachers an easy ride as well. Such was the real legacy of the sixties.

The quake that shook up American universities during the 1960s began to be felt fairly early in the decade. Most historians will select 1964 as the year of the quake, for that was the year of the well-publicized riots at the University of California's Berkeley campus. But there were rumblings before that. Clark Kerr, then the university's president, had apprehensively noted the previous year that "the undergraduate students were restless," although neither he nor anyone in the academic establishment of the time fathomed why this might be so. When the tumult was unleashed, many observers of the educational scene were quick to point out that Berkeley, of all the huge land-grant universities, had somehow become the archetype and glittering example of the large, impersonal learning factory where undergraduate students were merely being sent along as on a conveyor belt.

Berkeley in 1964, more than any other institution of its kind, had found ways to wall undergraduates off from the faculty and the academic community in general. For many years Berkeley had prided itself on becoming a world-class research university, and as such its professors were shielded from lower-level students, most of whom were taught in mammoth lecture classes, sometimes containing as many as a thousand students. A great deal of the instruction was by teaching assistants, and many students could pass through four years at Berkeley without having so much as a single human contact with a professor. Professors were permitted to have offices with no names on the door, marked only with a number the aloof inhabitants might reveal to students if the spirit moved.

After the 1964 riots, in which students seized and occupied Sproul Hall, after the establishment of the so-called Berkeley Free Speech movement, and even before the spread of similar movements to other universities around the country, the faculty senate at Berkeley appointed a commission to study the campus rumblings. Its report, known as the Muscatine Report for the committee's chairman, an obscure English professor named Charles Muscatine, gave more than a fair warning of how student activism would subsequently be dealt with by college faculties everywhere in the land: namely with fear, timidity, and surrender tinctured with huge doses of guilt. The students wanted something; something about the university was bothering them. What was it?

The truth is that, outside the political realm and beyond the cries for a different war policy, the students really didn't know what they wanted. The word they used, however—and it became the buzzword of the sixties—was *relevance*. The college experience must somehow be made relevant to the present generation of students. But what was relevance? The students didn't know, and apparently their professors didn't know either. All that was known is that there was a call for action, a call for reform, and if there is one thing that professors can't be seen resisting it is a call for reform. To be sure, they may eventually find a way to sneak around the back of this urge for reform, at least to the extent of keeping things comfy for themselves. But in progressive, forward-looking America it is not possible to resist publicly calls for reforms, especially when they are loud and strident. Therefore, professors frantically began searching for ways to placate the students lest noisy masses burst into the professors' offices or rip things up in the laboratories.

Of course, it was easy to take the side of the students where the war in Viet Nam was concerned. It was easy to join the raging chorus against the government and big business. It was easy for liberally oriented professors to mouth confusing and contradictory platitudes about "the greening of America." It was a little less easy to join with the students in condemning the university. The professors didn't precisely do that. Instead, the call to "reform" in the educational sphere meant surrendering to everything the students were clamoring for. In order to continue to be let alone by students, the

108

THE POISONED WELL OF LEARNING

professors needed to take the spine out of the university curriculum. If there were things that the students didn't like, too many onerous requirements, too many unpopular subjects to be studied, too many hurdles to be gotten over before graduation, these nuisances would have to be removed. However, academia would have to extract something in return. A place like Berkeley would not, in fact, give up gargantuan lecture courses. It wouldn't have the resources to do so without crimping the professor's style. No, such courses would stay. They are every bit as much in evidence today as they were twenty years ago. But new and imaginative ways would be found to make them popular with students. The rigor would be pumped out of them. A's would be handed out all around. The unpopular class would be thrown out or redesigned to meet new demands and appetites.

It was all done under this madly fluttering banner of "relevance." The faculty senate report at Berkeley clearly pointed the way that things would be going in American colleges and universities for the next decade. "Our student body is too large, too various, too changing to be susceptible to many universal formulations," said the report. We need to make the curriculum over so that it will be comfortable and presumably undemanding to the multitudes, something that can be done under the impressive-sounding but essentially hollow call for relevance. We must eliminate those courses "that have through obsolescence lost their contact with vital human concerns."

One could get into a long and futile debate over whether the new "ideas" of curriculum reform that spread throughout the land in the next several years were intellectually justifiable. It could be said by many (and has been) that the traditional curriculum was jettisoned without anyone ever having proved that it was not "relevant." It might be possible to demonstrate that the curricular innovations of the 1960s were mere acts of desperation, the results of sheer opportunism. One might argue that whatever was now called "relevant" was relevant only because certain numbers of people were insisting that it was so, and that it was necessary for professors and faculty groups to get on the bandwagon and hoot for "change" and "relevance." But one thing was certain about the developments in the sixties and can be documented with ease. The college curriculum was softened, defreighted. The reforms of this period may not have made the undergraduate experience better or more modern, but they certainly made it easier. Students were still riding down the conveyor belt, but now they were doing it in comfort.

Should the students or the professors get the credit for the so-called curriculum reforms of the 1960s? It is pointless to argue the issue: The two groups mapped out the territory together. Of these things we can be certain: It was a time when professors were looking for ways to sidestep conflicts with students. Students were looking for ways to render the curriculum innocuous. If they weren't going to be "engaged" in the work of the university, at least they could be relieved of its burdens. They could have easy entry into the job market or into law school, sent on their way with palms and flourishes.

Educational reform, it was called, and during the sixties it spread to every campus in the land. Not many stopped to observe at the time that all the reforms being asked for were of the defreighting variety. Pressure was put on to decrease the number of hours needed for graduation, to reduce the number of required courses, to unload courses students found too difficult. In this era there was a push to get rid of requirements that students master a foreign language or learn the rudiments of mathematics. There were new and clearly less demanding courses and "options"; if the introductory course for some science was difficult or annoying for large numbers of students, you instituted a baby- or TV-type course to take its place. Students were allowed to withdraw without penalty from courses they didn't care for, even up to the last day of class, and in some cases even after they had received a grade they didn't like.

Whatever the publicly expressed "ideal" behind the educational reforms that came on the scene in these years, one couldn't avoid the impression that the actual result was nothing but a clever gimmick to make the undergraduate curriculum softer, more pliable, than it had been before. Consider one very popular fad of this period, the pass/fail option, under which a student takes a course and is graded in the normal manner by the instructor but, unless the student fails, is given only an indiscriminating grade of "pass" on the official transcript. Accordingly, if the lowest passing grade is D, and the student achieves this grade, it will appear on the permanent record as P or Pass.

An example of the kind of reasoning offered for this little

innovation, and usually accepted by faculty committees and senates with bovine indifference, is provided by a University of Illinois catalogue I have in hand: Pass/Fail courses have been initiated "to encourage students to explore areas of interest which they might otherwise feel compelled to avoid because such exploration might lead to poor grades, and to reduce the sometimes detrimental overemphasis on grades". In short, the pass/fail option goes under the flag of a fair-minded liberalizing of the harsh trend toward excessive competition.

A noble-sounding aim, no doubt, but twist it however you like, the real result of the pass/fail course is to lighten a student's workload by one course each semester. That is to say, a pass/fail course is simply one in which the student needs to put in only the smallest amount of effort to get by, however idealistically the matter may be looked on in theory. The fact is, the students themselves did not perceive the pass/fail option as a way of broadening their intellectual horizons but only as a way of working less. It meant one fewer course to worry about per semester, or, if you like, one-fifth less effort, one-fifth less reading, one-fifth fewer tests.

One of the most fascinating developments of the sixties is that students during this time managed to bamboozle professors into accepting their own slyly transparent recipes for change; professors who, a generation or so before, would have given the Bronx cheer to any such proposals would ratify, almost without a whimper, all the manifestos handed up by students, transforming the debased student lingo of advocacy into high-sounding educational ideals and giving them a luster of respectability that at one time they could never have attained. During this period students were active participants at faculty and committee meetings, and their imagination and ingenuity as "political schemers" would surely challenge those of a Borgia.

Dipping into my archives of this period, I find a copy of an alumni magazine from a prestigious liberal arts college that contains a long article on what is called the college's "present curriculum review." Yes, here it is in the lingo of the day, and using all the popular buzzwords: faculty justification for "meeting the needs" of the present generation of students (they probably should have said "wants").

This news item, which apparently was written by a student and not by a reporter from the Alumni Office, begins by telling the presumably long-since-petrified alumni that, while their alma mater has not been a leader in the "liberalizing trends" that have become apparent in the colleges and universities, "neither has it remained dormant." And in the last two years, it boasts, "the college has been involved in a fervent and genuine dialogue on the curriculum and revision to it."

Among the reforms students apparently won for themselves were a reduction in the total number of courses required for graduation, from forty to thirty-six, and a new semester system described as "a 4-1-4 semester schedule (four courses each semester sandwiched between a month of independent study)." A strange kind of sandwich, this—it looks as though a month of independent study is sandwiched between two semesters, each with four courses instead of the old five—but in any case, the upshot is a lessening of the academic load. It's hard to see anything else as the result. There are shorter semesters (thirteen weeks instead of fifteen), fewer courses per semester (four instead of five), fewer courses required for graduation (thirty-six instead of forty), and a generous "study" period (vacation, need one ask?) between semesters. Comprehensive examinations in one's major, instituted a mere decade or so before, were mercilessly killed and disappeared from memory. Clearly there was a lot for the students to cheer about in all this.

Not everything the students wanted was accepted by the faculty. On the table were proposals to abolish *all* requirements except those specific to a particular major. The students particularly pummeled Freshman English and the foreign language requirements, two classic bugbears. The faculty stood pat on these things.

Still, for the most part, the faculty contemplated all of these proposals with serious nods and expressions of genuine sympathy. During the course of the debate a professor of psychology siding with the students reportedly said, "If a liberal education is to mean anything, it must mean an education designed for each student individually. And it should mean a program of studies designed *by* each student, not *for* him." All sounds wonderful, doesn't it? In the dialogues of such times the key terms have a lofty and impressive ring, and few saw them as the shabby dodges, the placebos, that they actually were. I suppose that the good professor of psychology never stopped to think that education, if it is to be anything, is first of all a process whereby the immature are to be shaped by the more mature, and that education at some point must also require the designation of the form and content of study by someone other than the student. Presumably the professor did not think that education is merely emoting at the end of a log, and he probably would hold that a student who selects a certain course—the professor's own course in psychology, let us say—has to expect to follow a course of study laid down by the teacher. But, befuddled by student rhetoric, he could not see that the same reasoning needs to be applied to larger units of study than the single course, and that this is why we have such a thing as a curriculum in the first place, and also one of the main reasons why we have faculties, faculty meetings, faculty studies—to preside over a *course* of studies.

In *The Closing of the American Mind*, Allan Bloom concludes that this era of curriculum reform in America's colleges and universities was a tragic chapter in our educational history. While it is now customary to say that some good was achieved during that period, Bloom laments that he could find little other than destructiveness coming from this era. The trouble with the things that were alleged to be *good* about the reform era—"greater openness," "less rigidity," "freedom from authority," "ability to do one's own thing," and all the rest—is that "they have no content and express no view of what is wanted of a university education." The result was "unmitigated disaster" for the universities. Bloom, who was teaching philosophy at Cornell at the time, recalled Plato's wonderful analogy of a ship sailing without a captain and without a sail, carried forward by any wind that happened to be blowing. During the sixties he was sitting on various committees and found himself voting futilely against the dropping of one requirement after another:

> The old core curriculum—according to which every student in the college had to take a smattering of courses in the major divisions of knowledge—was abandoned. One professor of comparative literature—an assiduous importer of the latest Paris fashions—explained that these requirements taught little, really did not introduce students to the various disciplines, and bored them. I admitted this was true. He then expressed

surprise at my unwillingness to give them up. It was because they were, I said, a threadbare reminiscence of the unity of knowledge and provided an obstinate little hint that there are some things that one must know about if one is to be educated. You don't replace something with nothing. Of course that is precisely what the educational reform of the sixties was doing.

Unfortunately, frontal attacks on the course of studies were not the only sad legacy of this so-called age of reform. There was consistent pressure against the rigors of higher education on all fronts. Students were doing their best to impose their ideas wherever possible, seeking to make their education as congenial and "soft" as it could possibly be made. If they couldn't partake of the academic community, if they were forced to be merely passive receivers, at least they could make the learning process as comfortable as possible. Accordingly, they went to work not only on the curriculum as a whole but on the content of individual courses, on reading lists and examinations, on their instructors and professors, always with the aim of lessening the impact of all aspects of instruction from grades to methods of teaching and the numbers of assignments.

The 1960s produced irresistible pressures to provide students with easier, less demanding courses, courses in which high grades would be virtually ensured. It became an age of "grade inflation," in which professors were pressured relentlessly for more generosity. Year by year college faculties offered higher grades as if they were handing out cookies. A look at the records of any college or university in the land from this period will show that the numbers of students receiving A's and B's in their courses doubled and then tripled. Indeed, it is not hard to find whole courses in some universities—undergraduate courses—where few if any students received any grade below C (C, after all, was intended as an "average" grade, yet students everywhere now came to look upon it as a "bad" one).

This shocking grade inflation took place at a time when it was universally agreed that students' academic preparation in high school was poorer than it had been in years, a time when SAT scores were in sharp decline. Students were getting worse, but their grades were continuing to go up. In the 1920s only 20 percent of the students at Harvard made the Dean's List. By 1978 this figure had risen to 78 percent. In the academic year 1974–75, the entering freshman class at the University of Michigan received the lowest SAT scores in decades, yet in their college class work they received the highest grade point average ever. In the University of Illinois the course known as Freshman Rhetoric, where in the 1930s only around 10 percent of the students received a grade of A, 80 percent of the students received a grade of either A or B, and in some sections of this course every single student received an A!

A preoccupation with grades, with competitiveness, became an almost pathological phenomenon in the student mind during the sixties, and this has continued unabated since. As a university teacher I frequently find students coming to me with a bald demand for an A, sometimes accompanied by mildly worded explanations that if they don't get an A they can't get into law school or medical school. Students, of course, are well aware that undergraduate education in this country has become an entitlement, that everyone is permitted to pass through, so they reach out without hesitation to the next logical step, which is that law school or medical school or a top job should also be an entitlement. They want a grading policy that offers no surprises, no challenges. To get this they have in effect made a pact with their professors: You give me the easy A and I'll leave you alone. I'll let you merely process me; I'll not demand that you actually interact with me.

It wasn't only the students who pressured professors for higher grades during this period. Using their own devious methods, and with their own morally indefensible ends, administrators were doing the same thing. As the tenure crunch became aggravated on college and university campuses during the 1960s and 1970s, administrators began to push professors to show that they were popular teachers. Needing more "quantifiable" information on the performance of professors (and evidence to unload them when it became financially necessary), administrators began to institute forms and questionnaires for students to "evaluate" individual teachers. Needless to say, the process was justified by administrators on the ground that they were now able to offer evidence that professors were attending to teaching as well as research. On the surface the evaluation of professors looked like a giant step forward in a sensible campaign to improve college teaching.

Actually it was a giant step backward. Student evaluation of teaching, which at one time would have seemed outrageous if not downright obscene, was just another of the transparent gimmicks of student control that emerged from the 1960s. It had as its real effect a new climate in which professors had to live in perpetual anxiety about the reports students would turn in on them, in which they had to adjust their teaching practices because students had a great deal to say about matters of promotion, raises, and tenure. Young professors, especially those awaiting tenure, had to be constantly on guard and wary of displeasing their students lest a poor report of some kind lose them their jobs. Accordingly, the teacher evaluation movement was just another addition to the long list of pressures put on professors during the 1960s and 1970s to "let up" on college students and give them an easy ride through the system. It never held out the promise of making teaching better, only easier.

With evaluation forms in hand, students now had a great deal more to hold over their professors' heads in matters of work requirements, examinations, and the like. Not being stupid, students immediately perceived that evaluation was a very useful game to them, and they learned to play it with predictability and finesse. On the other hand, and as a kind of comic footnote, in the years since the teacher evaluation frenzy swept the land in the 1960s, there has been no indication that students are the slightest bit happier or more satisfied with the overall quality of teaching than they were a few generations before, when teachers were far more demanding and didn't have to answer them. To be sure, college administrators now have larger quantities of (mostly bogus) quantitative data to use in pulling themselves out of promotion quagmires. But this actually did little if anything to raise the level of teaching. And at the present time the brightest students have figured this out. Although they appreciate the blessings of grade inflation and want these inflationary trends to continue, they privately distrust "teacher popularity" and see it as one more means whereby they are euchred out of a solid education. The graduate students also have picked up on this same phenomenon. Not long ago a graduate student of my acquaintance remarked that he was suspicious of the grades he had received in his seminars. "It's easy to give everybody an A in a seminar," he complained. "But giving an A absolves the professor of the chore of giving us detailed comments, suggestions as to what can be improved, how to submit for publication, and so on." Grade inflation has been a comforting gift to both students and professors over the last several generations, but the loss to education has been considerable.

Grade inflation, pass/fail courses, reductions in workload, elimination of requirements—these are among the tangible evidences of the decline in the quality of undergraduate education since the 1960s. Unfortunately they are only some of the more obvious signs of the defreighting of college education. Some may wish to argue that most of the "reforms" that have been mentioned constitute only minor changes or adjustments; taken one by one, they may well be, but put together in a heap they add up to vast and shocking corruption. And those who believe that undergraduate education has been eroded only in administrative detail are not seeing the bleak picture presented by the learning experiences of individual students. The old-time undergraduate course itself has not remained sturdy but has decayed from within—one might say that it suffers from dry rot. On the surface all seems well; a healthy plethora of courses are available to every undergraduate student; there seems to be an embarrassment of riches. But a great many college course that were once stars in the firmament have faded into black holes. While the well-oiled machinery of the educational system seems to be grinding smoothly away, it now turns out a cheaper, gaudier, and less-refined product.

12

Lost in the Wilderness: The Undergraduate Course Today

T HERE IS A GOOD DEAL MORE to this issue of the defreighting of the college curriculum. The students who went to work "reforming" the curriculum in the 1960s and 1970s, softening it up for their comfort, accomplished what they did at a time when universities had their own motives for helping them out. Responding to a vast influx of money to be spent on prestigious research projects, universities began pushing to the limit an already strong tendency to become research factories and think tanks. Fading quickly from view was the notion that university life should involve fraternization with the young in a community of learning. Professors in their lofty roles as "specialists" and "experts" gravitated toward any expediency that would keep students out of their hair, and this meant surrendering to all the new fads, to every demand that undergraduate education be rendered harmless, trivial, and unchallenging.

This situation had been brewing since the first graduate schools were founded but became oppressive only after World War II, as professors received the institutional blessing that allowed them to drift slowly away from their original roles as educators. Students would get short shrift. The function of advising students withered, became routine; sometimes it was carried out by departmental secretaries with rubber stamps. There were fewer opportunities for students to meet professors and interact with them in a personal way. Professors seldom entertained undergraduates in their homes as they did in the nineteenth century; many present-day professors are not even aware that such a practice ever existed. Professors, and even administrators, abdicated all responsibility for the behavior and social life of students.

Undergraduate seminars and tutorials became rarities. Lower-level courses were passed along to teaching assistants or other "adjuncts." The amount of teaching that was carried out in large lecture sections increased. As I pointed out in the last chapter, in some public institutions a lecture course with more than a thousand students has not been unheard of. The primary teaching function is sometimes accomplished by video presentations or slide-projector shows, which allow teachers to have all of their material canned for repeated use. In this kind of mass setting students are seldom asked to write papers or essays; they are subjected instead to computer-graded examinations, ensuring that the instructor never has to look over a single piece of work that the student has written. Worst of all, the undergraduate course itself becomes a petrified product; it is hollowed out, trivialized. Occasionally such courses may be fun, entertaining. The large lecture course may be assigned to the rare departmental spellbinder or cut-up. But in the typical university the basic course, whether given in the lecture hall or small classroom, has as its central purpose the dispensing of predigested pablum.

Undergraduate education in the past several generations has been dealt the low card. The prevailing formula is not in doubt: Graduate and professional programs are high-priority items, undergraduate instruction low-priority; research and publicly recognized "output" are the pure gold, teaching and human interaction the baser metals. Resources—both financial and human—go to the things that receive outside public prestige and recognition. The defects of teaching go unnoticed except by those who are in a poor position to complain about them.

But let's see, in terms of particulars, how these priorities short-change the undergraduate in the American university today. Let's say you are a young student entering the freshman class of a large prestigious university. You sign up for a number of courses to fill so-called basic requirements. One of these courses, let us say, is Introduction to Psychology—a course intended to fulfill a requirement in "social sciences." There is a large lecture section held twice a week, usually taught by some remote senior professor, with a little luck one whose voice can be heard by everybody. With a little more luck the professor might be capable of presenting the material with clarity and force. But the chance of your ever having any important contact with this worthy is almost nil. Rather, your human contacts will be with a junior instructor or teaching assistant (in many scientific courses a lab assistant) who meets with small sections of the large course one or two days a week. Teaching assistants may be more accessible than the senior professor—but not much. Chances are they are young, preoccupied, overbusy, entirely wrapped up in research or graduate work. They have taken up teaching burdens so they can pay tuition and grocery bills until such time as they themselves become senior faculty members and can give up the burden of teaching freshmen.

Addiction to the drug of graduate teaching assistants—many of whom are only a few years older than the students they teach—has been a long-standing dependency of the American university. In the beginning, when graduate schools were small in size, reliance on teaching assistants was a practice of modest proportions. Only the most senior graduate students, those about to complete their Ph.D.'s, were employed in this capacity. Universities in the early days were scrupulous in hiring teaching assistants and assigning them to the classroom. And the universities tended to be apologetic about the practice and usually promised that it was a stop-gap measure, one that would be kept in place only until more funds were obtained to hire "regular" professors. After World War II more money flowed in (so, alas, did more students), but universities expanded the practice of using teaching assistants in the classroom. It was now the norm, no longer a confessed aberration or inadequacy. Sometimes student teachers entered the classroom with absolutely no preparation in teaching and no proven ability in their field; occasionally they received not a word of guidance from the senior staff on teaching practices and procedures. Reportedly, foreign graduate students have been put in classrooms without being able to speak a word of

English! Shocked by such horror stories, a few state legislatures have recently passed laws requiring English competence among college classroom teachers.

What about these TAs, with whom beginning students may have their only contact? Are they good teachers? Well, sometimes they are. Sometimes, being young and idealistic, they put in superb effort. Unfortunately, as graduate students they are bound tightly to their graduate programs. They are struggling to master the jargon and mind-set of some field of specialization; they necessarily have a hard time standing free of it and putting themselves in the place of the freshman who is not yet there. They don't have the "larger picture," which one might hope the senior professor possesses. It is not fair to condemn the achievement of individual teaching assistants out of hand, but their ubiquitous presence is indicative of the low status that undergraduate instruction possesses in large universities.

Let's go back to that introductory course in psychology. What is wrong with it is not only that the lectures are too large or that contact teaching is turned over to inexperienced beginners. The deeper and more fundamental problem with a course of this kind is that it is not suited to liberal education at all but is rather a watered-down version of upper-level courses in psychology. It is, accordingly, as dead as mutton in the mind of the typical eighteen-year-old freshman. It is nothing more than a hurdle to be overcome. The teachers who dispense courses of this sort plainly don't believe in them. To be sure, they may believe that such courses are necessary cogs in the educational machine. They may see them as performing a useful function for their own department; they may be drawing a certain number of students into work in psychology. Who knows— someday a few students from this undifferentiated mass may choose to major in psychology, perhaps even go on for a Ph.D.

Mainly, though, when one is a professor of psychology (you can make it modern history or linguistics, if you wish) looking out into the sea of faces, what one sees is a huge horde of human blanks being processed in the name of liberal education, along with a few potential converts to one's own restricted monastery garden. If one has any oratorical facility or skills of persuasion, one's main goal will be to wow the second small group with the buzz words and abracadabra of one's own calling. What one never does, of course, is to show how and where psychology fits into the student's already existing culture.

Nor does the professor make any effort to allow the students to synthesize what they learn here with what they are learning elsewhere in their course of study. Seldom do students enjoy the opportunity to question what they are being taught. They are passive receivers. They may on rare occasions get a chance to ask a question, but it is likely to be something they need to know to survive and pass the professor's examination. The subject matter itself and its place in the broader picture of science or human culture are never brought into question. Only its sanctified technicalities are on the table. The professor, and usually the teaching assistants as well, make it perfectly clear that their interest is only in keeping the students rolling along the conveyor belt. They have not the slightest interest in the students' values or the structure of their minds. Only one thing matters: that so many facts, so many hard-coated concepts, are swallowed in a period of fifteen weeks.

There is a shared understanding on the part of all participants that this course is nothing but an antechamber to something else. Indeed even the professor and the teaching assistant may be waiting for something more important to come their way. A professor might have chosen the large lecture course because he or she likes to lecture and colleagues don't—a rare occurrence. Such a person may be well compensated by never having to grade papers or see students in the office. But I have known departments—and not a few of them— where the large lecture course is a kind of punishment meted out to those who haven't cut the mustard in the profession, to womanizers, dipsomaniacal misfits, or those in ideological disgrace. Teaching assistants, on the other hand, have few choices. They are at the bottom of the totem pole—and know it. They must toil away in this sweatshop until the time comes when they can make good their escape, when they may be given their own small seminars of advanced students. In the meantime, they see their sections of the vast course as bread and butter—stale bread and rancid butter.

Keep in mind that the prevailing opinion about these lower-level introductory courses is that they are "service" functions. They are only something to be endured by those who teach them and those who are obliged to take them. There is a shared belief in their unimportance. On the part of the teachers, whether professors or

TAs, the introductory course is a place where they bide their time until assigned a "high-horsepower" course in their own specialization—Behavioral Dynamics or Multivariate Correlational Techniques, let us say. This is the really hot stuff. This is the really important material.

Several generations ago the undergraduate introductory course—whether taught in the large lecture hall or small classroom—was held in considerable esteem in the American university . I daresay it still is in a certain number of institutions. For the most part, however, with the cancerous growth of professionalism in the academic environment, these courses have been trashed or gutted. The shell is still there, but the inside has been scooped out and filled with something else. The something else may be neat, carefully packaged material, much like the material in a textbook, but it bears only a faint resemblance to a genuine educational transaction. Naturally students know that they are receiving prepackaged food and respond accordingly, turning to other things—student activism perhaps, or the more inspiring culture of the dorm room or the rap session or the beer parlor jamboree.

As to the content of the once-esteemed general education course, universities have taken one of two alternate paths, both of which are inappropriate for undergraduate students. The faculties either opt for a "junior" or low-level version of the advanced technical or professional course, or they attempt to lure students with "fun" courses in which little is demanded and all may achieve good grades. It is in planning this sort of course that one hears the most chatter about "relevance," about "meeting student needs," about the urgency of "curriculum reform." But there really isn't much choice between watered-down technicalities or cheap popularization. *Neither* alternative is desirable for the average vigorous eighteen-year-old looking for challenge in the college experience.

Not too long ago I had an opportunity to talk with a philosophy teacher, an old acquaintance, employed by a major urban university. I asked him how his department managed to keep afloat during the sixties and seventies when students were "fixing" the curriculum and faculties were rooting out things that weren't "relevant." It wasn't easy, he admitted. Philosophy, after all, is a rigorous subject, a demanding one, even at the lower levels. The abstract nature of the subject seems to exclude those incapable of sustained thought. In the free-wheeling sixties, certainly, it excluded a good many of those who came to college for vocational purposes, those who wanted merely to be supplied with "information" for use on the job. My friend's department lost many undergraduate students in the sixties and seventies. Things looked bleak. Fewer students were becoming philosophy majors. For a time it appeared that half of the departmental staff might have no one to teach. No new professors were being hired.

How did they solve the problem? How did they get their share of undergraduate students back? To meet this crisis, so my friend told me, the department inaugurated a number of what he called "blue baby" courses—with names like Philosophy and Sex, or Philosophy and the Urban Crisis, or Philosophy and Cinema—the purposes of which were to lure the unwary undergraduate into philosophy's gentler precincts. Later, with a little luck, the student might be persuaded to tarry for the real thing—courses in symbolic logic or in the ordinary language conundrums of Wittgenstein or whatever other esoteric puzzlements may now be amusing the graduate seminars.

This gimmick worked, up to a point. A number of students started drifting back, although not with overwhelming enthusiasm. From an educational standpoint, however, a troubling question could be asked: What was the use of such courses, many of which remain in the curriculum in this and other universities? Students sense that these contrived courses are not real thing, and they react to them lethargically. I suppose it would have been impolite of me to suggest to my friend that there are doubts about the ability of the typical professional philosopher, even one who possessed a gift for popularization, to teach such a course relating to the generality of experience. In the years since World War II, philosophy has become thoroughly professionalized, thoroughly withdrawn from the cultural mainstream. There are few philosophers working today in the tradition of the classic American philosophers who held the field during the early years of the twentieth century—James, Royce, Santayana, Dewey, and others who wrote for the general populace *as well as* for fellow philosophers, and who took up large public issues in their writings.

Philosophy, that is to say, has become almost exclusively a game for philosophers, a thoroughly technologized subject. Its practitioners devote all of their hours to fumbling with fraternal wordplay, solving puzzles, writing for esoteric journals like *Mind* and *Analysis*. Little that they do makes philosophers suitable authorities on any aspect of general culture. This prompts us to ask, how can such people have anything of interest to say about sex or cinema or popular culture or any of the other things that they attempt to teach in their lower-level popular courses? There is nothing in either their professional background or their academic training to suggest that philosophers—now word jugglers, miniaturists, analyzers of microscopic topics—would have anything more enlightening to say about urban problems or marriage or sex than the typical bread-truck driver or bookkeeper. Philosophers *might* have something worthwhile to say about such subjects if they ever got to them in their professional work, but they never do. Their professional life is hermetically sealed away from the shared culture; they never abandon their fierce abstractions. Of course, they may in fact do so on the side, although they never let it be known lest it evoke derisive catcalls or raspberries from colleagues.

Bright and eager undergraduates know that the philosophy professor who decides to talk about the movies or the mass media probably isn't much better qualified to speak on these subjects than the students themselves. They know that the smorgasbord courses they are being offered are not really extensions of the professors' interests or passions. If you want to understand the philosophy professor's preoccupations and intellectual style, you look to the kind of thing that he or she writes for *Mind* (which, declared one British wit, ought to have been called "The Vacant Mind"). Philosophy originally meant "love of wisdom"; today that is a rather risible definition. Maybe a new word should be adopted that signifies a love of the academic subject of philosophy, the field of philosophy. There lingers in the term *philosopher* a kind of implied authority: wisdom lovers are assumed to possess the brain power and the expertise to deal with a broad range of intellectual problems, but there is little evidence in their own professional work to prove it.

In the last half century or more, the total absorption of professors in their narrow professional field has largely resulted in their forgetting how to deal with the students who need to get their bearings in the intellectual world. As we have seen, the allegedly prestigious figures in the university are allowed to escape responsibility for the teaching of lower-level courses. They seldom inquire what goes on in such courses and tend to surrender to whatever plans junior faculty, departmental drudges, committees, or even students have drawn up for them. I am familiar with many renowned professors in a multitude of fields who have not the slightest idea of what is going on in the introductory courses of their departments, simply assuming that whatever it is it must be good.

Every once in a while, when universities are under particularly heated attack for their handling of undergraduate instruction, fumbling attempts are made to show that things aren't really all that bad, although usually not much is done to make drastic changes in the system. Administrators pretend to take teaching abuses seriously and call for committees to study them. A few senior professors are asked to offer a beginning course for a semester or two. The administration puts out guidebooks or white papers on teaching. Teaching assistants are monitored and checked up on. Word gets out that instructors of beginning courses are being rewarded; at the University of Illinois we have annual awards and even banquets for the most popular teaching assistants. Popularity is determined by ratings and evaluation forms. The trouble with these questionnaires is that the woebegone undergraduate students have nothing to compare the general run of their instructors with. Measurements of popular and unpopular teachers are made within a system that is already in place and for which no alternative is known. The main problems, of course, are in the total system itself—its sickly and moribund courses, its gutted liberal arts tradition that is being kept on display in mummified form. And in the last decade or so the liberal arts mummies have turned to powder, as I will suggest in a future chapter.

So the liberal spirit of education today languishes in the shade. Its proper administration requires strong personal interaction between teacher and student, something that has long since disappeared from the modern university. Students are being given "a taste of something" in their undergraduate years, and once they are around for a while they will get on the track—so we are told by those in the know. The conveyor belt will haul them up. Well, undoubtedly the typical student does get a taste of something in today's undergraduate courses. It would be an exaggeration to say that these courses are totally worthless. However, it is usually junk food that students receive—fare that is distinctly below their capabilities for learning, and far below the capabilities of our universities, the richest and best endowed in the world.

13

A Fallen Giant of the Curriculum: Freshman English

IF YOU WANT TO FIND OUT why the quality of college education has declined so sharply during the last several generations, you do not need to turn to the abuses of the large lecture course, or to teaching by slide projector, or to teaching by adjuncts and graduate students; you can turn to the specific content of undergraduate courses themselves, to what goes on in these courses, what is learned from them, what they add to a student's general culture or to his or her passion for learning and for life. Consider a course nearly universal on campuses throughout the land: Freshman English, sometimes officially called Elements of Composition, Introductory Rhetoric, or by any number of other academic-sounding titles. As a close observer of this particular course for at least three decades, I have been aware of the ailments to which it has been susceptible at most universities. At one time it was believed that the course had a major role in the undergraduate curriculum, an important function to perform for college students. But its usefulness and its days of glory passed us by.

Freshman English at one time was as close to pure gold as you

127

could get in the undergraduate curriculum; it represented general education par excellence; it was intended as an introduction to higher learning. It gave a perspective on a new and presumably loftier dimension of education. The course was difficult and demanding, but at the same time challenging and invigorating. It called the student to acts of careful reading, serious discussions of ideas, disciplined and methodical writing. It offered an opportunity to leave childhood and adolescence behind and savor the world of the intellect, even if in relatively small doses.

In most universities Freshman English has fallen on evil days. It has been watered down or trivialized. Except in some small private institutions, the course is assigned to teaching assistants who have little idea of what it was originally intended to accomplish. Most often these TAs are graduate students in literature and so assume that the course is a first-step course for undergraduates who expect to enter the field of literature—a grievous, I think even tragic, mistake. In some universities, even prestige institutions, the course has been eliminated because it is too hard to administer. Some English departments, usually as a way to conserve precious resources, cut it back to one semester or "exempt" large numbers of students on the grounds that college freshman nowadays are bright and articulate and already know how to write—a foolish assumption that is belied by repeated complaints from other departments, as well as by the test scores of high school seniors. Others replace Freshman English with a course that smacks of professionalism rather than general education; of course, at its best it *was* a general education course, and the very notion of general education makes no sense in the research university. The fate of Freshman English, accordingly, has been what might be expected in a highly professionalized environment. The perceived need for writing instruction demands that the course be kept, but it is retained only in a mummified form; it is kept mainly for display. Those who teach the course, and especially those who administer it, have no belief in it.

Originally, though, Freshman English was an altogether different thing. The course got its start at Harvard back in the 1880s and 1890s in response to the deficiencies of the rapidly disappearing "classical" curriculum. Harvard called it English A in those days. The moving spirit behind the course was an eccentric New England Brahmin named Barrett Wendell who simply loved teaching in the "college" and had no desire to be a research professor. The reasoning behind the idea was impeccable. Like many of his contemporaries, Wendell perceived that something was wrong with the stale traditional curriculum of the high school; students did not come to college adequately prepared to think and express themselves. They may have had practice in something called "composition," but invariably what they learned was to compose Latin elegies and assorted pomposities in the vulgar tongue. Few of these students had even been exposed to a composition course that was related to conditions of everyday life. They had no idea how to write a sensible short essay, a piece of technical exposition, a business letter, or any forceful explanation of a simple point of view about the world of here and now. The Harvard freshman might be able to conjugate Latin irregular verbs but had no idea how to get up a modest argumentative theme that had a beginning, a middle, and an end.

Wendell's course was, for the most part, a writing course. Students also did some reading, and they discussed these readings in class. Sometimes they were called upon to write about the things they read. The readings were not necessarily confined to "literature"; there might be short works on topics as diverse as history, art, science, philosophy, public policy. The assumption was not that the course was intended to introduce students to the English Department or to literary studies; rather it was a portal to the educated mind. The readings were designed to be every bit as meaningful to the chemistry or economics student as to the potential English major.

But the writing segment was the heart of the course. And it was a tough and demanding introduction to writing. You had to write five hundred words every day. Sometimes it might be a theme, sometimes a personal essay, sometimes a letter or report. But you had to keep writing, keep learning to write. Papers were criticized in class, endlessly marked up by Wendell himself, used for points of discussion in individual conferences with students. Yes, five hundred words daily! An inconceivable chore for the student of today. English A was the bane of every freshman's life. But he came out a better man for it.

How could any instructor read that many themes from several classes of freshman students? How could one hold up under the workload and stay sane? In our day nothing of the sort is imaginable, but Barrett Wendell took on the burden with grace, even relish. Keep in mind that the college administration was not dunning him for publication linage or pestering him with endless committee assignments or mind-deadening forms and questionnaires. Wendell seemed to have had time not only for grading his load of daily papers but for joining the boys on the playing fields late in the afternoon. William Lyon Phelps, a graduate student at the time and later a distinguished professor of English at Yale, recalled those days of the 1890s when Wendell was polishing up his course in Freshman English. Phelps visited Wendell in his rooms (luckily for his peace of mind Wendell was a bachelor, like many college instructors in those days) and recounted these visits in his autobiography. In his cramped quarters at Harvard, Wendell carried on for many years "the all but intolerable burden of reading and correcting themes day after day. His room was filled with these compositions; they were all over his table and chairs, and when he lay down on the sofa, to get a little rest, he used a bunch of themes as a pillow. However picturesque and bizzare his own manner and way of expression, he never tolerated affectation in the compositions of his students. Ruthlessly he combed out ever bit of 'fine writing,' every trace of insincerity, and taught them how to express themselves clearly and with an economy of words."

It must have been a painful process for both teacher and student, not only because of the terrible burden of those daily themes but because of what was expected of the writer. The compositions demanded that the student make a transition to the adult world. No longer permitted were the vapid compositions of the high school years, the stilted language, the loose opinionizing. Freshman English was the place where college put a stop to incoherent thought patterns, weak logic, pretentious diction, the tortured exposition of the student newspaper editorial, the yells of the college yard, the higher grunting of the recitation hall. Here it was that one had to grow up—or be sent down.

Well, over the years, this splendid old course gave up the ghost. The daily theme disappeared, replaced by the weekly theme. I am familiar with a number of universities today where students are required to write only three or four short papers during a semester, while youthful and supposedly vigorous teaching assistants grumble about having to read and grade even these few. Of course, if you don't write regularly and in a disciplined way, you will never learn to write, so it is probably fair to say that the Freshman English course fails in its original purpose, which was to teach students to write in an adult fashion. To be sure, all students coming to college are literate, or presumably so, but higher literacy, literacy wedded to the processes of thought, is something altogether different. Some present-day students pick this up on their own, but they probably don't do so in Freshman English. Indeed, reading many Ph.D dissertations and articles written by professionals in learned journals makes one suspect that many allegedly educated people *never* learn to write.

What, then, goes on in the course called Freshman English, or Elements of Composition, or Introduction to Rhetoric? It still exists on most college campuses, but, like many other courses, it exists in a watered-down form. It may be reduced to something trivial and insignificant—a review of high school grammar, or a paltry progression of exercises in which students are encouraged to express their emotions or to tackle some current political or campus problem in a meandering and undisciplined way. Students may come to expect a grade of A or B in the course merely for the enunciation of any safe current platitude or accepted academic prejudice. Whereas freshman English was once a tough course, which flushed out the weak and incompetent, today it is seen by most undergraduates as easy, unchallenging, soporific. In some places it is still tough sledding, but more often than not for the wrong reasons. It may be rigorous in a bad sense, the teacher being a nitpicker along the lines of the high school schoolmarm. (It doesn't matter much what you say if you don't have any comma splices: so says the schoolmarm, male or female.) The ideal Freshman English teacher will know when to praise and encourage genuine student inspiration and when to balance such praise with demands for careful and precise use of the language.

There are a few obvious reasons why the course called Freshman English has gone astray in recent years. One is that a course that is required of every undergraduate student, or even a large portion of the freshman class, that cannot be administered as a lecture course and demands close scrutiny of a student's work is going to place a heavy burden on the resources of any large institution. Things are bad enough in the small ivy-covered liberal arts college with no teaching assistants; in such a situation every member of the English Department might have to teach at least one section of Freshman English. At a research university, administration of the course on a high level becomes a near impossibility. This is a course that requires frequent individual contact. Undergraduate courses in general receive low priority in staffing and financing. How can warm bodies be found to teach the course, let alone teach it in the grand manner of Barrett Wendell?

At the University of Illinois, for example, we have, at latest count, seventy-eight sections of the course officially called Principles of Composition. Every one of these sections is taught by a graduate teaching assistant. Nothing, of course, would prevent an individual of professorial rank from teaching the course if one had the desire, but none ever does. A number of years back, when suspicions were raised about the quality of the course by university officials, the head of the English Department taught one section of the course for a single semester, an event touted in the local newspaper as an indication of the university's commitment to undergraduate education.

Before World War II, even at large state universities like Illinois, Freshman English remained somewhat manageable. Some professors occasionally taught the course. There were considerably fewer sections, and when it was necessary to assign teaching assistants to them, only the more advanced doctoral students were used. Efforts were made to inculcate in these apprentice teachers the values and intentions of the course. Their grading practices and classroom performances were closely monitored. As huge numbers of students poured in to the university in the postwar years, and the university doubled and then tripled in size, staffing of Freshman English became a near impossibility. Under emergency appropriations dozens of new sections were added. Pressed into service were faculty wives, retired high school teachers, graduate students from other departments, and, of course, countless people who had just taken their college degrees somewhere and had never stood before a class in their lives!

Under such circumstances, what industry calls "quality control" became a virtual impossibility. A senior professor and perhaps an assistant professor were called upon to "administer" this monster, but they seldom had time to ponder what went on in the classroom, or what freshmen were being taught, or what kind of writing was going on. Nearly all of their working hours were spent figuring out ways to get live bodies on the podium, or listening to complaints about the most hopeless or incompetent teachers: the tin-horn despot, the monomaniac, the faculty wife nursing her babe in class, the alcoholic or pothead, the pamphleteerring activist, the low-level pedant, the aspiring high school teacher, and professional pettifogger, the dissertation grind who absents himself or herself for weeks on end, the fool who knows nothing about writing and fills students with such patent absurdities as "You must never begin a sentence with *and* or *but*."

Not too long ago I glanced at a freshman theme that had been graded by a teaching assistant. Nobody could say that the teacher had failed to do justice to the minutiae of writing: The TA had filled up the student's effort with dozens of squiggly marks. I noticed the presence of at least fifteen spelling errors in three pages; yet the paper, a half-rational diatribe about the American military presence in the Middle East, received a grade of A−. I ask the TA why the grade was so high. His response was that the student was "onto something big," and he didn't want to discourage him by including minor errors in the grading. The truth was, in Wendell's day, *either* the so-called minor mechanical errors *or* the flabby thinking would have been reason enough to downgrade (and probably fail) the paper.

It is hard to exaggerate the difficulties involved in riding herd over a motley and anarchistic army of young teachers who themselves have not worked their way loose of the Salingerized ego, who themselves probably never went through the discipline of learning to write, and who believe, like their freshman students, that the best way to express themselves is through a "good-hearted" but vague, undisciplined spilling out of emotions. Freshman English is obviously one place where the young need regular contact with minds that are more mature, more disciplined than their own. Unfortunately, conceived as a course that can be taught by anybody in the building, Freshman English has been able to persist only in a depreciated form.

Many large universities have played around with the course, occasionally finding variants of it that work somewhat less imperfectly. The University of Illinois had, until the late 1960s, a School of

General Studies, which offered its own variant of Freshman English. This course was taught by a corps of full-time, competent, and seasoned professionals. Most students "in the know" took this course in preference to the one administered by the English Department, which had long had a bad name around campus. Unfortunately, the university foolishly abolished its School of General Studies in the late sixties—universities have a tendency to get rid of things just when it is becoming most evident that they are really needed—and the superior version of Freshman English disappeared with it. But around the same time, some of the pressure was taken off the English Department in other ways, so that its own deficiencies could henceforth be disguised. The requirement was cut from two semesters to one, and many students arrived on campus having taken their first year or two at a community college. Such students were probably not taught the course on a high level, but they may have had it under congenial and at least partially intelligible circumstances.

One of the most nettlesome problems about staffing and teaching Freshman English in the setting of a research university is that the course calls for teachers whose devotion is to general education and who are themselves proficient writers. People outside of English departments always assume that the teaching of writing is in good hands when it is carried out in an English department. English professors, after all, nourish themselves on Shakespeare and Milton and Dickens—they *must* maintain a strong personal interest in writing; they *must* in some sense be writers themselves. Unfortunately these are completely unfounded assumptions. The English professor (and graduate student) sometimes is a competent and graceful writer, but in the present environment of professionalized literary studies and jargonistic criticism, it is far from a certainty. The English professor of today is more likely to be a conceptualizer than a writer, to confuse writing and theorizing, and to believe that the great writers of the world are variant literature professors who implant symbols and hidden meanings in texts. Many of them believe—as hard as this may be to realize—that Dickens and Hardy or Hemingway are plodding and unimaginative souls like themselves and were kept from becoming "literary critics," theorizers, only by virtue of having to spend much of their time writing novels and poems for other people's enjoyment.

The published writings in journals and critical organs that display the customary writing habits of literary professors are not reassuring when one considers the qualifications for those aspiring to teach college freshmen how to write. I open at random, and put my finger on a paragraph from, the *Publication of the Modern Language Association*, a leading professional journal for literature and language teachers. My finger has selected a passage that is characteristic and, as writing, neither better nor worse than the norm for such a journal. Here is the paragraph my finger sought out. It is apparently about Joseph Conrad's novel *The Nigger of the "Narcissus."*

> The three-phased drift in point of view—from the nearly omniscient, to a blending of the omniscient and the subjective, to the fully individualized—mimes a hypothetical historical drift from organic community, to a transitional balance between gemeinschaft and gesellschaft, to a society dominated by the class of special interests. Within this drift one hears the dialogic clashing of the various voices of those interests. Furthermore, the fictive narrative-author who emerges at the end of *The Nigger of the "Narcissus"* is an uneasy mirroring of the authorial persona Conrad himself was adopting in the third of the "three lives."

Whatever one may say of this paragraph, it should be readily apparent that it is *not* writing. Well, perhaps it is correct writing, "expert writing," scholarly writing. Clearly, though, it is not writing. It is what I prefer to call conceptualizing. I do not condemn it; I merely suggest that persons whose customary meditations and preoccupations are of this sort are not favorably placed when it comes to ministering to college freshmen, who need to be taught the virtues of clarity, simplicity, force, organization. These, after all, are the qualities that should be inspired in the incipient chemist, financial analyst, historian, lawyer, or child psychologist. But they are not likely to get these qualities from the contemporary English professor floundering in the quagmire of criticism.

Some of my readers may wish to defend the person whose work I quoted above (I have no idea whether he ever taught Freshman English or not). They may want to insist that this is writing for a narrow and a select audience, that the writer may actually know how to write with clarity, charm, and force when he so desires. My own experience casts doubt on this neat little excuse. I have found that the vast majority of those who have taken up residence in a fortress of abstractions and multilayered concepts seldom return to the world of ordinary human discourse, *do not* in fact write things for the average general reader, and are not therefore in a position to teach and evaluate everyday writing. It is, accordingly, a fallacy to assume that the English professor makes a better writing teacher than the professor of mechanical engineering or physiology. It is a fallacy— yes, maybe we should call it the "English professor fallacy"—that any person whose intellectual concerns are literature must himself be a writer. As to the value and significance of the passage quoted above, I pass no judgment. I leave that to those who float above the earth in such high-altitude turbulence. I merely suggest that the vocation and habitual preoccupations of the author would not put him in a good position to teach writing to eighteen-year-olds.

To make any sense at all, to have a raison d'être, the course that for many years has been called Freshman English must have two absolutely essential qualities. It must be part of the stream of general education, and it must be rigorously taught and administered. If either of these qualities is missing, the course can be nothing but a ghost, an empty shell, a purposeless rut. Unfortunately, in today's university, where the liberal and general functions of education have withered, and where basic courses are designed to pluck the largest numbers of chickens with the least amount of squawking, Freshman English goes its way as a harmless nonentity. It once had an important function; today it is neither a challenge nor a benefit to the typical American undergraduate.

14

Wars Over "the Canon"

THERE IS A GREAT DEAL of heated talk these days about "the canon," which is the fashionable word to describe the traditional pattern of liberal education, the books on the reading lists in the courses that supposedly constitute general studies. I don't remember this lubugrious-sounding word being used in my own younger days; we merely talked about the undergraduate college program, or the list of books that made up the expected reading in any given field of study. The traditional curriculum was never considered sacred or permanently fixed. The now-fashionable enemies of the curriculum, the great books, and the other long-cherished educational patterns have cynically picked on this pejorative term to suggest craftily that anyone who wants to maintain the status quo is somehow a rigid and hidebound traditionalist. The "traditionalists" are likened to cowled friars, their holy books chained to the walls, like those in some medieval monastery. Those who assail "the canon," those who think that the curriculum should change and grow with time, have taken advantage of an obvious and undeniable truth—that things must and do change—to work all kinds of mischief in higher education. They have done this in the name of "progress," a word with which we Americans have always been easily hoodwinked.

In any case, anyone who reads the daily newspaper or follows educational policy issues in the national media will be aware that there has been a lot of angry wrangling in recent years about this thing called the canon, that is to say, about the issue of what courses college students ought to take, what books they should be reading in those courses, whether they should be marching to familiar and mellow old tunes or to some that are new and strange-sounding. This wrangling, of course, mostly stays within the academy, although when news of certain developments leaks to the public the university may appear in a rather bad light, and a certain amount of political clamor may ensue. A number of authors who have studied the American university in the last few years have been incensed by the trashing of the curriculum in the name of something new, we know not what.

It probably ought to be made clear right away that the war over the curriculum or the canon is not a global war in the university; it really more resembles a street fight. It is almost exclusively limited to courses in Western civilization, that is, to the oft-maligned general education core. Beyond that it mainly concerns studies in the arts and humanities—literature, history, philosophy, sometimes architecture, sometimes the social sciences. You seldom hear the chemistry professor fussing about the canon or even using this emotionally charged word. You can rest assured that the medical faculty at the university will not spend many hours arguing about whether anatomy or principles of diagnosis should be in the course of studies; they will not be carping over the textbooks used in the classroom. Chemistry is defined by the present status of the science; so is medicine. In the training of a doctor there is little time to work everything in; the essential things are inescapable. Professors are agreed for the most part on what these things are, so there is no time for nitpicking arguments about what should be studied. Yes, there *are* discussions over the curriculum in these fields, just as there are in the faculties of business or agriculture or engineering, but they are seldom frantic or debilitating. They involve keeping the train running smoothly along the tracks, not blowing it up. Whenever you hear the word *canon* spoken, you can be forewarned that someone is seeking to dynamite the curriculum that is in place.

In short, the battle over the curriculum involves that tired old warhorse general or liberal education. What should students know of the civilized world around them? What is meant by shared culture? Which are the "great" books to which everyone should be exposed?

Sometimes the haggling over these things seems as silly and as frivolous as a puppy's worrying a bone. On the other hand, when we come to the realization that at issue is the already battered concept of liberal education, and that the dialogue goes on in institutions where the liberal tradition has already been trashed and a new generation of participants has no idea of what the issues are, we should conclude that we have come close to the heart of what has troubled higher education in the last half of the twentieth century.

But who are these people making war on the canon, and what are they fighting against? The answers are not easy and the issues are complex, but it is probably a safe generalization to say that the new curriculum fighters are people who are alleging, among other things, that the long-standing approaches to most academic subjects have become worn out, that they do not admit of new learning, that they neglect the many fresh things going on in the sphere of the intellect. The traditional canon, it is argued, does not open the door to studies of those who were once thought to be voiceless, for instance women and blacks, or to the wealth of knowledge coming into the educated world from popular culture—cinema, television, comic strips, folklore, let us say—or to the disenfranchised, to immigrant groups, to ethnic minorities, to working people, or the repressed generally.

Some of the fire and brimstone being generated over the canon became a matter of public debate in the late 1980s when the faculty at Stanford University scrapped its undergraduate Western civilization course, replacing it with another that supposedly would do justice to contemporary needs and demands. The rumblings at Stanford began in the spring of 1986 when members of the Black Students Union complained to the faculty that the year-long course in Western civilization was biased, that it was racist and sexist, that it did not address the concerns of minorities and women. Many other students took up the war cry, seeing yet another opportunity to go to work on cherished preserves of the curriculum and thereby eliminate onerous requirements. Over the next year there were meetings, rallies, pressure sessions of one sort or another. Television coverage aided the crusading students when the Reverend Jesse Jackson arrived on campus and led a march of five hundred students to the chant "Hey hey, ho ho, Western culture's got to go."

Caving in to student demands, as faculty conclaves usually do in such situations, the senate at Stanford voted 39–4 in March 1988 to modify its traditional course in Western civilization and add a cluster of courses called Culture, Ideas, Values, which eliminated the idea of a core list of great works such as the Bible, Plato, and Shakespeare in favor of a roster of courses including, for example, one called Values, Technology, Science, and Society. Since not all students would be taking the same course, a common thread in their educational experience was lost. They could still elect Great Works, if they so chose, and, as a sop to public opinion, the entire program of Culture, Ideas and Values was abbreviated to CIV, which provided a hollow reminder of the word *civilization* even though the word *Western* was studiously avoided. The faculty resolution specifically commanded that every one of the new courses must include "works by women, minorities and persons of color" and that at least one work in each quarter must be devoted to issues of race, sex, or class.

It goes without saying that the "revision" of the Western civilization course at Stanford was not the work of students alone; it took place in the radically altered milieu that has taken root on campuses across the country over the past several generations. (I should repeat again, the movement came mostly from younger faculty members in departments of language, literature, history, the arts. Neither the mood nor the substance of the movement means much to people in the scientific and technical fields.) There is a widely held belief that the canon was created by white males to study the works of other white males, mostly those in power. The study of literature and history has accordingly been invaded by a flotilla of new buzzwords and epithets, new pejorative isms—racism, sexism, Eurocentrism, phallocentrism, logophallocentrism. Coming under attack are traditions dominated by "powerful males"—even if they were starving artists or writers who lived their lives out in garrets, even if they never knew success or belonged to the power structure. If they were males, they were part of a silent conspiracy to deny recognition to women, blacks, Asiatics, immigrants, out-at-pocket poets, and sweatshop philosophers.

Academics in a number of disciplines have been working hard to bring their own studies into line with these new demands for populist and egalitarian remedies. The so-called New History, for example, demanded consideration of intimate details of the lives of ordinary people as well as monarchs, presidents, and prelates. New

History purports to be history from the bottom up rather than from the top down. Its assumption is that there are rich mines of gold in the study of haying practices in Vermont in the eighteenth century, or the home life of rickshaw drivers in Hong Kong, or the diaries of coal miners in Appalachia or slaves in the antebellum south. (The new historians are probably at least partially right in these assumptions; there is no good reason why history should not have been paying attention to some of these things all along.) In literature departments Marxist deconstructionists are at pains to debunk the idea that an ordering of texts, an identification and celebration of figures on Mount Olympus, is a rational enterprise. They insist that anyone who believes reading Whitman is more valuable than reading than poems of Sally of the Sawdust or Peg Leg Al is making a claim that can be justified only by fascistic and totalitarian methods.

The call for us to pay attention to people without authority, people previously unrecognized, people disenfranchised or stripped of power, has become the dominant leitmotif of scholarship in the humanities. It is not surprising that humanities professors would seek to unload all of the fashionable ideologies on college introductory courses, since many such professors are totally preoccupied with these ideologies in their own books, seminars, and professional meetings. If there is an unremitting pressure to include in the curriculum whole new courses of study with names like Afro-American studies, gender studies, or oppression studies, it is because these subjects are de rigeur in the rarefied atmosphere of graduate seminars in the humanities.

At a meeting of the American Studies Association in the fall of 1990, a glance at the program revealed an almost mind-boggling preponderance of papers with titles such as these: "New Perspective on Gender," "The Euro-American Imagination and Its Racial and Cultural Others," "History and Ritual in the Works of African American-Women," "The Aesthetics of Protest," "Consciousness, Ideology and Practice in Contemporary Black Popular Culture," "Out on the Rim: American Culture and the Pacific," "Southern Women's Humor," "Afro-Caribbean Ritual in America," "Beyond Salt of the Earth: Media and Chicano Labor Activism," "Black American Culture in Paris During the Cold War," "Ethnicity, Class and the Construction of the family in the 1940s and 1950s,"

"Women and Migration: The Social and Economic Consequences of Gender." These are not by any means peculiarities or bizarre exceptions to the roster of papers; these constitute the *mainstream.* They are characteristic of the regular, nay prevailing, preoccupations of the academic scholar in the humanities and social sciences.

What seems to be driving the scholars whose concerns are with such things as power, gender, and ethnicity? What is motivating those who, like the faculty at Stanford, have sought to replace traditional liberal arts subjects with new courses in Caribbean studies, native Americanism, and all the rest? Some have been quick to point out, like former Education Secretary William Bennett, that behind these new directions is not an idea or a vision, but rather a *program.* "This," said Bennett, "is not an educational agenda but a political agenda."

This same concern, that college students are being deprived of an education in the name of some kind of indoctrination, has also been urged in a recent book, *Tenured Radicals,* by Roger Kimball, a onetime teacher at Connecticut College and Yale and lately editor of *The New Criterion.* It is a major premise of Kimball's book that in the 1980s and 1990s the American university has come to be dominated by sixties-style dissidents who now enjoy the handsome paychecks and creature comforts of the university while continuing to push for the radical agendas of their own college youth. To be sure, says Kimball, the "tenured radicals" are no longer advocating physical destruction of the property, the tearing down of the walls brick by brick—why should they want to tear down an environment that is so agreeable to them? No, they are content to have "internalized" their own radical vision, helping it come to fruition in the college curriculum of today. How susceptible the present generation of students is to sixties-style radicalism is a tough question, but there is little doubt that the curriculum—the humanities curriculum—has been infected by a highly politicized agenda.

The trouble with all this, according to Kimball—and he is hardly alone, since most of the recent critics of higher education from Bloom to Page Smith have been alarmed by the same tendency—is that shoehorning in the political agenda has had the effect of squeezing the traditional curriculum out. The college curriculum cannot simply grow in size; there are already too many things to be learned, to many requirements to be endured. The pressure is always toward easing burdens and not adding to them. Accordingly, if gay studies is to be added, something has to be expunged—probably the Bible, Plato, Dickens, or the Declaration of Independence. And this, for the most part, is what has happened. "With a few notable exceptions," says Kimball, "our most prestigious liberal arts colleges and universities have installed the entire radical menu at the center of their humanistic curriculum at both the undergraduate and graduate level. Every special interest—women's studies, black studies, gay studies, and the like—and every modish interpretative gambit—deconstruction, poststructuralism, new historicism, and other varieties of what the literary critic Frederick Crews has aptly dubbed 'Left Electicism'—has found a welcome roost in the academy, while the traditional curriculum and modes of intellectual inquiry are excoriated as sexist, racist, or just plain reactionary."

It has been said, and by reasonable and cautious people, that one of the justifications for the various forms of New History, for women's studies, for black studies, is to instill pride in one's self, one's race, sex, or ethnic origin. If this were true the introduction of some of these new elements to the curriculum might well have the beneficial effect of creating a bonding of disparate elements of the community. Admittedly, there is ample justification for black studies, since blacks have for a long time been a lonely and isolated group on most college campuses. They need something to spark their imaginations and their sense of worth, so that setting aside something special for them does not seem at all unreasonable. In co-ed institutions, and even in all-female colleges, there is plenty of justification for women to have feminist viewpoint seminars. Even male-bashing groups have a kind of tonic effect, and only the most stubborn, humorless, and unregenerate male would take exception to them. The problem with such endeavors is that they attain their principal goals rather quickly and wear themselves down into humdrum sciences that have little chance of gaining the long-term attention of the brightest students.

Historian Arthur Schlesinger, Jr., an undeniably respected figure of the liberal establishment, welcomes these new entries to the domain of history and to the traditional curriculum, but with a strong caveat. He is suspicious that what has come along so far is of questionable value either to the field of history or to civilization. He finds a certain artificiality, a certain fakery, in using history to minister to the psychological needs of minorities. Furthermore, he believes that the correct way to remedy whatever defects there may be in history is not through creating what he calls "good citizenship history," or history of the bleeding heart, but rather by correcting whatever defects the historical literature already has. What we need is not new bad history written from a different viewpoint but rather better history. The trouble with so many of the new histories that have popped up—women's history, Hispanic history, and the like— is that they are not conceived as real history and not taught as such. "Let us by all means teach women's history, black history, Hispanic history. But let us teach them as history, not as a means of promoting group self-esteem." Let us not go under the assumption that watered-down pop history can be used as an injection of feel-good medicine. We have to guard, furthermore, against what Bertrand Russell called the fallacy of "the superior virtue of the suppressed." We must not believe foolishly that because some minority group has been neglected, it is automatically superior.

Above all, says Schlesinger, there is another fallacious assumption to which the new curriculum reformers have fallen prey. It is that they alone are custodians of a radical or democratic tradition. They alone have discovered the fellowship of humanity. Schlesinger denies the existence of a monolithic body of work designed to enforce the "hegemony" of some class or group. Most of this is a pure fabrication of the new canonists. "In fact, most great literature, and much good history, are deeply subversive in their impact on orthodoxies. Consider the American canon: Emerson, Whitman, Melville, Hawthorne, Thoreau, Mark Twain, Henry Adams, William and Henry James, Holmes, Dreiser, Faulkner. Lackeys of the ruling class? Agents of American imperialism?" Absurd. Most of what the new canonists purport to have discovered is already a major strain in our literature.

There are two other obvious defects in the thought of the new canonists, and perhaps both have the same root. The first is that so much of what passes for scholarship in the humanities, so much of what is now being foisted off on dispirited undergraduates, is just plain dull stuff. How wearisome it is to come to college expecting to be shaken up by the great thoughts and achievements of mankind, and then to be dragged through the low-ceilinged rooms of pedantry. The real problem with the new canon is not so much that it has politicized the college curriculum but that it has miniaturized it, has reduced it to low heaps of rubble. The danger to the academic establishment is not so much what worries Roger Kimball, namely that it has been stirring students up to a program of political activism, but that it doesn't stir them up to anything at all. The trouble with professors attempting to indoctrinate students with the fashionable academic ideologies is not that they will ignite students with their incendiary ideas but that they will turn students away from all ideas, will make them believe that *everything* connected with scholarship is trivial, tame, and humorless. Pedantification, not politicization, of the academic mind has been the problem in recent years.

Not too long ago I talked with a very bright young lady, a college senior, who early in her college career had selected women's studies as her field of concentration. She looked forward to this eagerly, believing that here was something she could identify with in a personal way, something that would give her college education a sharp focus. To use the favorite buzzword of the sixties, it would be "relevant." And yes, so it should have been. Relevance is in fact a quality that one *does* want in one's education; a personal note of usefulness and meaningfulness is an essential part of any truly liberal education. Alas, the young lady found not very much in women's studies that she could identify with, not very much that was relevant beyond a stark point of view that was stated in the first few weeks and then rolled out like bolts of fustian over four years of college.

Women's studies turn out to be semester after semester of "theorizing." You just apply the same old formulas to books and ideas that have been in the curriculum for years, without ever really getting enough of the cultural landmarks that had made books and ideas meaningful to civilized people in previous generations. You take a course in Shakespeare from a feminist point of view without ever getting the chance to enjoy Shakespeare, without ever learning why his plays have passed the test of time. The literature course treated from a feminist perspective is bogged down in the leaden mysteries of Marxism and deconstructionism, in all manner of pettifogging interpretations. True, you can use Shakespeare as a kind of sparring partner, as a straw man of the male establishment. There might be a little fun in that kind of activity—for a while. But one gets through this pretty quickly, and the repetition of it for four years is a bit boring, to say the least. What the student gets in the feminist interpretation of literature is one murky and trivial adventure in concept-spinning after another. The bare notion of a feminist perspective suggests a strong human element; yet the actual courses are dreary, as if is taking a course from a textual editor who had become mired in spelling variations, dropped commas, mysterious interpolations of text fragments. Instead of being a bracing and invigorating new subject matter, the feminist interpretation of literature turned out to be just some hypertrophied form of scholasticism. There is much ideological posturing, a considerable amount of verbal wordplay and sparring, muffled exclamations of "fi, fi, fo fum, I smell the blood of an Englishman," but not enough genuine adventure and exuberance to keep a lively undergraduate student awake for more than one semester.

Beside its dullness, the new canon has another obvious defect. The proliferation of new isms, relevancies, and soothing academic ego boosters really doesn't do anything to draw students together in any kind of community of interest. Nothing has come out of the ideological canon that can take the place of the classical curriculum of the nineteenth century or the Western civilization tradition of the earlier twentieth century. The classical curriculum or, say, the great books program had the virtue of giving students a common thread of recognition. When the college-educated student from New York got together with a college-educated student from California, they had something in the way of a shared culture; they had at least a modest ground of conversation.

Philosopher George Santayana was once asked what books college students should read, and he replied that it really didn't matter very much except that they should all read the same things. One of the main functions of higher education is to produce a unity of interest, a woven tapestry of human culture. Such a thing cannot be found in the menu of the new canonists. They have invented so many new subjects, so many tiny and trivial areas of specialization, they have been so intoxicated by "diversity," that there is no likelihood that a uniform curriculum could ever emerge from their undertakings. Every single university will have something different to offer. If a professor at Stanford decides that he wants to emphasize the economics of indentured servitude in the Spanish colonies during the seventeenth century; if another professor, at the University of

Virginia decides that she wants to fill her students with the intricate truths of African cargo cults—all that can result is a nationwide cultural dis–community.

The new canon cannot lead to anything even faintly resembling a unity of learning. The only unity that the new canonists seem to want is one of dispute and agitation, not of fraternity and human worth. Instead of education being used to draw people into a mutual harmony, you have a cacophonous anarchy of tribes, flags, isms, enclaves, and special turfs. It is impossible to imagine any consensus among the university conceptualizers as to what the new canon should consist of; they have merely insisted heatedly that nothing in the old one is any good. Arthur Schlesinger is correct in saying that the new canon results in a kind of cultural and linguistic apartheid, a very dangerous climate in a nation where the bonds of cohesion are already fragile.

Even if all of the theory spinners and ideologues of the academy were to get together and make their own nationwide standard curriculum, there is another reason why no unified and coherent culture could ever come out of it. Present-day specialized academic learning has neither the force nor the vitality to dominate the whole of the national culture. Nearly all students in college have read things on their own; they are exposed to the mass media and television; they have their own private and eccentric interests. They know that people of good sense and breeding esteem Shakespeare or *The Golden Bowl* or *Brideshead Revisited* more than they do the doggerel of a Kentucky mountaineer that some professor has picked up and is making a fuss about. They know that treating the works of Tugboat Annie to Marxist annotations is not really an achievement of lasting significance. Try as hard as they might, professors at the university cannot bamboozle them into believing otherwise. Alert students all know that the university is not the principal generator of literature, indeed, not usually a generator of it at all. The world's writers are not in the academy, and they do not draw their values from it. History is written about by professors but not made by them. The popular culture, insofar as it really is popular and not some contrived essence gotten up for a specialty journal, belongs to all the people, and the people don't need to be told how it holds them together. It just does.

The sorry thing about the new canonists is that while they talk a great deal about returning to the "real," or to the "soil," or to the "folk"—to things that bind people together—all of their achievements tend to pull in precisely the opposite direction. They mainly want to establish new and variant power monopolies of their own. They do not want to discover a unifying culture, and they seldom have a desire to speak in a language that can be understood outside the academy. Like the radicals of the sixties, they want to tear down all the houses they can find and take refuge in sand castles of their own devising. But it is an unrealizable dream. They have found the sand castles to live in, but they have not succeeded in bringing the whole world down to this level. Nor are they likely to do so in the future. On the other hand, they have succeeded in making the university a more plodding and uninspiring place, which, by itself, is quite a sufficient national calamity.

15

The Penumbra of Liberal Education

ONE OF THE MANY THINGS the new canonists and their allies have forgotten is that liberal education is not something having to do solely with the curriculum or with filling students' brains with certain kinds of information. The ideal of liberal education as it arose in ancient Greece, as it was filtered down to us through the Renaissance and nurtured in Europe over many centuries, was never an ideal of information dissemination and retrieval. It was always, and preeminently, an ideal of humanity. Its intention was to create a full human being, an individual blessed with character, intellect, and individual style. A century ago, in our diminutive ivy-covered colleges nobody would have understood why a big fuss might someday be made about the curriculum as if that constituted the whole of college education, or, for that matter, why people would do heated battle over competing lists of books. They would have seen such things as distinctly subordinate to the character of the teacher and the student. Education was aimed at producing civilized people, not information containers in human clothing.

It is easy to forget the purely individual and self-directed component of a liberal education whenever one gets into elaborate discussions and arguments about what it is that universities should be

149

giving to their students in the way of an education, what should be included in the canon and so on. It is easy to forget that whatever the contributions of a university, all truly educated people need to supply something of their own drive, their own force of imagination, their own individually acquired body of knowledge, and it is largely these things that constitute their character and intellectual makeup. A person who *only* followed a course of studies laid down for him or her—whether a traditional or a newly "relevant" canon, however perfectly concocted—would be an imperfectly educated individual. The curriculum is only one reference point for higher education. The individual aspiring to education has to supply other reference points out of his or her own experience, needs, and desires.

Everybody who has ever taught in a university is aware that some students are tuned in to learning, have an appetite for it, and others do not. Sometimes we state this distinction in very simplistic terms: These are the good students, and those are the bad ones or the mediocre ones. The good students are people who seem to pave their own way, who have naturally inquiring minds, who are interested in learning about the world around them, who read books they have chosen for themselves, not merely because they are forced to read them or because their titles are on a reading list that must be followed in order to pass an examination. These students read books because they want to read them, because ideas arouse their curiosity or enflame their spirit.

For these reasons, it is almost always impossible to make any generalizations about a standard or "correct" path to liberal education. It does not follow, for example, that the person who studies one of the traditional liberal arts majors—philosophy, literature, history, the classics, etc.—will be a more liberally "educated" person than the individual who comes to college to study something "vocational" like engineering or business. Yes, of course, it is nice for everybody to know something about the great works of literature, to have some brush with the guiding ideas of history, but I have known English majors who are dunderheads; I have known philosophy majors whose knowledge is completely of the canned or bottled variety. I have known students in the college of business or engineering who seek out an individual style and culture on their own and can be more truly described as "educated" than other students who have boasted that they have sacrificed cash value to receive a liberal education. I have encountered hundreds, nay, thousands, of students who have majored in liberal arts subjects simply because they heard they were "soft" and could assure them of high enough grades to get into law school. In any case, there is no clear evidence that students who major in some liberal arts curriculum and merely follow the canon (new or old) will be any better educated, that is, more liberally educated, than students who follow what is laid down before them in a pharmacy course or an agriculture course.

It is so easy to forget the all-important individual component in education that a great many educators and cultural leaders get caught up in a wasteful and distracting endeavor to fine-tune the college curriculum. It is easy to make intricate and invidious distinctions about what constitutes education, about what ideas, books, facts are needed to be stored in a person's mind if that person is to be considered "educated." Maybe it is only natural, maybe it is a part of human frailty, to ask questions such as "What makes for an education person?" "What are the essential characteristics of a 'learned' individual?" "Is there a particular body of knowledge that anyone must master in order to be a functional or contributing member of intelligent society?"

There are, of course, no absolute answers to these questions. This is because the questions themselves, while quite reasonable and sensible, are burdened with all kinds of hidden assumptions. They all assume a philosophy of education in which students are thought to be receptacles of information. To be sure, this has always been one way of looking at all education from grammar school onward—and an obviously practical way. A number of things need to be mastered if one is to read and write; there are certain tasks that must be mastered if one is to function in a complex social and economic world. So it must be true that there are a standard number of facts and ideas one must possess if one is to be considered "educated," a "college man," or whatever. Unfortunately the receptacle or storage box imagery, while never precisely incorrect, is simply inadequate, misleading, when it comes to pinning down what is meant by liberal education: education for selfhood and citizenship. Liberal education is a domain in which an individual has one foot in the established world of learning and the other foot swinging free, moving toward one's own selfhood, toward a world of one's own making. To assume that only the ground on which that first foot is placed constitutes education is to fall prey to a woefully impoverished notion of what higher education is about.

This point has been missed by a number of recent authors who have strenuously risen to the defense of liberal education but who mistakenly believe that liberal education is akin to something that can be contained in a storage cabinet. I look, for example, at the highly popular book *Cultural Literacy: What Every American Needs to Know,* by E. D. Hirsch, Jr., which at superficial glance appears to offer strong support for disciplined general education. Hirsch, who is a professor of English at the University of Virginia and has written and lectured widely on reading and literacy, argues what seems to be a very plausible theory, namely that the student who lacks a certain basic culture, who has failed to read in his or her formative years, simply cannot be an educated person. That is to say, a student whose stock of information is so limited that he or she does not know in which century the American Civil War was fought, or believes that Socrates was an Indian chief, or that Schubert was a rock star, or that Turkey is in South America or Toronto in Italy (Hirsch found this delicious piece of ignorance in a UCLA junior), such a student has not really made much headway in the world of learning. Such students clearly do not know how to read and *have not* read; so it doesn't make much sense to try to pound specialized knowledge into them. They have no frame of reference, no receptacle, for it. Unfortunately, diminished reading habits in the television age, along with failures in the primary and secondary schools, have brought to the colleges many who are crippled in precisely this way.

Some kind of cultural knowledge—cultural literacy, Hirsch calls it—is a necessary foundation for any person who claims to be educated. Obviously, "cultural literacy" is a vague and illusive concept, but at the back of his book Hirsch gives a sixty-four-page list of things that literate Americans should know—although presumably not every literate person will be familiar with every one of the well over four thousand items. At random I pick from this curious assemblage: Bard of Avon, Max Planck, Immanuel Kant, Marie Antoinette, Montreal, schizophrenia, London Bridge is Falling Down (song), Saint Francis of Assisi, thalidomide, two–China policy, Frank Lloyd Wright, work ethic, chutzpah, call a spade a spade, Rube Goldberg, caveat emptor, GNP, Pandora's box. The presumption is that a person who fails to recognize most of these things will be playing with only half a deck, will not be well positioned to play the game of life. To say the very least, such a person will not be what Hirsch would call an educated individual.

It would seem that Hirsch's list is not unduly demanding; and of course his appeal for a shared body of knowledge is reasonable. But it is interesting to note that a great many educators carped at Hirsch's list. They made the expected complaints that acquisition of such a general literacy called for a rigid and hidebound curriculum, that his body of information was "elitist." Keeping in mind that many of those who teach at all levels, from kindergarten through graduate school, are convinced that we live in an age of information overload where simply too much is expected of the young, it is little wonder that a big uproar met the demand that anyone claiming to be culturally literate should be familiar with a good many of the items on Hirsch's list. (Hirsch compounded the problem a year or so later when he published a much longer and more intimidating list in a book entitled *The Dictionary of Cultural Literacy*.) Hirsch also received more than a few rebukes from his university peers, from his colleagues in English, from new canonists, many of whom have sweated to prove that it is not essential to have read *Moby-Dick* and that such an achievement could be replaced by reading tracts of deconstructionist critics or the philosophical reflections of academic Marxists, stevedore philosophers, corner grocers, or any "plain persons" who may share their enthusiasm for overthrowing the present economic order. Hirsch apparently didn't want to wrestle with the academic establishment, and in the years since the publication of his books he has assumed an abject posture, attempting to curry favor with the new canonists. He travels around the country denying that he is an elitist, hedging on his own thesis that there can be such a thing as a standardized framework for literacy.

Well, there *was* something wrong with Hirsch's fundamental idea, but it was not what the new canonists believed. His books presented a distorted, cartoonlike version of general education. General education, if it is anything of value, is not a box stuffed with individual facts; a person's mind is not composed like a dictionary or an encyclopedia. A person's education consists of a network of facts, ideas, propositions, truths, sensibilities, moral attitudes, held together by his or her own outlook on the world—something that is built up over a lifetime. The network itself is more important than any individual point or item of intelligence. Indeed, when we read books like Hirsch's, we don't really know what is meant when we are told that to be culturally literate we have to be able to recognize the name Immanuel Kant. What is the allegedly educated person supposed to know about Kant? That he was a philosopher? That he was a German philosopher? That he was an "objective idealist"? If a person recognizes only the name Kant, if the name merely rings a bell, then the kind of knowledge that person has is probably not useful beyond what might be needed for parlor games and crossword puzzles, or perhaps for cocktail party chatter in university communities. The sad truth is that probably even the person who has gone through college and taken a course in modern philosophy has probably forgotten why Kant was a major figure in modern philosophy, why he is more important than Christian Wolff or Schleiermacher (who are not on Hirsch's "need-to-know" list).

Or what is the youthful learner supposed to have remembered about Marie Antoinette? That she was queen of France? That she said "Let them eat cake"? That she went to the guillotine? What should one know about schizophrenia? Probably a very large number of college graduates have heard the word, and of these the majority probably have a mistaken idea of what it is—"split personality," like Dr. Jekyll and Mr. Hyde perhaps; that is not in fact the technical meaning of the term in psychiatry. In any case, the idea that general education consists of thousands of shards of information, little nuggets, is completely mistaken. Every one of us has vast pockets of ignorance; things that are of extreme importance to us mean nothing at all to the person next door. There are probably large numbers of genuinely educated people in these United States who recognize the name of Immanuel Kant, perhaps as a German philosopher, but beyond that know nothing important about him, so that mere recognition of his name is little more than fragmentary debris blown up in a sandstorm. (The usefulness of Kant's name for cocktail party chatter is very much in doubt.) Mere recognition, in short, is a decidedly secondary ingredient in one's learning, and it becomes progressively more unimportant as one's maturity and individuality increase. What *is* important is the knowledge one possesses that is going to be put to actual use.

Although Hirsch's list is misleading, and appeals to meretricious tendencies to "quantify" that have long besmirched the field of education, one idea behind it is obviously worthy of notice. The educated person must be, in some very significant way, a person of broad general culture. The people who have made a contribution to learning and to the growth of knowledge have invariably been people with an insatiable curiosity; they are most often avid readers; they like to investigate things, to explore, to create on their own. Most of what they know they doubtless have learned without either help or hindrance from their teachers. Genius always pops up from little springs here and there, its effects not much changed by being subjected to educational institutions. But beside genius there is always a healthy strain of normal enthusiasm, of what Allan Bloom liked to call *eros*, and those who possess it will be alert to what is going on in the world. Such people will, in all likelihood, be driven to acquire a wide range of knowledge. Lack of a suitable framework of knowledge is usually a sign that an individual is just taking a ride on the educational conveyor belt.

Where educators like Kirsch go wrong is in assuming that somehow one needs a single corpus of knowledge to function as a liberally educated person. The truth is that the "single corpus of knowledge" concept is better suited to specialized education, is better suited to training than education. It *is* true that a definite body of information needs to be acquired to be an architect or a doctor. The body of knowledge needed to produce the liberally educated person is much more elusive; it is fuzzy at the edges. And it has to be.

Hirsch was not, of course, the first to conceive the idea of an organized body of knowledge to which all people seeking to be educated must subject themselves. Others have devised fashionable ideas of "core" learning over the years. Back in 1910, Harvard President Charles W. Eliot edited for publication the famous Harvard Classics, a collection of fifty volumes (sometimes called "the five-foot shelf"); later on, the so-called Great Books movement offered a similar educational style. The Great Books philosophy, when it included an attempt to synthesize the knowledge found in the world's great books—an approach recommended by our favorite American Aristotelian, Mortimer J. Adler—gave us something we could hold up as a lofty ideal. The five-foot shelf and "Great Books" program were noble efforts with much to recommend them, just as Hirsch's list of cultural nuggets has its appeal.

Two features of the Great Books program (and the Harvard Classics idea) are particularly laudable. The first is the one so highly esteemed by Mortimer Adler, namely that the program attempts to offer an intellectual *framework* for learning, an architectonic, so to speak, a well-planted tree to hang things on. The Great Books program offers a kind of map of the territory. Second, it provides a shared core curriculum, something that draws students together in the pursuit of learning. Of course, no single specific reading list or curriculum is necessary to achieve this end; one can imagine an effective list of readings quite different from that provided by the Great Books course. Still, this quality has widespread appeal not only within but outside the academy. Universities do not have a monopoly on culture, although the new foggers and the enemies of the canon often believe that they do.

But the trouble with the Great Books and similar programs is that they tend to overlook the deeply personal element that is in every truly educated individual. The well-known writer and drama critic George Jean Nathan once remarked (this back in Charles W. Wliot's day) that he didn't like people who had a "five-foot shelf" of uniform books in their houses. He suspected first of all that they were probably using it for interior decor or as a way of impressing their neighbors. Even more important, he said, he wouldn't want to know anybody whose bookshelves didn't hold something that represented a funky little interest, something offbeat or eccentric. In a "five-foot-shelf" of classics, he would be heartened to see stuffed in between them a "history of burlesque" or a few books on deep-sea fishing or butterfly collecting or the history of railway locomotives or books of Gothic romance—anything that reflected the personality of the owner rather than that of some gray eminence. None of which is to denigrate the value of a received body of learning; rather, this notion emphasizes the equal necessity of one's personal outlook, one's *own* list of favored books.

Keep in mind that the reason for education in the first place is to fire up the imagination of the individual and provide him with a culture of his own. Education is not merely a matter of transferring the words and ideas of some prescribed list of books into a person's brain. Of course, a well-rounded culture is a major goal of all of us, and, as such, it will be the source of personal involvement and inspiration. But we must always expect to encounter individuals who have vast pockets of ignorance and who put all of their drives and energies into some self-generated project, something unique that they have discovered for themselves. We are all familiar with monomaniacs, with one-track geniuses, who put their passions and energies into some interest that marks their individual style. The truth is, the energies they devote to these interests are every bit as important as the breadth of knowledge (provided, of course, these interests come from their own souls and are not merely canned goods, dollops of technical information they have acquired to become professionals). I have long been convinced that a great many of the most highly imaginative and creative people of the world wouldn't do very well if given a questionnaire about the Harvard Classics or about the Hirsch open sesame list, but that nonetheless this has not hampered them in the acquisition of their own drive and highly individual culture. I am convinced that the late great pianist Vladimir Horowitz would not recognize more than 20 percent of the items Hirsch finds so essential to education, yet it did not keep him from becoming the greatest pianist of his day. I suspect that by any sensible standards Horowitz was not only a pianist of the first rank, but a liberally educated man as well. His liberal education, though, was almost exclusively something spun out of his own interests and desires.

Of course, our universities (or music academies for that matter) are not in a position to produce the Vladimir Horowitzes of the world; such individuals will just appear from time to time. The main problem with these institutions is that as they are presently constituted they are not very comfortable havens for the cultivation of the ordinary individual either. The education of all of us grows out of our peculiar talents and desires just as much as it does from the breadth or quantity of our knowledge. Accordingly the modern university, which has lost its ability to interact with the individual person and expends an inordinate amount of its efforts on the standardized educational product, is indeed consumed by this function. Remember that the present generation of curriculum busters who claim to want to address the individual student are no more interested in doing so than the hidebound traditionalists they mock; they don't want students to go off on their own either but merely want to inculcate a *different* set of values that are every bit as rigid as those proposed by the defenders of the status quo. They say they want to "fire up" their students—but this just means firing them up to new canned ideologies even more rancid than the old ones they reject.

Beside their inability to come to terms with individuality, another fatal flaw in the approach to liberal education is found in most universities today. It is the belief, born of specialization, that liberal learning, because it is somewhat formless, must of necessity be thin or shallow. Something that goes to the very depths of a person's soul, that appeals to his or her most pronounced interests, cannot be shallow, but that it is so is an almost universal attitude in our universities today. Allan Bloom put it extremely well when he assailed the now nearly universal belief that "there is no higher level generalism." The total surrender to this dogma is endemic in the American university and is probably its most grievous defect today. General education courses are invariably taught without fire and enthusiasm; they are viewed as "service" courses, to which the lowest personnel are assigned; they often descend to mere popularizing; they are seen as mere "introductions" or stepping-stones to "higher courses" elsewhere. It has always been one of the most obvious perversities of large universities that they have small and elite seminars for graduate students. These advanced students could probably just as well be taught in large lecture sections since they are already riding on a clear track, whereas the most tender and impressionable minds in the university are massed together and fed on intellectual frozen pasta.

Thirty or forty years ago, even in the largest universities, general education still tended to have some eminence. Today, with notable exceptions, of course, the nutrients needed to keep the liberal arts tradition alive are just not there. Universities clearly have the resources to nurture tradition, but they put them elsewhere. It was easy to surrender to the belief that liberal or general education is soft, shallow, and introductory, so the universities gave way to those beliefs almost without a whimper in the 1960s. As we have seen, they did not "trash" the traditional and long-familiar general curriculum; they did not throw it out the window. It is still there, but in an embalmed form, a form that is bound not to appeal to the most able students. The new canons that have come along, emphasizing diversity, openness, selectivity, and political rectitude, are similarly embalmed, but with a different kind of embalming fluid. Liberal education must be broad, it must be fitted to the individual's interests, but it must also be administered on a high level. By the 1960s the universities abandoned this ideal, and they have been the worse for it in the years since.

Part IV

Student Life in an Impoverished Community

16

Toward a Rejuvenation of College Life

W<small>HEN THE EARLIEST UNIVERSITIES</small> began to make their appearance in the late middle ages, they were perceived as human communities drawing together individuals who had some common interest. The university was like a family, a collection of people who wanted to be together for this reason or that. It consisted of people who wanted to share life together for a period of time. The small ivy-covered colleges of America's early history were governed by much the same spirit and guiding principle, even though they did not aspire to become universities and sought to preserve their sense of community with a small and homogeneous student population.

The modern public university has been driven by quite a different motivating force. The original model of a university as a community faded before another and more energetic model, which conceived of the university in terms of productivity. Since the end of the nineteenth century we Americans have gravitated toward the idea that the university is like a giant department store, an emporium, a bazaar of some kind, a place where people come to shop for things. People come to the university to purchase goods that are pre-packaged or made to order. Students, for example, want to obtain degrees so that they can step out into a technologically complex

163

world, that requires specialized knowledge. They pay for those degrees and expect to receive them on time and at the right price, just like a person who buys a bolt of cloth in a dry goods store.

The giant modern university has many other customers as well. The government or the corporation may contract with it to study things, to provide information, to issue brochures, to tell farmers how to raise corn, to produce chemicals, computers, dental drills, or pollution control devices. The present-day university floats like a cork in a large sea of commercial ethic. It is charged with vast responsibilities. Naturally it fancies that it is somehow free and detached from the economic ocean in which it floats, just as a cork on the crest of a wave might fancy itself free to toss and turn however it liked. By this means or that the university is tied to the rest of society, and there is little denying that higher education, indeed all education, has prospered and grown to its present mammoth size because it provides things that society wants, because it does society's bidding.

Until the last half of the nineteenth century our colleges and universities were lacking in this drive to produce and to sell things. There was no compulsive element in their nature. It is sometimes said that in our early history a person went to college because he wanted to become a gentleman, or a scholar. But even these wants were not pressures. At that time, when the word *gentleman* had some meaning, clearly the quality was already in one's possession *before* one entered the college. The scholar, on the other hand, didn't need a university affiliation but could be any individual who acquired a library or followed any intellectual pursuit. It was no more considered absolutely necessary for a scholar to attend college or university than to work in the Boston Public Library or visit the cathedrals of Europe.

As long as the American college or university was not under the compulsion to produce, it retained its original humanistic drive. That is, it continued to be a community where people came together voluntarily, and where they related to one another in individualistic rather than purely mechanical ways. For the better part of the nineteenth century, students who decided to attend a college or university were taking themselves to a place where the principal goal would be to create some kind of bond between themselves and their fellow students and professors. The college had something of the atmosphere of home and family, and students were seeking out the peculiar stamp of another, a new, home and family. They were seeking to grow with the college community just as they had grown to maturity in their own families. Here everybody lived under a single roof, so to speak, even if there were several buildings. The atmosphere of the community was all important. Everyone was pulling in the same direction; all believed themselves to be dedicated to similar ends. These ends were kept so vague and undefined that one was not traumatized by a sense of failure if some specific goal had been missed. The only real failure was not becoming rooted in the college community.

The "giant bazaar" model of the modern university doubtless has some things to recommend it. It is purposive, hard-driving, and efficient. It permits people to request highly specific objectives and allows them to believe that they have achieved them. On the other hand, the marketplace has its weaknesses as a human institution. When one is simply a buyer, one can be cheated or shortchanged. One is an outsider, a passerby or a passerthrough. One does not form any kind of permanent identity with the institution or with a particular way of life. The student who comes to buy an education is an isolated being in an alien environment.

The same weakness spreads to all members or participants of the university community. The professor, who in a sense is a merchant or even an "executive" of the great bazaar, does not have any vested interest in the personal element of the business, only in the "bottom line," his or her own sales receipts. As we have seen, professors today do not bond intimately to the college or university where they work (although the institution of tenure gives them ample opportunity to do so); instead their main allegiance is to their special field of study, whether chemistry, literature, anthropology, or mechanical engineering. A professor sometimes forms alliances with students, but usually only insofar as they also are drawn to his or her particular end product.

We have already said quite a bit about the ways in which this tendency toward specialization has been injurious to the cultural life of the professor. The injury to the student, if anything, has been even greater. By and large the losses to the student have gone unnoticed precisely because the university as emporium has found ways to make the educational process appear beneficial and, most recently, attractive and easy as well. While the universities were whittling down their offerings and their standards in the years after World War II, they found new ways to make higher education appealing to the young. Expectations of performance and achievement were considerably lowered. Students were offered freedoms they had never enjoyed before. They were told that they could enjoy the benefits and the opportunities of the college campus with few corresponding obligations. In the old-time college the student was burdened with obligations both intellectual and moral. One could seek one's individuality, but perforce inside a community one was obliged to repay for the benefits enjoyed. Some of these obligations seemed like restraints unworthy of adulthood, but they were not altogether inappropriate in the kind of atmosphere where one was attempting to achieve mature citizenship.

A great many freedoms have been offered to students in the years since World War II: freedom to come and go without restraint and "parental" supervision, freedom of personal conduct—sexual freedom, freedom to smoke and drink, and many others that are universally taken for granted today—freedom from the traditional academic rules and regulations such as class attendance. All such freedoms seem beneficial at first glance until one realizes that freedoms *from* things are often only empty freedoms. In recent generations colleges and universities have taken off the old restraints, but they have assumed, probably wrongly, that students will fill the void with something positive. More specifically, they have assumed that students will use their freedoms for *educational* ends, to fulfill the sorts of objectives that universities are presumably designed for. But there does not seem to be a great deal of evidence that the sorts of freedoms that have been granted to students in the last several generations have led them to closer identification with the world of learning; rather they have tended to isolate them further from it.

The advantage of a university conceived as a community is that students arrive expecting to become involved with its intellectual and cultural life. They do not come to college believing themselves to be either passive receivers or people on whose shoulders no responsibilities fall. They believe that something should be expected of them. And the truth is—perhaps this is only human nature— people function best when something is expected of them. The role of passive receiver, of whom little is expected, is not really a treasured one. The average adolescent attending college wants to make a passage to adulthood; but adulthood does not simply mean liberation from the strictures and restraints of childhood, it means challenges and serious expectations. When the long-established guiding principle *in loco parentis* was replaced by the present belief that students should be given total freedom to live their lives away from meddlesome deans, proctors, counselors, and other professional busybodies, there was much rejoicing all around. But nobody ever stopped to ask whether students really wanted and expected that the university would pay no attention to their ideas and actions. Paying no attention means not caring, and after several generations of not having anybody care about them, many students have begun to be suspicious of universities that have eliminated a negative but added no positive in its place.

The American university cannot get back on the road to health until it does things to bring students back into the community. The resources are all there; there are pockets of goodwill in all our institutions of higher learning, even though countervailing pressures on professors and administrators in the last half century have kept them suppressed. If our colleges and universities can find ways to return to the network of shared human values and free themselves of their present preoccupation with the manufacture and sale of knowledge products, a great step forward could be made.

17

Students: The Lively Lonely Crowd

$\mathbf{D}$O OUR PRESENT-DAY STUDENTS get much out of their four-year brush with America's institutions of higher learning? Do they enjoy going to college? There is a lot of conflicting evidence on the point. Many recent critics of higher education have found that college students plod their way through the system because it is required of them, but that they respond to the system in joyless and perfunctory ways. Allan Bloom found the college students of recent decades intellectually frigid, disinterested, incapable of being awakened to the realm of the mind. In an excellent book published in 1987, *Campus Life: Undergraduate cultures from the End of the Eighteenth Century to the Present,* historian Helen Lefkowitz Horowitz found the students of the past decade or so to be "joyless workaholics," grinding through the requirements but essentially nonintellectual in their attitudes toward higher education and life in general.

On the other hand: Michael Moffatt, an anthropologist, lived for several years in the undergraduate dormitories at Rutgers University and studied student activities and lifestyles exhaustively as both a detached observer and respected confidant of his youthful subject, summing up his findings in a book called *Coming of Age in New Jersey.* He insists that if you ask most college students whether they

168

enjoy college, the majority will reply, "College is great; I've had a wonderful time; I'm sorry to be leaving." When you ask them what has been great, however, most will respond by referring to all the enjoyable parties, the games, the trips out of town, the beer busts, and the dormitory jam sessions, and so on. Moffatt found that when they are not going to class or hitting the books, the majority of college students spend most of their free time not in studying or engaging in cultural pursuits but in "fooling around." There are, of course, organized extracurricular activities sponsored by fraternities and sororities, and these take up a lot of time. There are also athletic activities, either personal or intramural, but Moffatt found, surprisingly, that only one in ten students took part in them. Mostly, student free time outside the classroom is given over "to the endless verbal banter by which maturing American youths polish their personalities all through adolescence, trying on new roles, discarding old ones, learning the amiable, flexible social skills that constitute American middle class manners in the late twentieth century." Ask typical undergraduates what they want to do with their spare time in college, and they will invariably respond, "Have fun."

"Friendly fun," according to Moffatt, consists of "such easy pleasures as hanging out in a dorm lounge or a fraternity or sorority, gossiping, wrestling and fooling around, going to dinner with friends, having a late-night pizza or late-night chat, visiting other dorms, going out to a bar, and flirting as well as more serious erotic activities, usually with members of the opposite sex." Activities that come under the general heading of "fooling around" make up the extracurricular lifestyle of the typical college student. And, of course, it is an enjoyable lifestyle. College students use the college or university campus as a place to slip smoothly and without severe psychic pain into the state of adulthood.

Typical American college students perceive themselves as belonging to two separate and distinct worlds—the academic world, the world of required studies to which one devotes grudging; and the world of these spontaneous extracurricular activities. The central problem of student life today is not that there are these two worlds—for clearly students, more than their elders, need to have fun, need to have ways to blow off steam—but that the two domains are walled apart, kept completely separate. It is one of the most obvious weaknesses of our American universities that they have done such a poor job of convincing the young that learning, that things of the mind, are also enjoyable. Here you have these great institutions of higher learning with their well-endowed libraries and laboratories— institutions that are the envy of the world—yet somehow the majority of students are not really drawn to them. They gather, for the most part, outside the walls, flitting about and enjoying themselves according to their own tastes. They may well acquire some culture during their college years, but they do not earnestly partake of the culture of the institution; they prefer a culture that they have invented for themselves. There are, of course, no reasons for condemning this separate student culture—probably there is a lot to be said in favor of it—but sometimes one suspects there might be more efficient means of achieving the same thing than expensive institutions like colleges and universities.

The wall between academic life and student extracurricular activities is not precisely a new thing and should not be blamed wholly on the neglect of the present-day American university. College students are well endowed with physical energies and have always had a vigorous and sometimes mischievous need to distance themselves from adults. They want to strike out on their own, and within tolerable limits they should be encouraged to do so. On the other hand, as long as there have been universities, professors and members of the community with a strongly intellectual bent have been troubled by the uproariously low tone of undergraduate life. Writer and literary critic Edmund Wilson, who attended Princeton from 1912 to 1916—by which time, admittedly, the suffocating old classical curriculum of the college had not surrendered much ground—was puzzled by the weak intellectual motivation of his fellow students. When not strictly following the particular course of studies laid down for them, they seldom read, seldom attended a play or a lecture; they seldom showed curiosity about anything except what was required. In several editorials written for the *Princeton Library Magazine,* Wilson chastised his fellow students for their apparent lack of cultural inspiration. Why, he asked, couldn't they be induced to attend a play by George Bernard Shaw, rather than only the "dismal farces" of the Triangle Club? Why couldn't they pick up a book by a serious modern novelist like H. G. Wells or Arnold

Bennett? Wasn't there anything at all between the daily grind and the weekend orgy?

If this problem was troubling back in 1915, it is alarming today. Wilson complained about the low level of the Triangle Club farces, but at least in some sense these were imaginative celebrations of youth. The students produced the shows themselves, and they grew out of bona fide cultural and literary traditions. The weekend "foolings around" and beer busting of recent generations of students have few if any moorings in definable intellectual traditions. In 1915 there were bridges (although sometimes weak) between the realm of learning and the realm of student pleasure. Today these bridges have virtually disappeared.

Probably in the Princeton of Edmund Wilson's time, certainly throughout most of the nineteenth century, serious extracurricular activities were a major part of student life on most campuses. At Princeton there were probably many students, even of the upper crust, who got little out of the college experience beyond what was afforded by clubs and sporting groups. Elsewhere around the country at the same time there were college students whose cultural interests did not extend much beyond those of their fraternity or sorority. But Wilson's charge against the student of his day failed to take account of important pockets of a cultural community. At the very center of what was once called the "college experience" were glee clubs, oratorical societies, debating societies, organized discussion and special interest groups. Outside the classroom students attended, much more than they do today, plays, lectures, book groups. They edited literary magazines and engaged in all manner of other activities that were not only cultural in nature but disposed toward an exercise of the imagination.

Anyone who looks at a typical college yearbook will notice that most of these older kinds of student activities still exist. There are still glee clubs and debating societies on nearly every campus. By and large, though, they engage the attentions of a much smaller portion of the student population than those of fifty or a hundred years ago. Today these traditional extracurricular activities are regarded as "sissy" or "square" by a great many students. They smack of adult or parental guidance. There isn't much "fun" in them. Like so much else in the university, they have become "specialized" activities, absorbing the talents of students who are forced into them because they are related to their major or because for some peculiar reason they are unavoidable. I know of many large universities that have quite good theatre groups, for example, but participation in them is mostly limited to theatre or drama majors. Truly amateur theatre groups are often few and far between, so that students who delighted in taking part in a drama group in high school are brushed aside at the university. (Naturally in the smaller college or liberal arts school this is less likely to be the case.)

For the most part, the influence of the older organized college activities has waned on campus even if most of them have not utterly disappeared. To be sure, some of them have been replaced in the affection of students by new kinds of activities, some of which are healthy and even conducive to creating a sense of community. In recent years students have shown a propensity for joining groups involved in civic causes such as those touching on the environment, racial problems, or urban renewal. During the sixties the attentions of college students were drawn to numerous forms of activism and protest, some of which were troubling to their elders. But it is also easy to forget that student activism did a great deal to harness adolescent energies. Many of my colleagues tend to believe that the political activism of the sixties was a far better use of student time than the panty raids and adolescent high jinks of the period just before. And there is probably a certain amount of truth in this. Student interests in political causes or social issues have sometimes provided commendable ways to channel incipient student idealisms. When one thinks of organizations like Save the Whales, Campus Chest, blood drives, or numerous environmental groups, when one considers the number of college communities where students have become involved in cleanup efforts, or recycling projects, or animal rights causes, or projects to paint and repair the houses of elderly citizens or aid the homeless, it would be a mistake to think such activities sterile or socially uncaring. And the fact that many of these activities have been student generated makes them especially valuable.

On the other hand, far too many of the newer kinds of student activities are not closely related to the intellectual life of campus. Also, many of the "save the world" causes are stereotyped and repetitive, consisting of getting up boilerplate statements and pamphlets, shouting canned and simpleminded slogans through bullhorns. Many of the critics of student activism of a few decades ago were unduly worried about the specific content of the ideologies being preached by the many bellicose individuals screaming epithets about the war, about the government, about corporations that manufactured napalm, or about Marine Corps recruiting. But a larger difficulty was that so many of the student "activist" issues gave little play to student imagination or creativity. The activists fed on dead slogans that were often as simplistic and mindless as anything ground out of baser regions of American politics and a good deal less ingenious. In short, these activities often harnessed only students' physical energies, not their imaginations.

The principal advantage of the older kinds of social activities associated with college life, even with their aura of parental authority, was that they had the tendency to draw students more intimately into the intellectual arena, tempted them with the kinds of preoccupations that gave the university its reason for being. Furthermore, the social reform boilerplate and the political bustle of recent decades had the effect of freezing students in a perpetual state of adolescent rebellion, whereas the older forms of student activities, which required some kind of individual input and impetus toward excellence, had the effect of furnishing a suitable ground between adolescence and adulthood and gave vent to both play and intellect.

There were, not too many generations ago, student activities that clearly drew students into the mainstream of college and university life, gave them genuine means of participation, made them believe that they belonged to the intellectual community in significant ways. For example, today I think it would be safe to say that few colleges or universities have first-rate literary or humor magazines. (For many years, I'm afraid, I haven't seen any humor magazines worth the paper they are printed on.) But as late as the 1920s a great many college magazines were imaginative, substantial, and literate. When Edmund Wilson complained about the intellectual isolation of students at Princeton in 1915 during his undergraduate years, he forgot that he himself was doing a superlative job of editing the *Nassau Literary Magazine;* he and his fellow student contributors— among them F. Scott Fitzgerald and John Peele Bishop—were producing a magazine of considerable merit that was neither stuffy nor puerile. There were numerous first-rate college literary magazines in those days beside the nationally known ones like the Princeton *Lit* or the Harvard *Crimson*. Around the country many aspiring writers won their spurs on high-quality magazines that were published even by small and undistinguished colleges. The literary magazine gave college students the opportunity to do something adult that was all their own.

So too the humor magazine. In the days when college education seemed to be designed for the young and not old fogeys in training, the humor magazine was a jewel of perfection on many college campuses. Some student humor magazines attracted a broad and enthusiastic audience among the reading public. In the 1880s a group of editors at the famous Harvard *Lampoon* went on after graduation to establish *Life* magazine (the *old* pre-Time, Inc., *Life*), which for four decades was perhaps the best humor magazine in America. Maybe it is true that we Americans have lost our native sense of humor, weighed down as we are by the cares of trade deficits, savings and loan imbroglios, and failed foreign policy, but it is pleasant to remember that at one time the young of our nation displayed a forceful and decidedly robust comic imagination. Spirited college youngsters like Robert Benchley of the Harvard *Lampoon* and S. J. Perelman of the *Little Brown Jug* cultivated talents in their college days that later flourished in commercial magazines like *Judge* and the *New Yorker* in the 1920s and 1930s. Today the quality college humor magazine has all but disappeared; the few that remain are unspeakably crude and juvenile—let's face it, just plain bad.

Alas, the loss of the old extracurricular activities is not the only evidence of the wide gap between today's students and the universities that serve them. It is only one kind of evidence of a much more deeply rooted problem. A wider, more generalized disinterest in things intellectual marks the student life of our time. Probably the majority of those who go to college today manifest little interest at all in what goes on in the intellectual environment around them. Outside of the books needed to pass examinations or write term papers, they read little. Research universities usually take pride in the fact that undergraduate students are privileged to breathe the air of these prestige institutions where much is supposed to be going on in every field of learning, and they have hoodwinked themselves into believing that much of this will rub off on students, even if they are not on close terms with the great creative minds who grace the premises. But there is little evidence that such is the case. A few undergraduates, to be sure, will become integrated into the intellectual life of the institution (once again it is highly specialized or segmented groups we are talking about), but the majority have come to take only what is needed to obtain a degree; they show not the slightest interest in anything else.

A survey of American undergraduates made in 1984 by the Carnegie Foundation for the Advancement of Teaching discovered that 46 percent of American students spent no time at all attending campus cultural events. Half the students spent no time in any kinds of organized campus activities, athletics excepted. Furthermore, and more gloomy, only a small handful of students spent more than an hour or two a week on leisure reading; 23 percent spent no time at all on unrequired reading during their entire college careers.

In my teaching experience at the University of Illinois I have discovered that although the university offers its students a great many cultural events—concert and lecture series, museums, film programs, opera and theatre companies, and all manner of others— many students make no use of these facilities. A number say that they would like to avail themselves of these opportunities if "they had time." (Free time they actually have, but they prefer to spend it elsewhere.) We have three museums at the university—a world-renowned art museum, the Museum of Natural History, and the World Heritage Museum—but a recent survey by a graduate student in education showed that more than half of the undergraduates had never paid a single visit to any of these museums during their college careers. We have one of the largest research libraries in the world, with over forty specialized departmental libraries, yet about half of the undergraduate students have not used any of these libraries except in connection with a specific course requirement. Many students used the reserve collections in which books for a particular course are set aside, but beyond that made no use whatsoever of the library. A year or so ago I spoke with a junior who did not even know where the main library was!

For these patterns of student isolation to be altered, the university, especially the large research university, must reorder its priorities, must seek new and innovative ways to reach out to undergraduate students. These efforts cannot originate with the students but must come from the faculties, since the students have been on their own for so long that they cannot be expected to take the lead. Even without radically altering their present total absorption in their specializations, there are probably things that faculties could do that would not be exorbitantly expensive and would make an enormous difference.

One thing I believe to be essential is that every student in a university have a "real" academic adviser, that is a full-time faculty member who is acquainted with that student, who knows at least something about his or her interests and peculiarities of mind. At the present time the advising function on most campuses is a perfunctory administration chore. I have known places where the "adviser" does nothing but rubber-stamp a student's program card—sometimes not even doing an adequate job of checking to see whether the student is fulfilling graduation requirements. I have even known students who have found the adviser's function so useless that they forge his or her signature on their program card rather than wait for an appointment. In any case, program approval is a poor excuse for "advising." Every student needs to have a faculty person who knows him or her by face and by name and interacts on a personal level.

Somewhat related to this suggestion is another, which is also not impossible to implement but undeniably calls for some redirection of resources. There needs to be at every university an investigation of all possibilities for one-on-one instruction. I believe that no better role model for this can be found than the tutorial system that has worked so well in British universities. This system, which was instituted with marvelous effect at Harvard by A. Lawrence Lowell, has since flourished in other places with similar success. At present many universities have some kind of provision for tutorial instruction of undergraduates, but sorrowfully this usually involves only a small number of students, most often those who seek it out or those identified as "honors" students. I would strongly propose that all undergraduate students be treated to the luxury of at least one tutorial course during their college career, more if possible. Probably this tutorial would be in the student's major field, but it could conceivably be in another area if one were inspired enough to seek out a professor with whom one could share something of interest.

We need to invent new and resourceful ways to bring students and their professors back together in some kind of community of desire.

In the small college of a hundred years ago, when the professor lived within stone's throw of those ivy-covered buildings, human interaction was not only natural but unavoidable. In the megaversity of today, ringed by parking lots, where students may be housed in the inner core and professors escape by automobile at four o'clock to the suburbs, personal bonds are difficult to forge. On the other hand, if professors were encouraged to find innovative ways to fraternize informally with students, a great step forward could be taken. Professors might once again be encouraged to entertain students in their homes; it might be better for universities to expend funds for this kind of socializing than to dole out money for professors to attend meetings of professional societies in some faraway city.

I have found that in most universities the faculty and administration are not very resourceful when it comes to finding ways to bring professors and students together on a plane of shared interest. Sometimes students themselves are a little better at doing so, even in the face of indifference from their elders. A number of years ago at the University of Illinois the Commerce Club instituted a program in which a small group of students invited a professor or two out to lunch, an event that resulted in the opportunity for general discussion as well as low-key camaraderie. More recently the Housing Division inaugurated a program in which a group of students invited professors out to dinner and a night at the theater or some other cultural event. This marvelous idea was marred only by the sadly small number of participants. Over two-thirds of the professors invited failed to show up, perhaps not wanting to waste time hobnobbing with undergraduates. But such reluctance might change if the university held up an entirely different set of priorities.

The trick, of course, is to get teachers and students talking about matters of intellectual concern; to find ways to form groupings that allow members of the campus community to relate on a higher plane. Many of those who have lived or taught in large universities are aware that fraternities and sororities plan occasional student-professor dinners or parties. Unfortunately, in the twentieth century the so-called Greek system is so resolutely unintellectual, if not anti-intellectual, that these events do not rise above the level of nodding socialization or dignified imbibing. What is needed are opportunities to allow student and teacher to plug into each other's minds on an informal and relaxed level.

There are a great many opportunities for a university to establish a pipeline between its intellectual offerings and everyday student life. In recent years many large universities have introduced orientation programs for beginning students, and in some places these have been extended to cover activities over a whole semester. A few universities designate a theme of some sort around which both courses and a multitude of events may cluster during the freshman year. If a topic like the environment is selected, students can also channel their energies to those activities outside the classroom that spark their interest. At the same time the topic can be taken up in freshman classrooms, say, where it may be treated in a more traditional academic way. A related idea is the all-campus convocation as a more or less regular event. At Washington University in St. Louis, for example, a weekly convocation featured poets or political figures from the local community. This sort of event has the added advantage of creating a bond between academia and the outside world—a bond that has been allowed to weaken in recent decades.

Sometimes novel ideas for energizing the community mushroom to the joy and satisfaction of almost everybody. Some years back a dean of students at Evergreen College in Washington State established a day at the end of the year called "Super Saturday," the purpose of which was to thank everybody for yet another academic year. Super Saturday grew to include a street fair, entertainment, barbecues, and a book sale. The day now provides an opportunity to solidify ties between the college and the larger community, and it has attracted as many as twenty-five thousand people. The faculty at Evergreen also hold potluck suppers in their homes, and there are annual retreats at a small lodge called The Farmhouse.

Ernest L. Boyer, in his recent book, *Campus Life*, has suggested that while it is important for every college or university to establish a just community, a disciplined community, and a caring community, it is equally important to become a "celebrative" community. That is to say, each must do something to sustain and cultivate the heritage and traditions of the institution. Sometimes this can be done through ceremonies and celebrations—a Founder's Day, for example, or an Annual Convocation. It can be done by finding ways to integrate students into long-standing traditions of one kind or another. Boyer cites the example of the famous Parade at Princeton

University in which alumni of the college, going back to the oldest grads, march with the seniors during graduation week.

Students should be made aware of the history and traditions of the institutions they are attending so that they don't immediately get the idea that the place was made by others and they are just passing through. Students should be taught something about the history of their college or university—its triumphs, its famous scholars, its architectural beauty. Is there significance in the ivy or an old oak tree or the configuration of paths? Is this the old parade ground where the ROTC drilled before being shipped off to World War I? A university must not only impart information; it must learn to share its rituals, its mellowed past, its individual style.

Some of these things may seem redolent of life in the small private college of yore, unfeasible for large public or research universities. Perhaps, but perhaps not. It has been the large universities that have been most often charged with indifference to undergraduates, and it has fallen to them to answer the charges, or at least appear to be doing so. In my own experience the large universities haven't really gotten the message yet. They know they are under pressure for change, and they grasp the main thrust of the complaints, but they have been so long frozen in inertia, so long dominated by graduate schools, by research priorities, by the publication treadmill, that they cannot make substantial improvements or changes in the quality of human education. Their usual approach is to put up some window dressing, change the drapes, so to speak, and then go back to business as usual. Anybody who has been around the American university for the last ten years has heard a lot about a new emphasis on teaching. There are prizes for best undergraduate teacher, and second best, and even third best. Guidebooks on teaching methodologies and evaluation abound, but for the most part they seem to be perfunctory efforts, incapable of touching the defects of an essentially cold and impersonal institution dedicated to the production of specialized particles of knowledge.

At the University of California at Berkeley, which got more than its share of brickbats for indifference to students back in the 1960s, thee is now an elaborate fall convocation to greet students—replete with music and refreshments. (Nearly all universities, however large, manage to put on a pretty good show when families and other taxpayers are on the premises—especially at graduation time.) As part of the fall reception of students, each freshman is greeted by a member of the faculty or staff and accompanied through a formal receiving line at the student union where each student gets a chance to meet the chancellor. Then the freshman is introduced to an upper-level student who acts as his or her host. A splendid idea, no doubt; unfortunately it is hard to see this effusive ceremony as more than a public relations extravaganza, after which the bewildered students wend their way back to the dorm and on to classrooms taught by teaching assistants and adjuncts.

The University of Illinois had a delightful and innovative idea for undergraduate education back in the late sixties, when it, along with other mammoth public institutions, was under fire for not addressing the needs of its lower-level students. The university established a learning-living program called Unit One. Students who selected the program were assigned to a dormitory where they were able to take part in an intimate and cohesive community; they even took some of their introductory classes in the comfortable and homelike environment of the dorm. Unit One offered advising and counseling. An artist-in-residence program brought in not only artists but people from all walks of life—labor leaders, business executives, a former presidential speechwriter, a circus clown, an experimental film-maker, a noted ballerina, a coal miner—all of whom received room and board in the dormitory during their period of residence. Unit One had a pottery studio and a photo lab and had full-time instructors in these areas.

Altogether Unit One was a marvelous idea. It eased students into the lonely and inevitable routine of trudging from one class or lab section to another. It brought students into close contact with people who seemed to care. It provided intimacy; it provided community. For a short time the idea was thought to be a good one around the university; indeed the very name, Unit One, suggested an intention to establish other learning-living programs elsewhere in the university. Unfortunately, this never happened. As soon as the era of student activism was over, the faculty of the College of Liberal Arts and Sciences, which ran the program, dropped it. With many students returning to the daily grind and sticking to the pursuit of the diploma, the Liberal Arts faculty saw no need for such "coddling" of students. The unit's funding was withdrawn, the money probably being used to hire three or four more research professors in organic chemistry or comparative linguistics or deconstruction criticism. The students in Unit One put up a protest to save the program, and they managed to keep it alive in an impoverished form. The Liberal Arts College wanted nothing to do with a program that reflected no glory on the various specializations, but the program continues to this day, run by the university's Division of Housing. Without strong faculty support it goes its lonely way as an anomaly, standing in a backwater of the academic mainstream.

In the last several decades nearly all universities have become aware that they are under attack for their indifferent and mechanical handling of undergraduate students. Administrators, at least the best of them, know that the general public does not share the enthusiasm of the academic community for high-powered research. They are now becoming aware that the public is wary of the canard that what goes on in the graduate school "rubs off" on or "filters down" to undergraduates. When things get hot and outside complaints become strident, small efforts at "reform" are made. Invariably, though, these are temporary or devious appeasements, window ornaments; they are cast aside as soon as the public is distracted by something else. The Unit One situation is a good example.

Furthermore, it has been my experience that even when efforts are being made to address this or that particular complaint about undergraduate education, things start to fall apart someplace else. Older excellences disappear or find themselves under attack. The University of Illinois, for example, took the foolish and inexplicable step of abolishing its Division of General Studies in the 1960s, just at the time it was becoming obvious that more of this sort of thing and not less was the order of the day. The Unit One program was instituted around the same time, so it might be possible to say that the university took a tiny (but well-dramatized) step forward, just as it was also taking a gigantic leap backward. Universities thus discover crafty and showy ways to prove that they are addressing areas of weaknesses, while at the same time doing everything to ensure that nothing in the status quo is really disturbed, to see that the education of undergraduate students continues to be an unimportant and marginal byproduct.

Liberal or general education, as we have often had occasion to say, is a difficult and delicate plant to keep under cultivation. In our present-day universities it is regarded as something of a troublesome weed, so there is little wonder that it struggles to survive between the cracks of the mighty edifice that much prefers to produce self-gratifying pleasures for professors, highly specialized research end products, individuals holding professional degrees who have the true stamp of the university on them. Liberal education cannot be cultivated without paying close attention to students, and this is precisely what the universities don't want to do. They have what they believe are more important functions, and until the public finds ways to demand something else, the primary educational functions of the universities will continue to be performed in mediocre and uninspiring ways.

18

In Loco Parentis—Then What?

ONCE UPON A TIME—not so long ago in fact—college students were treated like children. Their behavior was carefully monitored, their indiscretions scrutinized, their privacy regularly compromised. It was not that they were precisely thought to *be* children. Deans and professors of the old-time college were well aware that college-age youth stood between adolescence and adulthood and were thus full of exuberant animal spirits. The hope always was that you could find some sort of golden mean between allowing free rein to those spirits and establishing demands for civilized adult behavior. But whatever compromises were made between the need for restraint and the need for freedom, there was an underlying assumption that the regulation of student life was in some sense a duty of the college. Deans, proctors, advisers, housemothers, even professors, accepted, at slightly distant remove, the obligations of parenting. They assumed that the parents back home, usually paying the bill, had expectations that the college community was a civilized community and that certain standards of behavior would be maintained. The college not only imparted information but provided an environment for living.

All this has changed, as most of us know. Colleges no longer stand *in loco parentis*. They have abdicated responsibility for what students do with themselves outside the classroom. There are academic rules, academic standards, and these can be enforced—due dates for

papers, requirements of class attendance (in some places), or procedures for the taking of examinations. But over the past several
generations most colleges and universities have gravitated toward
the assumption (or at least the practice) that the only nexus between
the student and the institution is the classroom. The college students
arrive as fully formed adults, should be treated like adults, with few
if any demands on them as members of the community, with no
regulation of their behavior. Vanished into the recesses of history are
books to sign in and sign out, rules on drinking, gambling, or sex;
gone are snoopy proctors or housemothers who check up not only on
the behavior of students but on the orderliness or the contents of
their rooms; disappeared, too, are files and records in the college
office documenting the student's indiscretions and peccadillos.

The practice of closely monitoring student behavior had its roots
not in the medieval European university but in the denominational
colleges of early America. This practice was tied to the stern belief
that education was as much a moral as an intellectual dimension of
life. But inculcating the moral dimension by means of birch rod or
rule book had its obvious defects, as most people today will agree.
The presence of the rule book and the snoopy parental surrogate
tended to inspire the very sorts of behavior that they sought to
control. As a curious footnote of history, students in the small
college of the nineteenth century were much more uproarious, much
more destructive, than the students of today. Those in charge of the
college property had to be constantly vigilant against students who
overturned things, played all manner of pranks on fellow students
and professors, tarred and feathered the statute of the founder, or let
firecrackers resound in recitation hall and dormitory corridor.
Hazing was a particularly vicious form of student behavior in the
1880s and 1890s, and it was hard to stamp out precisely because it
was so strenuously opposed by college administrations. There is a
naturally rebellious strain in the adolescent, and when balked it
often seeks malicious and destructive forms of expression.

The surrogate parental role put very heavy demands on the
personnel of the college. Professors wearied of having to sneak
around the side of a building to see if a student was throwing a
firecracker or carrying a jug of hard liquor. At Princeton, President
James McCosh lamented, "I abhor the plan of secretly watching

students by peeping through windows at night and listening through keyholes."

Even more important, though, the old parental environment had detrimental effects on the students—just the opposite of what it had hoped to achieve. The poet Edna St. Vincent Millay, who arrived at Vassar just before World War I, found the rules and regulations stifling and childish. Having virtually reared several younger sisters, and become a published writer at the age of twenty-one, she could not fathom the college's restrictions on behavior. She wrote to fellow poet Arthur Davison Ficke: "I hate this pink-and-gray college. If there had been a college in *Alice and Wonderland* it would be this college.... We can go into the candy kitchen and take what we like and pay or not and nobody is there to know. But a man is forbidden as if he were an apple." Millay almost didn't graduate—too many infractions of the rules: smoking, missing chapel, being away without leave, ducking classes. Indeed, the faculty voted to withhold her degree, although this extreme action was vetoed at the last minute by President Henry Noble MacCracken, who had probably observed that Miss Millay was hardly a harum-scarum adolescent.

The watchful parental environment began slowly eroding in the late nineteenth century, especially with the growth of large public universities and the appearance of urban universities where students commuted to the campus. But the parental approach was still very much in evidence everywhere in the land as late as the 1960s. When I began my teaching career at the University of Illinois in the mid-1960s, there were still severe restrictions on student behavior. The university leaned hard on those found in possession of alcohol or drugs. Dormitories were segregated as to sex. Boys were permitted to visit girls only in the lounge of the girl's dormitory. A vigilant housemother guarded these precincts with an eagle eye to make sure no passions got out of hand. There was even said to be a "three-foot" rule, which required that three feet must be observable on the floor in front of every couple seated on a sofa or davenport. University police flashed lights into parked cars for evidence of sexual adventuresomeness and even scoured cemeteries and lonely lanes for glimpses of students necking or "making out." The university had a "security officer," an ex-FBI agent, who kept extensive records of student transgressions.

By the early 1970s this climate had completely changed, as it had almost everywhere else in the land. During and shortly after the period of student unrest, the University of Illinois threw in the towel and gave up all pretense of monitoring student morals. The security officer and his files of naughty behavior were no more. Unisex dormitories were in, and efforts to curb the sexual proclivities of undergraduates were a thing of the past. "Hours" and sign-in books for women became a memory. To be sure, in most places men and women were housed on different floors or different wings, and feeble efforts were made to keep the sexes apart. There continued to be some "rules," but they largely went unobserved, and university officials made only half-hearted attempts to enforce them. Many parents over the past two decades have been deceived by the seeming security of separate floors or separate wings for the sexes, but those in the know (including all administrators) realize that these "separations" are nothing but charades. The truth of the matter is that most colleges and universities no longer make efforts to control the sexual activity of students.

The new freedom for students has had a great many obvious benefits. The expectation that students will act more like adults when treated as such has paid dividends. The college students of the present are undoubtedly less frolicsome and mischievous than those of the past—a good thing, no doubt, although not a few of their professors also find many of today's students less creatively playful and imaginative in the hard-boiled, "all for business" university. Some of us even occasionally yearn for the days when student behavior seemed more colorful and childlike. For the most part, students have not grossly misused their new freedoms, and it would be difficult to allege that college students in America are an unruly lot.

But putting students off on their own except in matters academic has decidedly had many undesirable side effects. The highly segmented university, with its tendency to isolate people in watertight compartments—undergraduate students with their culture, graduate students with another, professors with yet another—tends to create a kind of moral vacuum, an empty space at the heart of things. Undergraduate students are not without society, of course, because they create their own society, and a lively society it invariably is. Yet most undergraduates, and even graduate students, feel themselves abandoned by the larger academic community. In fact, they often feel uneasy, even lost, in an institution that provides no expectations and affords no guidelines for behavior. Today's students, like students in the past, like all adolescents for that matter, push for freedoms, but they never expect them to be completely granted. They believe that somehow a university is a nurturing environment, and they expect to be cared for in some sense. Accordingly they exhibit a good deal of unease living in a place where little is given and little is expected except in the classroom.

Not too long ago a very sensitive and intelligent student of mine commented on the feeling of neglect and isolation that many students have on a large university campus. "Well, of course, we don't want professors to tell us how to run our lives, when to come in at night, and so on, but we think professors should be a little interested in what we know and think. They could say a little bit to us about our lives now and then." Educators have failed to learn the lesson that a great many parents of younger children have learned, sometimes after bitter experience: Even though the young don't want repressive governance, they yearn for control when it comes in the form of intelligent dialogue and intimate discussion. The intellectual mix of college students is in a fluid state, has not jelled, in spite of all their protestations to the contrary. They want to know how the world is ordered, what values are esteemed, and they do not totally resist gentle prodding from their elders. They want to know not only how things are but how they should be. Lack of such a formative spirit, which was traditionally one of the defining characteristics of education, leaves students bobbing in a sea of indecision and moral emptiness.

One of the hardest things for today's college students to accept is that beyond the classroom, and beyond certain bureaucratic "services," there is not a great deal for them at the university. In the classroom they are provided with learning, and often they are provided with the professor's attitudes and moral viewpoints, but they are expected to swallow these whole. If they have personal or psychological problems, they have access to a counselor or psychologist or social caseworker trained to deal with personal problems, but seldom do they have an adult to turn to who can discuss with them who they are as individuals, where they are headed in the world, how knowledge imparted to them in some particular course may be relevant to their needs. It is often asserted, and widely believed by educators, that all such things will be resolved with the passage of time, that the bent twig will eventually straighten itself and take the form of a solid oak. That is probably true. But at a time when the young are desperately seeking aid in forming their intellectual world and their moral attitudes, they get virtually no help from the university.

The new freedom from rules and regulations has not been as universally appreciated by students as many administrators believe. I have found many students displeased with the moral vacuum of the campus environment. A number of years ago I had a young lady in class, a student with a serious intellectual bent, whose life in the modern, rule-free dormitory had proved to be something of a personal nightmare. Nearly every night, when she wanted to study in her room—a space not really a great deal more commodious than a broom closet—her roommate insisted on enjoying the ultimate excesses of passion in the upper bunk with her boyfriend. (So much for the separation of the sexes on male and female floors!) The student was told by the housing administration that there was no remedy for this kind of situation; you just sort of learned to live with it. She could not break her room contract or insist upon having a different roommate and was eventually able to tear loose from her nightly voyeuristic experience only by going to a mental health counselor and insisting that she would have a nervous breakdown if she weren't moved.

University administrators insist that such situations can be worked out by students managing their own lives. They will have to do so in the adult world, so why not now? The trouble is that students eighteen to twenty-two, although adult in appearance, are not fully developed in their attitudes and values, not fully able to handle the stresses and strains or their interpersonal lives. They seek, in somewhat milder, perhaps disguised form, the kind of guidance they have been receiving at home. At one time this was provided not just by the implacable book of rules and regulations but by the quasi-parental guidance of real people who controlled the environment. They kept the reins of power not merely because they were authoritarian, but so that students could have a rich and tranquil environment in which to think and work.

Unfortunately, when you remove the prop of moral and personal support from college students, when you surrender to the notion that freedom has no content, has no corresponding obligation behind it, you are drifting toward an unstable and brittle human community. And this is what has happened for the most part over the past several generations. The university community has been in a condition of moral ambiguity and confusion, something that has at last begun to trouble the educational establishment.

By the late 1980s the moral climate on the nation's college campuses became so alarming that the Carnegie Foundation for the Advancement of Teaching initiated a study of campus values and campus life. The report that came out of this study, edited by Ernest L. Boyer and entitled *Campus Life: In Search of Community,* notes that college presidents and administrators, as well as civic leaders, have grown uneasy over the last few years about deteriorating conditions in the social life of the nation's campuses. There are, for example, strong concerns about increasing drug and alcohol abuse on most campuses today. There is a growing worry about crime on campus, statistically borne out by a steep increase in the number of crimes reported on or near college campuses—rapes, assaults, robberies, muggings. More subtle and elusive, perhaps, there seems to be a breakdown of civility: more incidents of abusive language, racial tensions, and sex discrimination, more demonstrations against minority groups and gays, more rowdy behavior in many campus settings, not even excluding the classroom.

The trouble is that since the sixties the universities have not been well positioned to do anything about problems of this sort. Once you have accepted the idea that students are free, that all forms of behavior outside the classroom are beyond the pale of regulation, you have no solid ground on which to stand when it comes to dealing with social problems on campus. Once the old rules and regulations are cast aside, there are few ways to get a grip on the excesses of student behavior, except when they involve blatantly criminal acts—assaults, perhaps destruction of property. Even here, most colleges, since they no longer have adequate forms and procedures for discipline, leave such matters to the police and outside civil authorities. Not long ago the wire services exploded with a story about a university student who was accused of three separate campus rapes, but only after he was actually convicted in a court of law was disciplinary action taken against him—he was expelled!

In many instances universities have completely abandoned control over illegal behavior and over such other behavior as is covered by the few regulations found in what remains of the old college book of rules. The rule books of recent years, for example, are couched in such obscure or ambiguous language that they invite students to reach the conclusion that they don't mean what they say, or rather that they simply won't be enforced. Underage drinking, for example, is prohibited, but the university really won't do anything about violators. This quickly becomes common knowledge. To take another example, I pick up the handbook for students currently in use at the University of Illinois and find the following pronouncement on the use of marijuana:

> The Senate Committee on Student Discipline recognizes the importance and the danger to the student of any violation of laws on marijuana and any controlled substances. It emphasizes the grave seriousness of these violations involving manufacturing, processing, distributing or selling marijuana or controlled substances, particularly within the university community, and expects the disciplinary system to deal with these violations in an appropriately serious manner.

These, of course, are all weasel words. The university "recognizes" the danger of students using or dealing in controlled substances like marijuana, not apparently because the university takes a stand against it, but because the law does and students may get in trouble with the law. Everything is couched in the hypothetical: "the university recognizes," it "may" take action, etc. Well, it *may*, but of course it doesn't. No cases dealing with marijuana use come before the campus disciplinary committee at Illinois, and I can recollect no recent instances where a student convicted of a marijuana offense in a court of law had his offense taken up by a campus disciplinary committee.

Maybe this is the way it should be. But the way in which the long-disdained marijuana laws are dealt with in most universities is dramatic evidence of the powerlessness of campus administrators when it comes to student behavior in general. At the University of Illinois some years back, students planned a campus marijuana jamboree called "Hash Wednesday," an event that has been held annually every spring since. An ever-diminishing number of the faithful show up every year and take a few symbolic puffs, although since marijuana use has diminished many more students are found quaffing beer, a more popular student lubricant of the present moment, on the occasion. Campus administrators sit nervously watching from their offices, and one year, after some bad newspaper publicity and a little blowing from the state legislature, a contingent of police dragged away a few scruffy-looking students as a public relations gesture; but in most years nothing at all has happened on Hash Wednesday. The annual event usually turns out to be a dull, tedious, and meaningless protest—so dull that only a few students bother to show up for it. They have essentially won their battle, so there is nothing important to protest.

Now, it may be that the university officials use precisely the right approach where marijuana is concerned. It could be that they are right in their apparent agreement with the students that the marijuana laws remaining on the books are silly, unjustifiable, and unenforceable. The marijuana problem may not be worth bothering about. But the larger problem of which it is merely an illustration is a good deal more troubling. Some years ago, when the universities gave up attempting to regulate student behavior, they placed themselves in a position where getting back any kind of control, or setting any kinds of standards, became a near impossibility.

In the last few years college administrators have had to swallow the realization that the quality of social life on the nation's campuses has sharply declined. Increased alcohol use among students has caught the attention of the general public to the point where its dangers are not lost even on administrators and faculty committees who prefer to remain oblivious to such matters. But having thrown away the old rule books, having abolished disciplinary committees, having abandoned procedures for the regulation of student conduct, the college or university finds itself in a perilous position. It is powerless to deal with whatever serious social and behavioral problems actually do arise.

In some states new laws have recently been passed that threaten to mete out strong penalties to colleges and universities that do not control underage drinking in dormitories or other campus facilities. The reasons for these new laws are alarming enough, although in many places they are regarded as meddlesome by administrators who complain that they can no more be expected to enforce such laws than they can enforce archaic laws on fornication. On the other hand, at the present time university administrators are being urged by their own campus communities to do something to control certain kinds of behavior because they happen to fly in the face of current academic mores. Racism, sexism, harassment, assaults on gay rights, abusive language and behavior are excoriated by professors and by student groups, all of whom pressure administrators to take action against these violations of current campus moral attitudes. University police are well aware that many instances of rape, including "date rape," are alcohol related. Accordingly pressures from women students have made administrators worry about reducing not only the number of rape attacks on campus but alcohol use as well.

Recently there have been news stories about institutions where officials have been jostled into action and have expelled or disciplined students who posted messages identifying women with four-letter words or spray-painting racial epithets—as well they should. But spray-painting itself is not the cause of alarm, apparently. In the Viet Nam War era it was considered to be only a minor offense to spray-paint antiwar slogans; this was thought to be part of our cherished freedom of expression. These "political commentators," after all, were the campus sages of their day. But spray-painting of campus buildings should be regarded as a serious offense *whatever* the slogan. Unfortunately, in this era of noninterference in student morality no uniform and consistent approach to such behavior has been possible, with the result that administrators mostly stand by helplessly when they are called upon to deal with acts that offend the fashionable campus sensibilities of the day.

The nation's colleges and universities have been governed in recent years by a kind of doctrine of selective barbarities. When barbarous acts are turned on particular people, ideas, groups, and doctrines that the academic community currently believes need protecting for one reason or another, the disciplinary rod comes out. All other uncivil behavior stands under the umbrella of freedom of expression. This is reminiscent of the kind of irrational discipline exercised by some parents of small children: The strap or rod comes out wildly and unsystematically whenever the parent happens to be agitated.

Unfortunately, as soon as you introduce the idea that there is no universal standard of civil behavior, as soon as you let it be known that everybody is free to select his or her own moral path without consideration of its effects on fellow students or other members of the community, then you are more or less powerless to curtail *any* kind of student behavior. Colleges and universities that for years have been saying to students "We don't care anything about your behavior outside of class" are now hardly well positioned to tell students how to act. In the rare instances when they try to do so, the effects are more often than not both comical and frustrating.

Not too long ago, in response to serious drinking problems, a large university in the southwest passed a new rule forbidding alcohol consumption on campus. In their turn, the students presented an ultimatum that said, essentially, "If you don't let us drink, we'll go off campus and drive drunk." The administration backed down in the face of this ultimatum (one administrator at the place called it "blackmail"), and the rule was rescinded, although the university countered with a mandate that a chaperon or uniformed policeman be present at all parties where alcohol is served.

In place of the old doctrine *in loco parentis,* the present-day university has substituted a kind of "crack the whip when really pestered" form of student control, which is every bit as degrading to all participants as the system of intricate control it replaced. Such an approach leads to flare-ups and recriminations, such as the threat made by the student body to drive drunk. It can generate new forms of adversarial conflicts between students and the university. But in the long run the intermittent and largely unpredictable moral spasms of college officials, the sporadic whip-crackings, don't do a great deal to improve the quality of social life on campus. What is needed is some agreed-upon belief that you can't have a workable community of individuals unless you insist upon restrained, civilized behavior. Civilization cannot survive only on gusts of free expression. Free expression can't prosper outside a common ground of civility and respect for the rights, beliefs, and peculiarities of other people.

Ernest Boyer urges American universities to return to some sort of coherent standards, or at least expectations, of civil behavior and sense of community. According to Boyer and the Carnegie Foundation, the university should be a just community, a disciplined community, and a caring community. To achieve the disciplined community, the university must "define with clarity" its expectations of student behavior. A university must be a place where there are appropriate rules governing campus life, where individuals acknowledge their obligations to the group. The foundation also urges an "honor code" governing both scholarly *and* civic dimensions of campus life. "Such codes convey a powerful message about how honesty and integrity form the foundation of a community of learning." This hints at a rediscovery of the old and long-abandoned notion that behavior and learning are not isolated parts of human life, not realms that are hermetically sealed off from one another. It suggests a return to the ideal that the educated person is a caring person with responsibilities not only to some narrow field of study, not only to the university, but to a larger human community.

It is rather interesting, perhaps even startling, to note that half of the students responding to a Carnegie survey supported some kind of code of conduct; at liberal arts colleges 60 percent of students did. A majority of students believed that known drug offenders should be dismissed or suspended. Quite remarkably, two-thirds of students surveyed believed that the drinking age should be raised to twenty-one in all states! There is widespread evidence, too, that students are more concerned than their elders about antisocial behavior. The majority of students are in favor of regulations concerning privacy, freedom from noise in dormitories, cheating, and plagiarism. Every student has been confronted by one or another kind of antisocial student behavior—for example, the tearing out of crucial pages on a reserve library book the night before the exam. A great many probably wish that universities cared more about controlling such behavior than they presently do.

But lack of control of student behavior is really not an isolated issue on college campuses today; it is just part of a much larger problem: the widespread inattention to student life; the indifference to general student culture except when it comes within the realm of classroom performance. Problems of discipline on college campuses have gotten a certain amount of scrutiny in the last few years, even though in all probability the majority of students do not cause serious problems to the institutions in which they reside. They pass through the system glumly, sluggishly, like coal miners trudging to the minehead. They ask little of their professors, and for the most part they are not a nuisance. But the indifference of their elders has largely institutionalized in them a kind of social lethargy. They may have fun during their years in college, they may enjoy their brush with higher learning, but most of their zest for life has been of their own creation. Their moral and personal life has been without institutional direction. To the university community they remain unassimilated, passing through an insensate system of points and credits, term papers and examinations, without joy and without personal fulfillment. Having long ago given up personal and moral guidance of students, universities now have a difficult time establishing it again.

19

Old Wine in New Bottles

I HAVE BEEN TRYING to suggest throughout this book that the American university as we know it today is not an ideal community in which to deposit young people in their late teens and early twenties. The young may enjoy themselves on campus, they may in fact do a great deal of growing up while away at college, they may even learn a lot, but for the most part they don't truly interact with the academic world. Most rapidly conclude that they are sojourners at the university, not key players, that the university seems to be made by others and for others—researchers, espousers of trendy political causes, grant seekers, elusive pedagogues, distracted graduate students working on their Ph.D.'s, tunnel-vision specialists, administrators clinging to their tiny patch of ground like a drowning person clinging to flotsam. That is to say, the young come to college looking for interesting and inspiring adults who will help them to make a spirited transition to adulthood, but for the most part they must abide the kind of process-teaching that they have been accustomed to throughout their lives.

I have also been suggesting, like so many other recent critics of higher education, that the failure to draw the young into a community of learning is a failure of what has traditionally been called a liberal education. Liberal education is elusive, as much a matter of style as of substance. It has little to do with the persistence on

196

campus of liberal arts subject matter. You can have mammoth colleges called the "College of Arts" or "College of Liberal Arts and Sciences" with dozens of departments in them, but there may be scarcely a jot of the liberal arts spirit in such colleges or the departments which make them up. Indeed in the large research university the liberal arts college is often just a variant trade school, which churns out historians to take up teaching posts in history just as the business school churns out economists or the pharmacy school churns out pharmacists. The liberal arts, the humanities, do not really come to life without the liberal arts style, and the liberal arts style in education is one that engages and enflames a person's individuality and desires within the framework of some purposive community of learning.

When I say that the liberal arts spirit comes to life only in some kind of community, I mean that people must be able to talk to one another regularly and intimately; that they must be on the same wavelength. It has sometimes been observed that higher education, technically advanced education, is able to make a nuclear bomb or some other weapon of mass destruction, but that only a liberal education provides the means to decide whether to use such weapons. This is not, of course, because liberal education gives people a specific kind of information, but rather because it gives them the framework, the mucilage to hold together the information they do possess. The framework is at one and the same time something that the student has created for himself or herself and a set of shared values, a disposition to understand, evaluate, and stand open to the ideas of others.

Earlier in this book I suggested that a long time ago we made a great mistake with the American university when we constructed it on the Germanic rather than the British model; I should say more precisely that we built our universities on the Germanic model with our own particularly nasty twist, the added insistence that universities be judged in terms of their productive output. The British model for higher education is based instead on the ideal of disinterested learning, a kind of learning accumulated slowly over time by people who come together in a kinship of learning and attempt to find a transfusion point for learning. It does not envision education as transferring little parcels of information from one person to another.

As I indicated, the British model for higher education assumes that whatever excellence and purity there is in the university is found in undergraduate colleges. Graduate schools, fields of specialization, are merely outgrowths of the undergraduate, liberal tradition and must not be allowed to gain the ascendancy over it. In the Germanic model, on the other hand, undergraduate education, general education, is a dreary and pale shadow of the specialized disciplines, a kind of kindergarten of the university. What we have is a "trickle-down" style of undergraduate education. Undergraduates get the drippings or leavings of the table from the graduate schools. No idea that has ever taken hold in the American university has been more harmful and destructive than this one. The Germanic model, which has created our so-called research universities, has not given us anything out of which we could create a human community of learning; instead it has given us rigid walls, upward ladders, a confusing array of offerings to students, a forbidding and meaningless collection of beehive segments, a Mandarin snobbery based on specialization, an unhealthy desire to hoard one's subject matter, one's private preserves and achievements.

Now, in the British model, so well exemplified by the centuries-old traditions of Oxford and Cambridge, a college is not a collection of specialized departments but a community of individuals. Instead of an engineering college or a business college or the typical specialty-oriented liberal arts college, you have small, usually residential, colleges within the confines of the larger university— Magdalen, New, or All Souls colleges at Oxford, let us say, or King's College or St. John's College at Cambridge. These "colleges" were all first and foremost human communities. If they also housed "experts," all to the good, but that little accretion trailed along afterward. One found professors, of course, but also an eccentric and somewhat disarming collection of other academic personages: readers, fellows, and wardens. As a new student, when you went into lunch you were never quite sure whether you were sitting next to a somebody or a nobody, a big wheel or a little wheel. In the American university, built on linear and hierarchical principles, it has been essential that everybody appreciate the difference between the big wheel and the little wheel. In the intimate dining halls or reading rooms of Oxford and Cambridge an eighteen-year old might not be aware that he or she was sitting next to a Nobel Prize winner.

Canadian writer and humorist Stephen Leacock, in one of the most lovely essays in the English language, "Oxford as I See It," expressed the belief that Oxford was the greatest university in the world because of the peculiar vagueness of the organization of its work. Oxford just sort of puts people together in a loose and quixotic fashion, presuming only that they want to learn together, to be together. If they don't really want to learn, there is some provision for that, too; both students and teachers are welcome to drift off into thin air if they so choose. The professor, however, said Leacock, is never a "live wire" sitting in an office dictating letters, applying for grants, or trying to get work as a "consultant," or "executive." These Oxford professors, said Leacock, are the only kind of professor worth having—"men who can be trusted with a vague general mission in life, with a salary guaranteed at least until their death, and a sphere of duties entrusted solely to their own consciences and the promptings of their own desires. Such men are rare, but a single one them, when found, is worth ten 'executives,' and a dozen 'organizers.'"

Leacock, who visited Oxford a number of times in the early years of the twentieth century, was delighted that nothing seemed to have changed there for hundreds of years, that the buildings at Brasenose College had not been renewed since 1525. At Christ Church College he was shown a kitchen that had been built at the expense of Cardinal Wolsey in 1527; during his visit four cooks were busy roasting an ox for the students' lunch. None of the colleges at Oxford seemed to be competing with one another to see which one had the spiffiest laboratories or the biggest dynamo.

When Leacock asked students what was so special about the methods of teaching at Oxford, he found that most of them praised not the lectures, not the libraries, not the presence of "star professors," but rather the presence of a person called the tutor. But precisely what was it that the tutor did? "'We go over to his rooms,' said one student, 'and he just lights a pipe and talks to us.' 'We sit around him,' said another, 'and he simply smokes and goes over our exercises with us.' From this and other evidence I gather than what an Oxford tutor does is to get a little group of students together and smoke at them. Men who have been systematically smoked at for four years turn into ripe scholars....A well-smoked man speaks and writes English with a grace that can be acquired in no other way."

There is a certain coziness in all this, a great deal of human warmth, certainly a leisured pace that we have never tolerated in America, the land where everything must be seen to pay dividends and show evidence of immediate utility. The tutorial system, whereby one is smoked at, where education seems to consist of a process of breathing in, is undoubtedly expensive, inefficient, and slow-paced—more reasons why it has been so hard to maintain in "progressive" America. But it is first-rate. It works. Equally inefficient perhaps, from our viewpoint, is the notion that the professor's first loyalty is to the college, to the immediate environment of learning, to the four walls of the place; only after one sees what one can do for one's college does one start to worry about one's specialized expertise. Oxford dons owe primary loyalty not to a specialty but to a small group of individuals, to the fellows of the college—at least traditionally. It is as important a part of their function to be a person, and a member of a family of scholars as it is to be someone who packs away a lot of learning. Furthermore, a kind of whimsicality, even eccentricity, is not only tolerated but esteemed. That is to say, the image of a professor in the great British universities is more that of the charming eccentric than that of specialist. Such people are fun to be around for their own sake.

Also the eccentric, the individualist, the person of independent mind, is more likely in the long run to be a productive and useful scholar than the hard-nosed professional chained to a system where productivity and specialization alone are glorified. This is probably only common sense, since the unfettered person of learning is more likely to throw off sparks than an intellectual serf trying to please some coterie or professional association or current school of political thought by dredging up ideas and platitudes that are standardized and safe. But under the old collegial system even a scholar who is not productive can add a great deal simply by contributing to the atmosphere of the institution, to civility, to mannerliness and the much-needed quality of pure distractedness.

Doubtless something like the British model of higher education persists in America in a number of our good small colleges and private universities, although even there it often tends to be infected by the Ph.D. bacillus that has swept the country in the twentieth century. Some universities, particularly the privately controlled Ivy League schools, have felt the need to preserve some of the traditional purity of undergraduate education. During his presidency at Princeton, Woodrow Wilson, who wisely eliminated the fraternity system there and put eating clubs in their stead, inaugurated the preceptorial method, which required every student to have a preceptor, essentially a tutor, who would be the student's counselor or friend. Wilson's idea was that the student's education would proceed by a kind of "intellectual contagion"—much like the "smoking in" Leacock mentioned as the essence of the Oxford style. You can't have higher education, Wilson believed, without a combination of the intellectual and the personal element.

Similarly at Harvard, during the presidency of A. Lawrence Lowell, an effort was made to counteract the graduate school approach of former President Charles W. Eliot by establishing a number of undergraduate "houses" built in a comfortable but elegant Georgian style. These offered not only a home but an intellectual center of gravity for the students. Lowell followed Woodrow Wilson in instituting a preceptorial system at Harvard, although the simpler British term *tutor* was used. In more ways than one the Harvard house system was patterned after the style of the colleges at Oxford and Cambridge. Each house was under the governance of a faculty "master" and graced with common rooms and oak-paneled dining halls where students could eat in a dignified and spirited intellectual environment. Mainly, though, the Harvard houses attempted to provide the sense of intimacy and community that British universities long ago found to be so necessary to high-quality undergraduate education.

Large public and land-grant universities, alas, were bitten much harder than Harvard and Yale by the Ph.D. bug. They were always having to *prove* that they were in the forefront of research and scholarly productivity. They were correspondingly less willing to provide quality programs for undergraduate students that would siphon off scarce resources from their "research" function. Nonetheless, during the 1920s the progressive educator Alexander Meiklejohn, who had previously introduced a solid foundation for general education while president of Amherst College, inaugurated an experimental college at the University of Wisconsin, which featured, among other things, a required two-year program in the liberal arts. The large land-grant universities for the most part did not embrace the "college within a college" idea, although there have been other experiments with it from time to time. After World War II, and following the strong publicity given to the general education movement in the 1940s, Michigan State University instituted such a program in its Justin Morrill College.

Even in the vast and bureaucratic University of California system there was a little experimenting along these lines, though it never came to happy fruition. While wrestling with the problems of "bigness" at Berkeley in the 1960s, Clark Kerr, doubtless nagged by feelings of guilt about the treatment of undergraduates on his gargantuan campuses, prevailed upon the California regents to establish a campus at Santa Cruz that would adopt something like the collegiate model of Oxford and Cambridge. The students would be called "members," and the faculty would be called "fellows." The fundamental idea was a good one. Unfortunately the experiment was unable to shake itself free of standard American academic conventions and institutionalized rigidities. Historian Page Smith, who became the founding provost at Santa Cruz, lamented that this attempt (and another like it at San Diego) failed because the colleges "were eaten alive by the entrenched disciplines" in standardized old-line departments. That is to say, if you still have young assistant professors having to claw their way upward on the academic ladder, if you still have petty politics and backbiting, if specialization continues to be the *ne plus ultra* of academic life, you are not going to be able to soften the major abuses of the American university. All you will have is window dressing, something on display. Of course, said Smith, bricks and mortar of the residential colleges are still there, proof positive that the idea can be physically carried out in a large public university. The trouble is that you can't really graft a close-knit human community onto a system that is built on notions of intellectual aggrandizement and bloodthirsty forms of competition among Mandarin "experts."

There are numerous other reasons why it has been difficult to hold up the model of the classical British university in the American milieu. The styles of Oxford and Cambridge have themselves decayed; they were not preserved in many of the new British universities—the so-called red brick universities, for example. Even more important, it has often been said the Oxford-Cambridge model is not suitable in democratic America because it is "elitist" and tied to the snobbish and antiquated British caste system. Such a view, for example, was held in one of the best books on education to come out of the sixties, Harold Taylor's *Students Without Teachers: The Crisis in the University*. Taylor, a student of John Dewey's and greatly influenced by the ideas of Alexander Meiklejohn, was president of the progressive women's college Sarah Lawrence during the sixties and was a strong believer in breaking down the artificial barriers between student and teacher, clearing away all of the bureaucratic and political rubble that interferes with learning. Taylor naturally would have approved of the sorts of things that Page Smith was hoping to do at Santa Cruz, but unlike Smith he did not like to make the analogy with Oxford and Cambridge. The British curriculum, he insisted, was archaic and steeped in illiberal traditionalism. The system as a whole was paternalistic, elitist, and heavily dependent on the existence of a student body that "has already been inducted into a tradition before it arrives in the university. Furthermore, the reason the British system worked so well in the past and is appealing to the visiting Americans, both students and scholars, is that it is not as heavily organized as the American system."

In view of Taylor's own sympathies, his interest in free universities, colleges without walls, student-originated instruction, and the like, his doubts about the British model seem a bit odd. By all means what *is* wanted is a system that is less organized and rigidly composed than the one we presently have. The leisured pace, the tutorial system, the eccentric calendar are all hallmarks of the British system that could well be adopted here or, at the very least, allowed to point the way to some unpressured and comfortable style of our own.

Taylor's worry about the dangers of importing elitism is equally strange. It is true that Oxford and Cambridge have for centuries been the private preserve of the genteel classes. It is also true that the English educational system shunts off its vocational or working class types to the red brick universities—except for the highly talented scholarship holders. However, even though there may well be invidious class distinctions at Oxford and Cambridge, there isn't the slightest danger that they would be or could be imported to America. Furthermore, much of the social elitism found in British universities is the product of an overactive egalitarian imagination in America and of cultural gaps produced by television plays and inferior works of fiction.

In truth, the Oxford style of education is far less inclined toward elitism than that presently encountered in our own supposedly egalitarian universities. It is far more tolerant of idiosyncratic behavior, of individuality; it is far more democratic in the best sense of the word. The American university—with its corporate ladder; its "distinguished professors"; its star system; its "prestige" holders of chairs; its brutal compartmentalism keeping apart students, graduate students, professors, administrators, its monstrous heap of titles, degrees, honorifics; its snobbish collection of ivory tower specialists—is not only more elitist in substance than anything in Britain, but probably more elitist than universities found anywhere else in the world.

Elitism and Mandarism are among the most virulent diseases that plague the American university today, although for some unfathomable reason American university professors fancy that they are totally free of them. It is one of the strangest ironies that nowhere do academics rail against elitism more than in America, yet nowhere are invidious and alienating distinctions carried to such extremes. In England elitism in the universities is often little more than a mannerism; it is mostly reduced to whimsical traditions and comical residues of times past; in America, where we constantly raise war whoops against elites, we actually embrace *academic* elites with fond enthusiasm. How much nicer it would be to have a system where social stratification, belief in kinds and levels of excellence, is so confused and archaic, so bemused and ineffable, that one doesn't have to waste any energy worrying about them. In the American university we worry about little else.

Anyway, if there should be anything not quite to our liking in the British model for higher education, there remains much to admire in it. Better it is by far than a system created in the mold of the giant corporation with its organizational charts, its line and staff organizations, its crude pigeonholing, its star players and gaudy go-getters, its vast army of titled grubbers. In the American universities even the large number of Marxists suffer from the Mandarin disease. They dissipate their energies trying to identify and scotch nonconformist ideas, to label what is "politically correct," to point out those who do not belong in the circle of the elect. They speak in jargons so thick that they will not be understood except by those of an in-group. Their self-proclaimed affinity for the disadvantaged and their supposed interest in "plain folk" is nearly always a sumptuous fraud, belied by the fact that they seldom have real ties to such people and would probably be laughed away by any whom they chanced to meet. In short, in the American university the most blatantly antielitist theorizers are themselves rabidly elitist. They do not speak or communicate in plain English, and they have little desire to associate with people outside their own humorless cliques.

More important, whatever defects there may be in the British caste system, we are hardly under any obligation to import to our universities. There is little chance that we would. All I have been recommending is that our massive, highly organized, highly compartmentalized universities give up the practice of centering themselves around the role of the specialist, the expert, and return instead to some sense of human community, and to educational institutions and programs that are devoted to it. If we want to have liberal arts education as a living thing, we have to have the liberal arts spirit, and this can survive only in intimate human groups where people converse and interact with one another in intimate ways. Small living units within the larger university, if administered correctly (that is, not simply used as publicity gimmicks), will get things back on track.

Of course, none of this will work if the present system of total domination by specialists is allowed to prevail. This does not necessarily mean abolishing the present academic departments, although at the legendary St. John's College, which was built around the Great Books program, there has been proof that it is quite possible to get along without the traditional academic departments—the History Department, the Philosophy Department, and so on. What is essential is that our universities somehow find a way once again to produce a class of professors who owe stronger obligations to general education than to some narrow field of specialization. I would not go on to suggest draconian measures—for example, the abolition of Ph.D. programs in the humanities until such time that the disease of expertitis subsides—because I know there is little chance for such a proposal to be adopted. But I have long agreed with Edmund Wilson that the Ph.D. as we know it is an imported monstrosity and that a triumphal step forward could have been made if it had been junked during the first wave of anti-German feeling during World War I.

Even though this is not a realistic solution since it would be resisted with all of the fury the American university possesses, even if such a step is not in the cards at the present moment, it might point us in the right direction. And if undergraduate instruction were reformed, reorganized along the lines of traditional Oxford and Cambridge, the universities might be able to ensure the prestige and worthiness of the liberal arts professor in ways that are not brutally tied to a system of specialization.

It could, for example, become clear that liberal arts professors have a different set of obligations than the narrow specialists. Instead of being rewarded for churning out tiny evidences of productivity, instead of being chained to the publish-or-perish treadmill, instead of having to fight the silly battles of academic politics, they could be appreciated without being evaluated and quantified; they could pursue individual intellectual interests, whatever they might be, without having to answer for them. This again is following the Oxford model: Find good people, people you are comfortable with, and let them pursue their interests. One who in midcareer decides to switch from philosophy to modern history ought to be permitted to do so without penalty. The usual bromide of the academic establishment is that any such freedom will not work because the professor will just lie back and settle into a lazy sinecure, will get stale. The trouble is, in the humanities the vast majority get stale anyway; they are not really all that productive over the course of their lifetime because they are caught in a trap. There is some belief that if they were allowed to create their own personal specialty, they might turn out to be more productive in the long run, that is, if we even have to admit the relevance of that glorified American desideratum "productivity."

Of course, they've talked a great deal in the universities about making the arts and humanities more interesting. This, they say, is one of the justifications for the so-called new canon, which promises to be more attractive to undergraduates. Naturally there have been political motivations, too, usually shoehorned in under the guise of revitalizing and modernizing the curriculum. It is said that the "old" curriculum does not address the needs of minorities, or women, or people of the third world. Many of those who bellow for a new canon think that by politicizing liberal education they have discovered a new way to make it interesting. But those who make these claims never stop to think that it may not be the traditional books that are dull but the manner of teaching them. (Plato dull? Shakespeare dull?) What you have at the present time is a tired system that drops the great books or classics of civilization on people's heads like bricks. This isn't what students are looking for, and this is not what they need.

I will be the first to admit, by the way, that in most universities the undergraduate core curriculum is stifling. The arts and the humanities seem sick unto death. It is interesting, though, that most Americans still thirst for knowledge in these very areas. A compelling report published by the National Endowment for the Humanities in 1988 gives convincing evidence of the diminished attractiveness of the humanities as currently dished out by the universities. On the other hand, it also points out that a growing number of Americans are buying books, visiting museums, joining cultural groups, attending concerts and plays. Our adult citizens yearn for art, literature, and history, apparently. Americans, who twenty years ago were said to have spent twice as much on sports as on cultural pastimes, now spend more on culture—$3.4 billion, as compared with $3.1 billion in 1986. Library demand for books in the humanities is up sharply, as is television viewing of serious cultural programming. Since 1957 there has been a 660 percent increase in the number of visitors to the National Gallery of Art in Washington. All this time, college enrollments in the arts and the humanities were going down, down, down.

I hardly need say that university people blame it all on the demands of vocationalism. They insist that college students don't major in literature and history because it won't get them a good job. Well, I suspect that a perverse devotion to vocationalism *is* at the root of the problem—but that this doesn't come from the students. It is the pedantic style of the liberal arts education that is at fault. It is the professor, we remember, who wants somehow to shine as a specialist in eighteenth-century studies and to stiff-arm anything outside that area. It is the professor who wants to mask ideas with jargon and deadly abstractions. So typical individuals today, seeking education in the arts or humanities, don't look to professors but to the mass media, to television, to museums, to the public library, to their own book selections. If they want to know something about the novels of John Galsworthy or Evelyn Waugh, they listen to what Alistair Cooke, not some professor of modern British literature, has to say about them. (Wouldn't it in fact be nice if our colleges and universities were staffed by people possessing the charm, the clarity, and the force of an Alastair Cooke rather than the fetching, clawing, and mincing pedantifiers who today predominate in our universities' faculties of humanities?)

As far as getting an exciting curriculum is concerned, there is no better way to achieve it than to have a lively and captivating professor. As long as one is required to teach materials that are dreamed up by political action groups and academic coteries, as long as one's habit of mind is steeped in the minutiae of professionalism, there is no way that one can revitalize one's own teaching. The only good teaching comes from one's individual passions and desires. This is why I have been suggesting all along that liberal arts professors ought not to be rewarded for displaying conformity to the herd mentality. They should be free-wheeling individuals who owe their main allegiance to the art of teaching within the context or framework of their own eccentric designs. This is the real justification for recommending a return to something like the Oxford-Cambridge model for undergraduate education. Of course, you ought to be able to teach black literature or women's studies, if ideas, books, persons in those areas really drive you out of bed in the morning, or if you find a student with whom you can share such subjects. But if you are only dishing these things out in a mechanical way because they are currently in vogue, then they are sure to be at least as deadly as anything held over from the supposedly worn-out canon—and in my own experience much more so.

What I have been suggesting is that the old and respected thing called liberal education can't be revitalized without totally overhauling the relation between students and teachers, and without giving a new charge and a new freedom to the liberal arts professor. A new or refreshed relationship between student and teacher, I believe, can be accomplished only in smaller and more intimate environments where teachers and students can talk to one another as human beings, that is to say, where knowledge is imparted through dialogue and the Socratic method, rather than through the dumping of hard lumps of information. All of this calls for increasing utilization of smaller classes, tutorials, individual contact; it calls for more time for personal and informal relations between student and teacher. It also calls for opportunities for the students to do something for the professors, to make some changes in them.

In *Students Without Teachers*, Harold Taylor suggested that it might not be a bad idea to allow students to take up the teaching role on occasion, to instruct other students and sometimes even professors. Of course, nothing of the sort could be completely formalized; the majority of students are not yet in a position to make this effort, and others never will be. But when students have themselves become inspired by something, when they have done research or reading on some subject dear to their hearts, why not? Certainly graduate students could be used to teach other graduate students in specialized areas—how much better than asking them to deliver canned materials to freshmen. Any more flexible system of the administration of teaching, anything that would smash the rigidities of doing things the same old way, would be a great step forward.

This does not imply a move toward complete aimlessness in the undergraduate curriculum. I am not suggesting that we need to throw out the traditional curriculum, the solid old Western civilization courses, or the great books. Anybody who has read this far will understand that I am in favor of maintaining these traditions. And I believe that they should be administered rigorously and at a high level, not reduced to pop or frozen lasagna. On the other hand, you can't have rigor and solidity without individuality and without dialogue, without student and teacher relying on one another and inspiring one another. Not only must the professors know why they are teaching, the students must be aware all along of how what they are being taught relates to whatever else they know and how it dovetails with their preexisting values.

None of these things can happen, of course, unless the professors put themselves on the level of the undergraduate student, unless they come to a sympathetic understanding. And doing so doesn't just mean teaching more undergraduate courses or making a few cosmetic changes in methodology. It means, as I have said all along, a change in the style of college and university instruction. The professor needs again to become a generalist, to pay first allegiance to the liberal component of education. This is best done in the setting of small colleges or other units within a large university that are specifically devoted to undergraduate learning. It need not, in fact, be destructive of specialized learning. I believe that a historian who has to teach the social history of England in the eighteenth century in an inspiring and spirited way to eighteen-year-olds is more likely to write an imaginative book on that subject than one who fusses over the dreary obscurities of the seminar room or makes elaborate and pompous declarations in working papers and missives to professional colleagues. Universities need to do a great deal more than they presently do to see that liberal arts professors speak and write to and for general audiences. They should reward such contributions as much or more than those aimed at co-specialists and other grapplers of the fine point.

The main kind of reform needed in the American university today is one that motivates the professor to be a different kind of person, that encourages him or her to emerge from the ivory tower of remote specialization and return to the mainstream of general culture. This will not be easy to accomplish, since all of the impulses in the university establishment pull in the opposite direction. Rewards and prizes are handed out to professors precisely in proportion to their ability to please professional colleagues in their own field or related coteries, precisely in proportion to their ability to publish in esoteric journals and limit the scope of inquiry to some sacred patch of ground.

What the professor needs to be urged to do, on the contrary, is seek for ways to find the transfusion point between the life of the academy and the wider human culture. The best place to look is among undergraduate students, who, so to speak, are on loan from the broader society. Universities should now make concerted efforts to see that professors become intimately involved in undergraduate life—not by making superficial and posturing attempts to emphasize the quality of classroom teaching, such attempts invariably being useless, but by expecting that professors will become involved in undergraduate life, and rewarding them for it. This means not only teaching in the narrow sense but personal involvement.

University administrations can begin to bring such reforms into being by demanding the reversal of the present emphasis on specialized courses and on graduate work at the expense of general education and undergraduate programs. If the university pumps prestige into undergraduate instruction and drains it away from the graduate seminar, if it ensures that the professor who seeks out basic

courses with wider vision will get smaller classes and other prefer-
ments; if the rewards for teaching the narrow graduate course are
lessened and the opportunities for it cut back, professors in time will
cease to think that the more "advanced" and "technical" things are
the better for them professionally. As things are, professors are
invariably given released time for supervising theses and dissertations, a fussing and hairsplitting chore that tends not only to invite
the graduate student into the inner sanctum of pedantry but to
reinforce the professor's own crimped habits of mind. If, let us say,
the English professor is given time off or assigned to smaller
numbers of students for teaching the course in Freshmen English, or
Introduction to Literature, if it is understood that such services to
the university will be seriously considered at promotion time, the
chances are that eventually the present distortion of instructional
values will be corrected.

Naturally it is not only in the purview of the classroom that there
needs to be a change of emphasis in the activities of the professor.
The modern university needs the efforts of professors redirected
toward campus life in general. The university should see that
professors put their highest priorities on activities that benefit *this*
college, *this* university, not the nationwide guild or profession. The
professor who organizes an undergraduate club, or acts as official
adviser for a literary magazine, or speaks to small groups, or takes
occasional lunches in undergraduate dorms, should be given priority
when it comes to promotion or financial advancement. This does
not need to suggest that one may not be rewarded for producing a
major book or for making some important discovery (of course, one
should be and will be), but much more emphasis should be placed on
intimate and local concerns and much less on the publication of
trivial papers, or on the deadly shuffling and pandering that
produces rounds of working papers, seminar papers, narrowly
focused university press books, and professional correspondence, or
on applying for grants, or on making convention appearances. The
university should let it be known that, at least in the humanities if
not in the sciences, grantsmanship and other such outside busy work
will receive small recognition in comparison to modest efforts on
the homefront. It is much better to go rowing with the students late
of an afternoon than to be putting out the hook to some national
organization far away.

Most universities today make extravagant (but mostly fake) claims that they recognize the importance of teaching and public service as well as research, but with not a great deal of effort they might actually do so. Professors could be asked to demonstrate what efforts they have made toward undergraduate learning and culture. They might be asked to tell what contributions they have made to the university community or the community at large. Has a professor of music volunteered to conduct a local chorus, or to act as its librarian? Is a history professor a leading light of the local Civil War roundtable, or a participant in a Civil War reenactment? Scholars should be at least equally encouraged in such activities as they presently are in coughing up working papers or other tentative explorations.

Even when the professor is importuned to conduct specialized research, even when urged to publish, something quite different should be expected than the present demand for the recondite and the obscure. The professor should be at least as highly praised (and probably more so) for publishing a book with a prominent trade publisher than for publishing an esoteric monograph with some university press. An invited column in the *New York Times* or *The Wall Street Journal* should carry as much weight as a narrow-scope article in some professional journal, or more. Several generations ago it was understood almost everywhere on college campuses that an article in the *Atlantic Monthly* was a greater achievement than one in *Comparative Studies in Society and History*. Today there would be no such tacit understanding. But there should be. Not too long ago I spoke with a colleague in psychology who seemed to be working on what seemed to me a rather novel concept in his field. I asked him why he didn't submit an article to a publication like *Psychology Today*. He informed me in no uncertain terms that *Psychology Today* is just "trash." I was not in a position to comment on that judgment one way or the other; on the other hand, if *all* outlets for the psychologist to reach the outside world are nothing but trash bins or sewer pipes, then it should be clear that there is something drastically wrong with our national culture. If there is no valid avenue of commerce, no conduit, between the specialist and the general culture, if psychologists know no other language than that which reaches other psychologists, we are in deep trouble indeed.

A major goal of the university today should be finding ways of cutting off support for noncommunicative and inward-turning research. This is going to require innovative ways of encouraging the independent professor, one whose first allegiance is to the broader culture rather than to the special discipline. In his recent book *Prof Scam* Charles Sykes concludes that we need to do something to produce once again the free-standing professor, the truly "renegade" professor, perhaps—the individual who knows that "every genuine idea, every article written in lucid, clear prose, employing logic, reason, insight, and wit is a subsersive act within the academic culture—a shot fired across the bow of the obscurantists, sorcerers, and witch doctors of profthink." Puncturing the idol of research will go a long way toward accomplishing this, says Sykes. The elimination of the blanket requirement for specialized research "would in effect cut off the life support systems to the centers of profthink. Dozens of the more outlandish sects would collapse since they are not sustained by any intellectual substance but by the demands of academic careerism." A result of cutting off the life support systems of profthink, and all the other forms of intellectual solipsism, would be a reinvigoration of the campus community as a transfusion point between society and the realm of learning, the reestablishment of some common ground between everyday life and the world of the mind. This common ground has been allowed to lie fallow for much of the twentieth century, and the time to cultivate it is now.

In recent years it has often been remarked of the United States that our social, economic, and political institutions have become brittle, rigid, and inflexible. This nation that prided itself for so long on its "youth" has been witness to the stiffening, the lethargies, of old age. Nowhere has this been more apparent than in our universities, which have become rigidly standardized and intellectually hidebound. These institutions tend to be less innovative, less willing to change, than even the most stuffy bank or corporation, or any similar institution professors love to scorn. Sadly, whenever they talk about bringing things up to date and revitalizing the curriculum, professors seldom mean that at all; they invariably mean creating something even more rigid and intransigent than what was there before, only with different people or different power groups doing the planning.

In any case, to survive in health the American universities are going to need to give up certain entrenched practices, most especially elitism conceived along specialty lines, and return to the notion that education's first function is to keep education youthful. Merely keeping the faculty well provided for, keeping laboratories well supplied, providing prestige to research professors will not be enough. We've been giving top priority to these things for the better part of a century while faith in our system of higher education has continued to decline.

Obviously, a grand and glorious system of higher education is still in place in the United States, and there are many excellent traditions behind it ready to come to the rescue. There are plenty of people in the academic world ready to do the job. But we need to be willing to throw out long-standing practices that have become stale and repetitive. We Americans have proved ourselves capable of doing things differently when we have had to compete with people who have built automobiles another way or found better ways to make steel ingots or computer chips. If our institutions of higher education can shake loose from some of their lethargies, they may well do us proud in the years ahead. If they can find ways to recapture their own youth and vitality, they may be able to shake off the symptoms of early senility. If not, they will become more and more a dead weight in American life.

Bibliography

Allardyce, Gilbert. "The Rise and Fall of the Western Civilization Course." *American Historical Review*, June 1982.

Allen, G. W. *William James*. New York: Viking Press, 1967.

Arrowsmith, William. "The Future of Teaching." *Improving College Teaching*. Washington: American Council on Education, 1967.

_____."The Shame of the Graduate Schools." *Harper's*, March 1966.

Ashby, Sir Eric. *Any Person, Any Study: An Essay on Higher Education in the United States*. New York: McGraw-Hill, 1971.

_____.*Masters and Scholars*. London: Oxford University Press, 1970.

Astin, Alexander. *Achieving Educational Excellence*. San Francisco: Jossey-Bass, 1985.

_____. "Involvement: The Cornerstone of Excellence." *Change*, July/August 1985.

Atlas, James. *The Book Wars: What It Takes to Be Educated in America*. Knoxville, TN: Whittle Direct Books, 1990.

Barnett, Ronald. *The Idea of Higher Education*. Bristol, PA: Society for Research into Higher Education and Open University Press, 1990.

Barzun, Jacques. *The American University*. New York: Harper & Row, 1968.

_____. "College to University—And After." *American Scholar*, Spring 1964.

_____. *The Culture We Deserve*. Middletown, CT: Wesleyan University Press, 1989.

_____. "Doing Research: Should the Sport Be Regulated?" *Columbia*, February 1987.

_____. *Teacher in America*. Indianapolis: Liberty Press, 1981.

Becher, T. *Academic Tribes and Territories*. Milton Keynes, Eng.: Open University Press, 1989.

Bell, Daniel. *The Reforming of General Education*. Garden City, NY: Doubleday, 1968.

Ben-David, J. *American Higher Education: Directions, Old and New*. New York: McGraw-Hill, 1972.

"Bennett Says Stanford Was Intimidated Into Changing Course." *New York Times*, April 18, 1988.

Bennett, William J. *To Reclaim a Legacy: A Report on the Humanities in Higher Education*. Washington: National Endowment for the Humanities, 1984.

Bloom, Allan. *The Closing of the American Mind*. New York: Simon and Schuster, 1987.

Boas, George. "Freshman Adviser." *Harper's*, July 1930.

Bok, Derek. *Beyond the Ivory Tower: Social Responsibilities of the Modern University*. Cambridge: Harvard University Press, 1982.

————. *Higher Learning*. Cambridge: Harvard University Press, 1986.

————. "Toward Education of Quality." *Harvard Magazine*, May/June 1986.

Boorstin, Daniel. *The Americans: The National Experience*. New York: Random House, 1965.

Booth, Wayne. *Mere Rhetoric and the Search for Common Learning*. Washington: Carnegie Foundation for the Advancement of Teaching, 1981.

Bowen, Howard R., and Jack H. Schuster. *American Professors: A National Resource Imperiled*. New York: Oxford University Press, 1986.

Boyer, Ernest L., *Campus Life: In Search of Community*. Princeton, NJ: Carnegie Foundation for the Advancement of Teaching, 1990.

————. *College: The Undergraduate Experience in America*. New York: Harper & Row, 1987.

Boyer, Ernest L., and Arthur Levine. *A Quest for Common Learning: The Aims of General Education*. Princeton: Carnegie Foundation for the Advancement of Teaching, 1981.

Bracey, Gerald. "The Time Has Come to Abolish Research Journals: Too Many Are Writing Too Much About Too Little." *Chronicle of Higher Education*, March 25, 1987.

Brown, Cynthia Stokes. *Alexander Meikeljohn: Teacher of Freedom*. Berkeley, CA: Meikeljohn Institute, 1981.

Brubaker, John S., and Willis Rudy. *Higher Education in Transition: A History of American Colleges and Universities, 1636–1976*. New York: Harper & Row, 1976.

Califano, Joseph A. *The Student Revolution: A Global Confrontation*. New York: Norton, 1970.

Caplow, Theodore, and Reece McGee. *The Academic Marketplace*. New York: Basic Books, 1958.

Chase, Alston. "Skipping Through College: Reflections on the Decline of Liberal Arts Education," *Atlantic*, September 1978.

Cheney, Lynne V. *Humanities in America: A Report to the President, the Congress and the American People.* Washington: National Endowment for the Humanities, 1988.

Chickering, Arthur W., et al. *The Modern American College: Responding to the New Realities of Diverse Students and a Changing Society.* San Francisco: Jossey-Bass, 1981.

Collier, Peter, and David Horowitz. *Destructive Generation: Second Thoughts About the Sixties.* New York: Summit Books, 1989.

Commager, Henry Steele. "Science, Nationalism and the Academy." *Academe,* November/December 1985.

The Condition of the Professoriate. Princeton, NJ: Carnegie Foundation for the Advancement of Teaching, 1989.

Cremin, Lawrence A. *American Education: The Colonial Experience, 1607–1783.* New York: Harper & Row, 1970.

Crews, Frederick. *Skeptical Engagements.* New York: Oxford University Press, 1986.

Dewey, John. *Reconstruction in Philosophy.* Boston: Beacon Press, 1957.

Douglas, George H. "Dark Days for the State Universities." *Colorado Quarterly,* October 1972.

————. "Whatever Happened to Freshman English?" *Educational Forum,* March 1973.

D'Souza, Dinesh. "Illiberal Education." *Atlantic,* March 1991.

Edman, Irwin. "Unrequired Reading." *Saturday Review of Literature,* November 4, 1950.

Education at Berkeley. Berkeley: University of California Academic Senate, 1966.

Enarson, H. L. "University or Knowledge Factory?" *Chronicle of Higher Education,* June 18, 1973.

Fashing, Joseph, and Steven Deutsch. *Academics in Retreat.* Albuquerque: University of New Mexico Press, 1971.

Feyerabend, P. *Farewell to Reason.* London: Verso, 1987.

Fifty Hours: A Core Curriculum for College Students. Washington: National Endowment for the Humanities, 1989.

Finn, Chester E., Jr. "The Campus: An Island of Repression in a Sea of Freedom." *Commentary,* September 1989.

————. "Higher Education on Trial: An Indictment." *Current,* October 1989.

Flexner, Abraham. *Universities: American, English, German.* Oxford: Oxford University Press, 1930.

General Education in a Free Society. Cambridge: Harvard University Press, 1945.

Goodman, Paul. *The Community of Scholars*. New York: Random House, 1952.

Graff, Gerald. "Colleges Are Depriving Students of a Connected View of Scholarship." *Chronicle of Higher Education*, February 13, 1991.

Grant, Gerald, and David Riesman. *The Perpetual Dream: Reform and Experiment in the American College*. Chicago: University of Chicago Press, 1978.

Grant-Robertson, Sir Charles. *The British Universities*. London: Benn, 1930.

Green, Kenneth C., and Alexander W. Astin. "The Mood on Campus: More Conservative or Just More Materialistic?" *Educational Record*, Winter 1985.

Greenberg, Daniel. "Publish or Perish—Or Fake It." *U.S. News & World Report*, June 8, 1987.

Gribben, Alan. "English Departments: Salvaging What Remains." *Academic Questions*, Fall 1989.

Hacker, Andrew. "The Decline of Higher Learning." *New York Review of Books*, February 13, 1986.

Hairston, Maxine C. "Required Writing Courses Should Not Focus on Politically Charged Social Issues." *Chronicle of Higher Education*, January 23, 1991.

Havemann, Ernest, and Patricia Salter West. *They Went to College: The College Graduate in America Today*. New York: Harcourt Brace, 1952.

Heath, Douglas, H. *Growing Up in College: Liberal Education and Maturity*. San Francisco: Jossey-Bass, 1968.

Hechinger, Fred, and Grace Hechinger. *Growing Up in America*. New York: McGraw-Hill, 1975.

Herring, Hubert. "Education at Bennington." *Harper's*, September 1940.

Hirsch, E. D., Jr. *Cultural Literacy*. Boston: Houghton-Mifflin, 1987.

Hirsch, E. D., Jr., Joseph F. Kett, and James Trefil. *The Dictionary of Cultural Literacy: What Every American Needs to Know*. Boston: Houghton-Mifflin, 1989.

"History Convention Reflects Change from Traditional to Gender Studies." *New York Times*, January 9, 1988.

Hofstadter, Richard. *Anti-Intellectualism in American Life*. New York: Alfred A. Knopf, 1963.

Hofstadter, Richard, and Walter P. Metzger. *The Development of Academic Freedom in the United States*. New York: Columbia University Press, 1955.

Hofstadter, Richard, and Wilson Smith, eds. *American Higher Education: A Documentary History*. Chicago: University of Chicago Press, 1961.

Hollander, Paul. "From Iconoclasm to Conventional Wisdom: The Sixties to the Eighties." *Academic Questions*, Fall 1989.

Hook, Sidney. *Academic Freedom and Academic Anarchy*. New York: Dell 1969.

_____. *Out of Step*. New York: Carroll and Graff, 1988.

Horowitz, Helen Lefkowitz. *Campus Life: Undergraduate Culture From the End of the Eighteenth Century to the Present*. New York: Knopf, 1987.

Hutchins, Robert Maynard. *The Higher Learning in America*. New Haven: Yale University Press, 1936.

Ingalls, Zoe. "Higher Education's Drinking Problem." *Chronicle of Higher Education*, July 21, 1982.

Jacoby, Russell. *The Last Intellectuals: American Culture in the Age of Academe*. New York: Basic Books, 1987.

_____. "Radicals in Academia." *Nation*, September 19, 1987.

James, William. *Memories and Studies*. New York: Longmans Green, 1911.

Jencks, Christopher, and David Riesman. *The Academic Revolution*. Garden City, NY: Doubleday, 1968.

Kahn, E. J. *Harvard Through Change and Through Storm*. New York: W. W. Norton, 1968.

Katope, Christopher G., and Paul G. Zolbrod, eds. *Beyond Berkeley*. New York: Harper & Row, 1966.

Keller, Phyllis. *Getting at the Core*. Cambridge: Harvard University Press, 1982.

Keniston, Kenneth. *The Uncommitted: Alienated Youth in American Society*. New York: Harcourt Brace, 1965.

Kerr, Clark. *The Uses of the University*. Cambridge: Harvard University Press, 1963.

Kett, Joseph F. *Rites of Passage: Adolescence in America 1790 to the Present*. New York: Basic Books, 1977.

Kidder, Rushworth M. "Academic Writing is Convoluted, Jargon-Ridden, and Isolated from the Messy Realities of the World." *Chronicle of Higher Education*, January 30, 1991.

Kimball, Roger. *Tenured Radicals*. New York: Harper & Row, 1990.

Koepplin, Leslie, and David Wilson, eds. *The Future of State Universities*. Elizabeth, NJ: Rutgers University Press, 1986.

Komarovsky, Mirra. *Women in College: Shaping New Feminine Identities*. New York: Basic Books, 1985.

Kuttner, Robert. "The Poverty of Economics." *Atlantic*, February 1985.

Ladd, Dwight R. *Change in Educational Policy: A General Report Prepared for the Carnegie Commission on Higher Education*. New York: McGraw-Hill, 1970.

Lasch, Christopher. *Culture as Narcissism: American Life in an Age of Diminishing Expectation*. New York: Norton, 1978.

Leacock, Stephen. "On the Need for a Quiet College." In *The Leacock Roundabout*. New York: Dodd, Mead, 1972.

————. "Oxford as I See It." In *The Leacock Roundabout*. New York: Dodd, Mead, 1972.

Levine, Arthur. *Handbook on Undergraduate Curriculum*. San Francisco: Jossey-Bass, 1978.

————. *When Dreams and Heroes Died: A Portrait of Today's College Students*. San Francisco: Jossey-Bass, 1980.

Lewis, Lionel S. *Scaling the Ivory Tower: Merit and Its Limits in Academic Careers*. Baltimore: Johns Hopkins Press, 1975.

Lilge, Frederic. *The Abuse of Learning: The Failure of the German University*. New York: Macmillan, 1978.

"Literary Critics Meet and Find Politics Everywhere." *New York Times*, January 1, 1990.

Loftus, David J. *The Unofficial Book of Harvard Trivia*. Boston: Quinlan Press, 1985.

Lowell, A. Lawrence. "Examination of Subjects Instead of Courses." *Harvard Graduates' Magazine*, June 1912.

————. *What a University President Has Learned*. New York: Macmillan, 1938.

Lynn, Kenneth. "Son of General Ed." *Commentary*, September 1978.

McConnell, T. R., et al. *From Elite to Mass to Universal Higher Education*. Berkeley: University of California Center for Research and Development in Higher Education, 1973.

McDowell, Edwin. "What Students Read Without Being Told To." *New York Times*, July 9, 1990.

Martin, Warren Bryan. *A College of Character*. San Francisco: Jossey-Bass, 1982.

Mayhew, Lewis B. *General Education: A Guide for Colleges*. New York: Harper & Row, 1960.

Mencken, Henry L. *Prejudices*, 5th ser., New York: Knopf, 1926.

————. *Prejudices*, 3rd ser., New York: Knopf, 1922.

Mitchell, Richard. *The Groves of Academe*. New York: Little, Brown, 1981.

Moffat, Michael. *Coming of Age in New Jersey*. New Brunswick, NJ: Rutgers University Press, 1989.

Mooney, Carolyn J. "Scholars Decry Campus Hostility to Western Culture at a Time When More Nations Embrace Its Value." *Chronicle of Higher Education*, January 30, 1991.

The More Effective Use of Resources: An Imperative for Higher Education. New York: Carnegie Commission on Higher Education, 1972.

Morison, Samuel Eliot. *The Founding of Harvard College*. Cambridge: Harvard University Press, 1935.

————. *Three Centuries of Harvard, 1636–1936*. Cambridge: Harvard University Press, 1965.

Moser, Charles A., ed. *The University at Bay*. Washington: Acropolis Books, 1974.

Neu, Jerome. "So Very PC at UCSC." *Wall Street Journal*, December 21, 1990.

Nevins, Allan. *The State Universities and Democracy*. Urbana: University of Illinois Press, 1962.

Newman, John Henry. *The Idea of a University*. New York: Doubleday, 1959.

Nisbit, Robert. *The Degradation of the Academic Dogma*. New York: Basic Books, 1971.

————. "Humanities." In *Prejudices*. Cambridge: Harvard University Press, 1982.

Nuechterlein, James. "The Feminization of the American Left." *Commentary*, November 1987.

Oakeshott, Michael. *The Voice of Liberal Learning*. New Haven: Yale University Press, 1989.

Ollman, Bertell, and Edward Vernoff. *The Left Academy: Marxist Scholarship on American Campuses*. New York: McGraw-Hill, 1982.

Ortega y Gasset, José. *Mission of the University*. London: Kegan Paul, 1946.

Oshansky, David. "What's Wrong With the History Journals?" *Change*, March 1973.

Peddiwell, J. Abner. *The Saber-Tooth Curriculum and Other Essays*. New York: McGraw-Hill, 1939.

Peterson, Houston. *Great Teachers*. New Brunswick, NJ: Rutgers University Press, 1946.

Phillipson, N., ed. *Universities, Society and the Future*. Edinburgh: Edinburgh University Press, 1983.

Pierson, G. W. *Yale: The University College, 1921–1937*. New Haven: Yale University Press, 1955.

Plumb, J. H., ed. *Crisis in the Humanities*. Baltimore: Penguin Books, 1964.

Purnick, Joyce. "Women Stereotyping Women." *New York Times*, July 11, 1990.

Reeves, M. *The Crisis in Higher Education*. Milton Keynes, Eng.: Open University Press, 1988.

Riesman, David, and Nathan Glaser. *The Lonely Crowd: A Study of Changing American Character*. New Haven: Yale University Press, 1950.

Ross, Murray G. *The University: The Anatomy of Academe*. New York: McGraw-Hill, 1976.

Rudolph, Frederick. *The American College and University: A History*. New York: Knopf, 1962.

———. *Curriculum: A History of the American Undergraduate Course of Study Since 1636.* San Francisco: Jossey-Bass, 1977.

Sanders, I. T., "The University as a Community." In J. A. Perkins, ed., *The University as An Organization.* New York: McGraw-Hill, 1973.

Sanford, Nevitt. *The American College: A Psychological and Social Interpretation of Higher Learning.* New York: Wiley, 1962.

Schlesinger, Arthur, Jr. "When Ethnic Studies Are Un-American." *Wall Street Journal,* April 23, 1990.

Scott, P. *The Crisis of the University.* London: Croom Helm, 1984.

Shaw, Peter. *The War Against Intellect: Episodes in the Decline of Discourse.* Iowa City: University of Iowa Press, 1989.

Shills, Edward. "The Sad State of the Humanities in America." *Wall Street Journal,* July 5, 1989.

Short, Thomas. " 'Diversity' and 'Breaking the Disciplines': Two New Assaults on the Curriculum." *Academic Questions,* Summer 1988.

Sinclair, Upton. *The Goose-Step.* Pasadena, CA: Upton Sinclair, 1922.

Smith, Page. *Killing the Spirit.* New York: Viking Press, 1990.

Snow, C. P. *The Two Cultures: And a Second Look.* Cambridge: Cambridge University Press, 1974.

Storr, Richard J. *The Beginnings of Graduate Education in America.* Chicago: University of Chicago Press, 1953.

———. *Harper's University: The Beginnings: A History of the University of Chicago.* Chicago: University of Chicago Press, 1966.

Sykes, Charles. *The Hollow Men: Politics and Corruption in Higher Education.* Washington: Regnery Gateway, 1990.

———. *Prof Scam: Professors and the Demise of Higher Education.* Washington: Regnery Gateway, 1988.

Taylor, Harold. *Students Without Teachers.* New York: McGraw-Hill, 1969.

Thayer, V. T. *Formative Ideas in American Education.* New York: Dodd, Mead, 1965.

Thomas A. Edison College. *Opening Doors.* Brochure, n.d.

Thomas, Russell. *The Search for a Common Learning: General Education, 1800–1960.* New York: McGraw-Hill, 1962.

Tocqueville, Alexis de. *Democracy in America.* Ed. Phillips Bradley. New York: Knopf, 1984.

Trilling, Lionel. *Beyond Culture.* New York: Viking Press, 1968.

Trow, M. "Reflections on the Transition From Mass to Universal Higher Education." *Daedalus,* vol. 99, 1970.

U.S. Department of Education, National Center for Education Statistics. *The Condition of Education.* Washington: U.S. Government Printing Office, 1985.

Van Doren, Mark. *Liberal Education*. Boston: Beacon Press, 1959.

Veblen, Thorstein. *The Higher Learning in America*. New York: B. W. Huebsch, 1918.

Veysey, Laurence. *The Emergence of the American University*. Chicago: University of Chicago Press, 1965.

Wegener, C. *Liberal Education and the Modern University*. Chicago: University of Chicago Press, 1978.

Whitehead, Alfred North. *The Aims of Education and Other Essays*. New York: Free Press, 1967.

Wilson, Edmund. "The Fruits of the MLA." *New York Review of Books*, 1968.

———. *The Triple Thinkers*. New York: Oxford University Press, 1963.

Wilson, Woodrow. "What Is College For?" In *The Papers of Woodrow Wilson*, ed. A. S. Link, vol. 19. Princeton, NJ: Princeton University Press, 1975.

Winston, Roger B., Jr., et al. *Developmental Academic Advising: Addressing Students' Educational, Career and Personal Needs*. San Francisco: Jossey-Bass, 1984.

Yaffe, Elaine. "What Are Today's Students Really Like?" *Colorado College Bulletin*, February 1985.

Young, Michael. *The Rise of the Meritocracy, 1870–2033*. New York: Random House, 1959.